MW00619095

toon
Qu'Apelle River
Regina
Assiniboine River
Riding Mountain
Lake Manitoba
Portage la Prairie
Brandon
White Horse Plains
Red River Settlement (Winnipeg)
Willow Bunch
Estevan
Boissevain
Pembina R.
Turtle Mtns
Neche
Pembina
Bottineau
Belcourt
Dunseith
Rolette
St Joseph (Walhalla)
Cavalier
Plentywood
Scobey
COTEAU
Souris River
Des Lacs
Buffalo Lodge Lake
Towner
Trenton
Williston
Minot
Velva
Devils Lake
Poplar
Ft Union
Ft Buford
DU
Grand Forks
River
Washburn
Fort Clark
MISSOURI
Sheyenne River
Yellowstone River
Missouri
Bismarck/ Mandan
Fargo
Moorh
Heart River
Little
Missouri River
Ft Abercrombie
Wahpeton
McIntosh
Sisseton
Grand River
Belle Fourche
Dupree
Ft. Pierre
BLACK HILLS
Belle Fourche R.
James River
Cheyenne River
White River
Sioux Falls
Yankton

BECOMING LITTLE SHELL

BECOMING LITTLE SHELL

A Landless Indian's Journey Home

CHRIS LA TRAY

MILKWEED EDITIONS

© 2024, Text by Chris La Tray
All rights reserved. Except for brief quotations in critical articles or reviews, no part of this book may be reproduced in any manner without prior written permission from the publisher: Milkweed Editions, 1011 Washington Avenue South, Suite 300, Minneapolis, Minnesota 55415.
(800) 520-6455
milkweed.org

Published 2024 by Milkweed Editions
Printed in Canada
Cover design by Mary Austin Speaker
Cover photo by Chris Chapman, Northland Studio
24 25 26 27 28 5 4 3 2 1
First Edition

Library of Congress Cataloging-in-Publication Data

Names: La Tray, Chris, author.
Title: Becoming Little Shell : returning home to the landless Indians of Montana / Chris La Tray.
Other titles: Returning home to the landless Indians of Montana
Description: First edition. | Minneapolis, Minnesota : Milkweed Editions, 2024. | Includes bibliographical references. | Summary: "From Montana Poet Laureate Chris La Tray, a singular story of discovery and embrace of Indigenous identity"-- Provided by publisher.
Identifiers: LCCN 2024002120 (print) | LCCN 2024002121 (ebook) | ISBN 9781571313980 (hardcover) | ISBN 9781571317445 (ebook)
Subjects: LCSH: La Tray, Chris. | Ojibwa Indians--Ethnic identity. | Little Shell Tribe of Chippewa Indians of Montana--Biogaphy. | LCGFT: Biographies. | Autobiographies.
Classification: LCC E99.C6 L3624 2024 (print) | LCC E99.C6 (ebook) | DDC 305.897/333--dc23/eng/20240229
LC record available at https://lccn.loc.gov/2024002120
LC ebook record available at https://lccn.loc.gov/2024002121

Milkweed Editions is committed to ecological stewardship. We strive to align our book production practices with this principle, and to reduce the impact of our operations in the environment. We are a member of the Green Press Initiative, a nonprofit coalition of publishers, manufacturers, and authors working to protect the world's endangered forests and conserve natural resources. *Becoming Little Shell* was printed on acid-free 100% postconsumer-waste paper by Friesens Corporation.

For the Little Shell Chippewa
and for Landless People everywhere

CONTENTS

INTRODUCTION
2022, WESTERN MONTANA / xi

CHAPTER 1
1977, FRENCHTOWN, MONTANA / 1

CHAPTER 2
2019, MISSOULA, MONTANA / 14

CHAPTER 3
2011, PLAINS, MONTANA / 23

CHAPTER 4
2013, MISSOULA, MONTANA / 35

CHAPTER 5
2022, FRENCHTOWN, MONTANA / 45

CHAPTER 6
2014, SIX MILE, MONTANA / 62

CHAPTER 7
2020, COUNCIL GROVE, MONTANA / 74

CHAPTER 8
2017, GREAT FALLS, MONTANA / 86

CHAPTER 9
2017, BROWNING, PABLO,
AND MISSOULA, MONTANA / 97

CHAPTER 10
2017, ULM, MONTANA / 109

CHAPTER 11
2021, HELENA, MONTANA / 119

CHAPTER 12
2018, GREAT FALLS, MONTANA / 138

CHAPTER 13
2020, GREAT FALLS, MONTANA / 149

CHAPTER 14
2019, BRITISH COLUMBIA, CANADA / 162

CHAPTER 15
2019, FRENCHTOWN, MONTANA / 179

CHAPTER 16
2019, LEWISTOWN, MONTANA / 195

CHAPTER 17
2020, CHOTEAU, MONTANA / 210

CHAPTER 18
2021, MISSOULA, MONTANA / 223

CHAPTER 19
2019, MISSOULA, MONTANA / 236

CHAPTER 20
2020, GREAT FALLS, MONTANA / 248

EPILOGUE
2021, BUTTE, MONTANA / 266

NOTES / 273

BIBLIOGRAPHY / 285

ACKNOWLEDGMENTS / 291

INTRODUCTION

2022

WESTERN MONTANA

IT'S A MIDSUMMER MORNING in 2022 in Western Montana, and dark clouds boil and roil and threaten thunderstorms. After days of swelter the precipitation is welcome, but the threat of wildfire by lightning is real.

I'm driving my gray 1999 Nissan Frontier pickup. I merge onto Interstate 90 westbound where it intersects with US Highway 93, at the western edge of Missoula. These two routes—I-90 east-west, 93 north-south—are swarmed with tourist traffic every summer. These yearly visitors are here because this place is beautiful. The valley, formed by the confluence of the Blackfoot, Bitterroot, and Clark Fork Rivers, is bordered by rolling mountains. Below the conifer-covered tree line, despite summer settling in with a vengeance, their slopes still show a hint of spring's green where they aren't patched in yellow arrowleaf balsamroot. Looming over the valley to the west, the bare conical peak of the highest point of this segment of the Rocky Mountains is just visible beneath the ceiling of clouds: Ch-paa-qn, her name a Salish word that means "shining mountain" or, depending on who you ask, "gray, treeless mountaintop."

Other Indigenous words are on my mind today. There are countless shiny cars, hulking SUVs, and gigantic pickups pulling trailers loaded with canoes and kayaks and bicycles. I note names like "Tacoma" and "Denali" on their bumpers, same with RVs called "Yukon" and "Winnebago." There are others, too, Indian names all, in a place not that many Indians remain.

I've thought about Indians my entire life. I grew up with the vague knowledge that my father's side of the family was Indian (Chippewa, specifically) as my grandmother would speak of it at times. I have a dim memory of being four years old and sitting on the faded linoleum kitchen floor of our little farmhouse in Huson, assaulting a coloring book with crayons. When asked why I depict a pair of children with red skin, I say it's because they're Indians. My visiting grandmother, Ruby Katherine (Doney) La Tray, sitting at the table, asks, "Is my skin red? No? But I am an Indian. And so are you."

I was very young and now I'm not, but the memory has stuck with me.

It wasn't until my grandfather, Leo Stanley La Tray, died just shy of eighty-three years of age in late September 1996 that pieces started falling into place. I was twenty-nine years old. A decade earlier, fresh out of high school, two friends and I headed west on the same Interstate 90 I'm traversing today, on our way to Seattle to become rock stars. I hadn't seen my grandparents since making the move. By 1996 I was married with a three-year-old son who would never meet his great-grandfather, living closer to Tacoma than Seattle, and working a job that required a long, traffic-infested commute that was slowly killing my will to live. The dreams of rock 'n' roll glory were over. I like to tell people my bandmates and I arrived in Seattle with bags full of spandex and leather when the city was on the cusp of dressing all their musical heroes in flannel and ripped jeans.

My friends and I didn't fit that bill. It's likely we weren't all that good either, but I'll never admit to that.

In 1996 I made the drive to Plains, Montana, for the funeral; it was the first one of a family member I'd ever attended. Though I barely knew my grandfather, I was one of the pallbearers. It was a beautiful fall day in early October. I left my Washington home in the wee hours of morning, crossed Snoqualmie Pass eastbound through the jagged and magnificent coastal Cascade Range at sunrise, then blew through the croplands of Eastern Washington as the day expanded in my windshield. The sun was bright, the foliage was changing to vivid reds and yellows, and the air was crisp and clean the entire way. It was a perfect day to travel. I loved to take long drives then and I still do now, especially alone.

Arriving at the small Catholic church in Plains—St. James Catholic Church, a structure with white siding trimmed in pale greenish blue that was built in 1919, six years after my grandpa was born—I was amazed to find the nave crowded with Indians. I took my seat in the front row, beside my dad, and stared around in a state of puzzled awe. During the service, which I barely remember—it seemed to be more about Jesus than my grandfather—Dad kept poking me in the ribs and trying to make me laugh. When we exited the church and prepared to join the procession to the cemetery, Dad leaned in and asked, "So, what did you think about all those Indians?"

"There were a lot of them," I said, for lack of a better answer. What I didn't say was how astounded I was.

Dad didn't talk about my grandfather very much, and when he did it wasn't flattering. For example, Dad had two baseball mitts he'd saved from his childhood. Oversized, shapeless hunks of leather sewn together like artifacts from another era, they seemed useless compared to the streamlined, shiny gloves I used during my Little League career. I remember Dad holding one of those old mitts one time, thumping his fist into its center, a slight smile on his face. "Your grandpa gave me this," he said. "It's the only goddamn thing he ever gave me."

After the service, while everyone else proceeded immediately to the cemetery, Dad and I stopped at the VFW bar just up the block from the church—VFW Post 3596, where my WWII veteran grandfather's lifetime membership had finally ended. Inside, Dad told me over a couple quick beers, "I'm not sad. Not even a little bit. That sonofabitch never did a thing for me."

~

Something my dad and his father had in common was the denial of any Indigenous heritage. Suggesting my dad was Native made him angry. I could never understand why. I was the opposite. I wanted to be Indian. I wanted that identity and I took it for myself, even if it had to be largely locked up. To me it was cool. Who wouldn't want to be an Indian? Who wouldn't want to be Chippewa? Growing up, if there was anything I knew about the answers to those questions, it was this: don't ask Dad for them.

My grandfather's funeral was a turning point in my curiosity about my family history. Here was a collection of people I'd never known but was clearly connected to. Who were they? Why didn't I know them? Why was I never allowed to know them? What was our family's story? I went home with more questions, only now I could see much more clearly where I came from, even if nobody in my family talked about it.

Whenever anyone asked my dad about other La Trays in Montana—there are many of us, particularly in northern border-hugging Hi-Line towns like Havre and Great Falls, or even Deer Lodge, where Montana State Prison is—he would deny any relation. I never heard him utter the words "Little Shell," "Rocky Boy's," "Turtle Mountain," or even "Chippewa," that I can recall, nor "Métis" (pronounced MAY-tee) all words for people and places critical to my life now. My dad spent his life denying his Indigenous heritage and, through his choice, mine as well, sometimes vehemently.

Referring to my dad as Indian in any way, in most contexts, bordered on fighting words. If pressed, his calmest response was to refer to the entire idea of "Indian-ness" as complete bullshit. When he passed away in 2014, Dad left me with a lifetime of questions about who he was and where he came from. No, who *we* are, where *we* come from. I'm certain he had the answers to many of these questions, but he chose to take them with him to his grave. I decided I would do what I could to find them on my own. If not from him, then through people who lived a similar experience. Through the story of our people.

This book is an attempt to answer some of those questions, to tell the story of my own family heritage, certainly, and why my dad felt the way he did about his heritage. If I've learned anything at all, it's that I'm not the only one to grow up in these kinds of circumstances. I'm also not alone in trying to find my way back to who I was all along: a proud Indian.

I'm not a scholar. I'm not a historian. I don't have an academic bone in my body. I'm a storyteller, and this is a story that needs telling. I feel compelled to share the story of the Métis people of Montana with the world, to tell the story of the Little Shell Tribe, the longtime landless Indians of Montana. Because it's clear we're largely unknown, not just to the wider world but even in Montana, the first state to recognize us as a legitimate tribe, despite our centuries-old association with a larger Indigenous family. Like the stories of all Indigenous tribes of the Americas, it's a sad story. Yet it's a story brimming with grit and determination, a story full of facts and dates shared as best as I've come to learn them; other storytellers may unearth different versions.

This version of the story is mine. It is a story still unfolding.

BECOMING LITTLE SHELL

CHAPTER 1

1977

FRENCHTOWN, MONTANA

IN THE SUMMER OF 1977, I was ten. One afternoon I was with my cousin, Casey, who's four or five years older than me. We went to the Triplex theater (since torn down) at the south end of Brooks Street in Missoula, where three movies were playing: *Viva Knievel!*, a vehicle for Butte, Montana, motorcycle daredevil Evel Knievel to play both action hero and movie star; *The Island of Doctor Moreau*, based on the 1896 H. G. Wells sci-fi novel and starring Michael York and Burt Lancaster; and *Star Wars*. We paid for one movie, then hopped the fuzzy red velvet rope barriers between auditoriums as each show ended until we managed to watch all three in one soda and popcorn–fueled debauch.

It was glorious. Knievel had humbled himself hurtling over the lip of the Snake River Canyon in nearby Idaho in a makeshift rocket a couple years earlier, but he was still a superhero to me. (This despite my mom's insistence he was an asshole. She denies ever having said that, but time has revealed she was right all along.) I'd thrown myself over my share of makeshift jumps on my bicycle while trying to emulate him, usually resulting in a tangled wreck of skinned knees and frustration. Knievel seemed cool. His costumes looked like something a member of the rock band

KISS might wear. I was into them too; their *Love Gun* album, which came out that summer as well, was the first record I ever bought with my own money.

Star Wars had it all: Heroes. A not-so damsel in distress. Laser gun fights and lightsabers. An iconic character who was essentially a dude in a Sasquatch costume who yelled a lot. And perhaps the greatest cinematic villain of all time, Darth Vader. My mind—and everyone else's, it seemed—was blown.

Yet as much as I loved *Star Wars*, it was evil genius Dr. Moreau and his experiments transforming man into beast that sparked my fantasies the most. After watching the movie, I roamed the wide, dry fields and stands of ponderosa pines near my home with renewed vigor, my two dogs—a large white German shepherd named Sinbad and a Doberman named Jonah—as companions, a set of plastic vampire fangs clenched between my teeth. In my imagination I was a half man / half wolf hero, the sworn enemy of the diabolical Moreau. Armed with superpowers of strength and agility, my canine companions and I rooted out Moreau's evil plots with abandon for hours at a time. A solitary kid for the most part, I tried to get my recess friends to play Dr. Moreau with me once the school year started, but they weren't interested, having not seen the movie. I shrugged it off; playing *Star Wars* was fine with me too.

My childhood in Western Montana lacked any trace of what many tend to think of as a "typical" Montana upbringing. When I was born in Missoula at St. Patrick Hospital on April 4, 1967, I was the third and final child to join the family. My sister Mitzi is two years older than me, my sister Nikki five. My mom was twenty-two at the time of my arrival, my dad twenty-seven. It's hard for me to imagine them so young. Dad neither hunted nor fished, so I never did either. The idea of my dad strapping on shorts and sandals to go hiking like I do now is laughable. (My mom is an avid hiker, though to my recollection that came somewhat later.) We never visited Glacier or Yellowstone National Parks, though neither is particularly distant from where I grew up by western geography—three and maybe five hours' drives respectively, which is practically next door by our way of thinking. We spent many summer nights sleeping outside, but I recall only one actual camping trip; I passed the night crawling in and out of the camper to puke outside because I'd taken ill. I think Fritos were involved. Maybe that's why my family never made it back into the bush. Possibly why I still look askance at Fritos too.

~

There's a substantial breakfast crowd at the Reno, a combined bar and restaurant just off the highway that bisects the town of East Missoula, where I'm dining with my mom early one morning. My mother, Becky, is seventy-four this morning in 2019, and beautiful. Her hair is silver with a purple streak on the left side, and her dark eyes are bright and quick to laugh. I adore her. The Reno is within walking distance of where she lives, and we often meet here for breakfast, a meal that's enjoyed at any hour of the day and arguably both of our favorites. Over the clatter of dishes all but tossed onto tables by an overstressed and surly server, Mom tells me of her early days with my father.

She was still in high school when they met. Dad, fresh from the navy, worked as a mechanic at a heavy machine supply store in Missoula called Miller Machinery. My mom's mother, Doris (she was my grandmother but never allowed us to call her anything but Mom; for clarity's sake, I'll refer to her as Doris), worked in the office. After school, Mom would drive to the shop in Doris's car to pick her up after work. Dad would often saunter out and visit her, much to Doris's dismay.

The dismay was for one of a couple possible reasons, my mom tells me, lathering red jelly onto a slice of sourdough toast. "It was either one, because he was Indian, or two, because he was Catholic," she says. Or maybe both.

I don't recall my grandmother Doris ever being religious in the way some people remember their grandparents. I don't recall any religious paraphernalia in her house, and of my three grandparents I knew, she was the one I spent the most time with; she was part of my life. I particularly remember her as an avid sports fan. We watched Atlanta Braves baseball on Ted Turner's Superstation in her tiny little green house one block away from Dornblaser Field where, until 1986, when their current stadium was completed, the University of Montana Grizzlies played their football games, the end zone cannon shaking the entire neighborhood every time the home team scored a touchdown. Doris occasionally took me to Harry Adams Field House on the UM campus for Griz basketball games too.

We didn't share musical tastes. She expressed woeful disappointment when I, at eleven or twelve, showed up at her house one day in a KISS T-shirt. It was black, of course, and bore the purple-tinted illustration of Paul Stanley, the "Starchild," from 1978, when each member simultaneously released a solo album. Paul was my favorite member, and I wore his image with pride. On seeing it my grandma Doris, as was her way, scowled, shook her head, closed her eyes, rubbed her hands together, and repeated with utter disappointment, "Oh, honey. Oh, honey."

Mom says Doris wasn't religious at the time my parents met either. Growing up in Missoula (my mom was born in Henderson, Nevada, but moved to Missoula when she was a toddler), Mom tells me Doris would take her and her older sister, Pat, to Sunday school at the Christian Science church but never attended any services herself.

"She so totally disliked Catholics though," Mom tells me.

Doris's father was Czech and Catholic, and Mom thinks that was the source of Doris's dislike. He was a district attorney in

Nebraska who left his wife and family for another woman. Doris never forgave him, even as she embraced the Bohemian side of her father's cultural background and ignored that of her mother's family, who were Danish.

Maybe Doris's disapproval of my mom and dad's budding romance was casual racism toward my dad's Indian-ness, or his Catholic background, or both. Who knows? More likely it was concern for my mom and dealing with men. Doris was already divorced from my mom's father (whom I met only once), and there was that buried trauma related to her own father. Still, reflecting while gnawing on a particularly gristly piece of breakfast steak and washing it down with another swallow of bitter coffee, I don't remember Doris and my father ever having a conversation in the years when the family still gathered—during holidays, for example—and Dad was even there, which he often wasn't due to his work schedule.

In her final years during the first decade of the 2000s, Grandma Doris shopped at the same local grocery store I often did: Pattee Creek Market, in the southeast corner of Missoula. I would see her pushing her cart around the aisles, gray and frail, hunched over the handle but still relatively mobile. Usually I approached her, but there were times I just watched her for a few moments before gathering my own necessities.

Doris died two weeks before Dad did in 2014, and I miss her. It was a rough time for my mother, and I admire her strength through the weeks and months that followed.

~

At our shared meal at the Reno, my mom is relating stories I've never heard before. She tells me that when they first met, my dad was living in a place called the Shamrock Motel. Long gone, it was out on East Broadway on the far eastern edge of Missoula, near where Van Buren Street meets Interstate 90 now.

"He called me up one time, midevening, and I could tell he was upset," Mom says. Dad wanted her to come over because there was something he needed to talk to her about. Evidently there had been some altercation, Mom suspects, likely in a bar, and somebody said something to him that got under his skin. Something that made him question the feasibility of their relationship.

"I went over there and he said, 'Will you ever be ashamed of me?'" Mom says. "I said, 'What do you mean?' and he said, 'Will you ever be ashamed of me because I'm dark?'" Even then, Dad didn't say anything about being Native, being Chippewa, anything like that. He was just "dark."

"I don't think I ever, ever heard your dad say anything about being Indian," Mom continues. "I never really thought of your dad as Indian either, but that's probably because I was too close to him. Because when he would first come to talk to me, I knew right away he was Indian."

Mom and Dad got married on June 29, 1964, in Missoula. Six months shy of three years later, and just shortly before I was born, Dad left Miller Machinery for a job at a paper mill in Frenchtown, a small community a few miles west of Missoula. The mill was a sprawling industrial installation near the banks of the Clark Fork River. He ultimately worked there for more than forty years, under four different owners. Shut down now for more than a decade, the mill is a Superfund site in all but official designation, much of it torn down and hauled away for scrap. I can see its remains from the front porch where I live today. In its day it was a noisy place, bright as a small city at night. It would belch a rotten egg smell into the atmosphere that, before environmental regulations tightened, hung over the entire valley. The scent still lingers in my memory as something that permeates my father's work clothes, his boots, even his black plastic lunch box.

One particular memory of that odor sticks in my mind: As a kid, I played with superhero action figures—characters like Tarzan, Batman, and Captain America—that were held together on the inside by elastic bands that would inevitably break, causing an arm or a leg to fall off. Dad would take them to work and repair them for me. In my mind's eye I picture him there, sitting on a bench next to the loud, steaming machines or at a table in the break room, holding these toys in his rough hands, one finger eternally twisted out of shape from an injury he suffered on the job early in his employment. I would be overjoyed when my heroes returned to me, patched up and ready for more action, even if they did smell like the mill.

What would that scene have looked like? My dad, still a young man, repairing these toys. In my imagining, it's a tender moment, regardless of what was going on around him. He didn't have to do this, and yet he did.

In the fall of 1971, my family moved twenty or so miles west of Missoula to an old farmhouse in the town of Huson. At the time it really wasn't a town; it still isn't. Back then there was a small store with a tiny post office attached, and a bar. The store is gone, but the bar's still there: Larry's Six Mile Bar and Grill, famous for its fried chicken with some pretty good fry bread on the side. There are more homes now, clustered at the dead end of Mullan Road where it peters out at a curve in the Clark Fork River, and there's a large organic vegetable and flower farm run by friendly acquaintances of mine. But otherwise, the place isn't much changed from when we lived there. Most of the people who address their mail "Huson" live in the hills and mountains to the north of the interstate. The town remains little more than a zip code.

A coworker of my father's owned the house we rented; we were only there a year. Long enough for me to turn five. Long enough to be left with a few vague memories. I remember warm milk fresh out of the cow from the dairy next door, cream still floating on top. (My sisters and I hated it.) I remember a morning my dad had to take his rifle and perform a mercy killing of a stricken cow at that dairy, which we weren't allowed to watch though we did manage to wander out later to stare at the carcass. I remember digging for treasure in the weed-choked sand embankment alongside the road that passed by our house and dead-ended just after the dairy farm. I remember being outside well into the dusk on endless summer nights.

I have fond memories of the place, though if I'd known then what I know now, it might've been different.

"Of course your dad didn't tell me at the time," Mom says, "that the house had had a murder-suicide in it the year before we moved in."

On Halloween night 1972, we moved again. This time we landed in Frenchtown and the house where I spent several of my most formative years, like the one I spent playing Dr. Moreau with my dogs. It was another old farmhouse in the center of a broad expanse of empty fields and rolling hills. I remember being told—by my sisters, maybe, or my folks—that it was the "second-oldest house in Frenchtown." The oldest was allegedly that of our landlords, the Hamels, at most only a couple miles distant as the crow flies, on the other side of I-90, near the heart of Frenchtown proper.

A line of ponderosa pines ran north-south, for a mile or so, perhaps a quarter mile east of our house, split down the middle by an irrigation ditch. The trees and ditch are still there, but the area is much changed and inhabited now, most notably by the sprawling campus of Frenchtown High School, which relocated and opened there in 1981. But during our time there we largely had it all to ourselves, with only a couple relatively distant exceptions, for miles extending up into the limb of the Rockies that marks the northern boundary of the Missoula Valley.

We had two television channels, both fuzzy, so we found most entertainment outside. Domestic animals were always around. Besides the dogs and a few cats we had a couple horses, chickens—including a pair of aggressive banty roosters my sisters and I lived in terror of because they were prone to chasing us—and several goats. During 4-H season, we raised pigs. Certain times of year, a neighbor grazed his cattle in the fields around us, and walking the half mile to the bus stop was sometimes a gauntlet run to avoid an enraged mother cow defending a frightened calf.

During irrigation season in the summer months, a small lake of subwater would rise in a depression to the northeast of us. It wasn't very deep; at most, it reached my adolescent waist. It got a little swampy, too, but that didn't stop me from swimming in it when it grew hot outside. There weren't any fish, but my sister and I would catch tadpoles, then bring them home and put them in an old aquarium to watch them turn into frogs over subsequent days.

Frogs and tadpoles weren't the only wildlife around. Sleeping outside in the backyard, watching the night sky—pointing out shooting stars and wondering if they were actually the Soviet Sputnik satellite—we would see bats flitting around, catching bugs. They nested in the eaves of our old house. We weren't afraid of them.

Badgers denned nearby; they made my dad nervous. Gophers. More birds than I can list. Deer. Rumored sightings of black bears and mountain lions not far distant.

Coyotes were common, making their presence known two or three at a time by sitting atop a rise just north of the house, as well as by their giggles and lamentations and yips in the night. Great hawks regularly soared overhead, and our dogs would charge out into the fields below them, barking and carrying on as if the airspace over the yard was the most inviolable, dearly protected zone under their jurisdiction. Another surefire way to send the dogs into a tizzy was when a jet speeding by overhead caused a sonic boom—the sound of an aircraft breeching the sound barrier. It was a little terrifying. The entire house would shake, and the dogs would go nuts. I guess such speeds are illegal in the United States now, as I haven't heard a similar blast in years.

Summer days fading into nights outside didn't always lead to bucolic campouts. These were the seventies; my ear for stories of UFOs and monsters and cattle mutilations would make me wake wide-eyed with fear should I hear an airplane or, even worse, a helicopter pass overhead in the darkness. With the 1975 release of *Jaws*, I was scared whenever I swam in nearby Frenchtown Pond—or "the Pit" as locals called it, from its early days as a gravel pit before it was filled with water—for fear of teeth from the deep. In the wake of that predator-as-villain film, which I watched in terror in a crowded theater as my aunt Pat gripped my leg like she was about to tear it off and defend herself with it, there were a rash of copycats. One example was a movie called *Grizzly*, whose ads featured breathless copy describing the beast as "18 feet of gut-crunching, man-eating terror!" I asked my dad how tall eighteen feet was, and he pointed high up on the side of the house and said, "About that high." For many nights after I lay in my sleeping bag staring at the side of the old place, dumbstruck that an animal could be so gigantic, waiting for it to come drag me away.

I was an avid reader with a rich imagination. I preferred stories brimming with animals and adventure, like Jack London's *The Call of the Wild*, which I particularly loved. I also loved sports, including football, basketball, baseball. Soccer, too, when it hit my radar the summer between fourth and fifth grade and I started playing in the fall through the Missoula YMCA program.

All through my early childhood I was always Chippewa. I didn't think about it; I was Chippewa because Grandma said so, and that was good enough for me. I was too young to worry about why Dad said we weren't. It was just one of those adult contradictions a child lives with, and Dad's close-mouthedness about it made it even less of a big deal. When kids played cowboys and Indians on the playground, I was one of the Indians because I was Chippewa. With the exception of that summer of vampire teeth, when I prowled around in the woods and fields, I was a Chippewa warrior, whatever that was. That's how I saw myself even as I got older and started reading Robert E. Howard's Conan the Barbarian books and comics, and Tolkien's *The Hobbit* and *The Lord of the Rings* books. I couldn't be a strapping, loinclothed barbarian or a dour ranger keeping the borderlands safe from horrors lurking in the wilderness. But I could be Chippewa.

I had Indian toys, like a big plastic Geronimo action figure (complete with club and shield and headdress) to go with a General Custer figure (complete with sword and hat and rifle and pistol), and a cowboy called Johnny West (complete with a plastic palomino horse). There was the Lone Ranger and Tonto, in toy, cartoon, television, and movie form; I wanted to be Tonto.

One Thanksgiving morning, I saw a cartoon version of James Fenimore Cooper's *The Last of the Mohicans*, and it blew my mind. A recent rewatch of the show struck me with its awfulness, but as a kid I absolutely loved it, so much so that the memory of sitting on the floor in front of the TV watching it is still etched in my mind. I've made a tradition of watching the 1992 film version starring Daniel Day-Lewis as an annual part of the celebration.

There weren't any Indians in my life, though. There were a few Indian kids in school I was aware of; a couple families who, based on the names I remember and where they lived, were probably Salish or even Blackfeet. They were mostly quiet kids who kept to themselves. At home, outside of my parents and sisters, the only extended family I interacted with were from my mom's side—my grandma Doris, my mom's two sisters, and two cousins. From my dad's side my grandparents were occasional visitors, and we sometimes drove up to Somers to see them at their house on the shore of Flathead Lake. Dad's brother and sister—my uncle Gib and aunt Sharon—visited even more infrequently. Finally, I remember a visit one time from one of my dad's cousins, a woman named Barbara Doney. My only recollection of that occasion is that her boyfriend, playfully chasing me around outside, was nearly mauled by Sinbad, our protective, and gigantic, white-and-black German shepherd.

Toys, movies, and television shows were the only Indians in my life. What I knew of Indians as a people were what any other seventies kid who got a public education in an overwhelmingly settler community knew of them. Tales of the first Thanksgiving, some nods to Sitting Bull and Crazy Horse, possibly Tecumseh.

Back then I had my share of racist ideas about what to expect from Indians. I remember an afternoon outing when I was probably about nine years old. My entire family—Mom, Dad, my two sisters, and me—piled into a VW Bug and made the trek out to Arlee, which was close to the nearby Flathead Indian reservation, by way of logging roads that go up and over the mountains. I can't recall any reason for the trip; it was just something to do, the type of family adventure I have very few recollections of. But I was excited because we were probably going to see Indians. Real Indians. I remember sitting in the back seat, bouncing up the battered gravel road, expecting at any moment to see a dark face peer from the shade and woody tangle behind one of the dusty ponderosa pine trees, a feather jutting from long black hair. I was focused the way I might be today driving through any region boasting wildlife, alert for an elk, a moose, or best of all, a bear or mountain lion.

I carried other screwed-up ideas of what to expect once we hit Arlee. Before I was a teenager, I heard nothing but horrible stories about Arlee and other nearby Indian communities. The Arlee powwow, held every Fourth of July weekend, was described as a drunken free-for-all. High school sports teams from "real" towns barely escaped the town with their skin intact, residents and athletes alike pounding the outside of their buses as they tried to leave.

When we hit Arlee on this family drive, all this racist hearsay from the mouths of people older than me made me expect to drive past bars with passed-out Indians sprawled in every doorway. The reality I learned that summer day was that Arlee was just another hot, dreary, little Montana town. Just like Frenchtown. Just like most of Missoula.

CHAPTER 2

2019

MISSOULA, MONTANA

IT'S A BRIGHT AND SHINING summer morning in 2019, and I'm in Deer Lodge, Montana. I'm poking around the confines of the Browsing Bison bookstore, just up the street from the Old Montana Prison, an imposing compound surrounded by high brick walls. It was built in 1871 when Montana was just a territory, and then served as the state prison from 1889 until 1979. It's now a historical landmark and museum. I visited once on a junior high field trip and it freaked me out. I probably won't ever visit again.

The front of the Browsing Bison blooms with glorious natural light from the large windows facing Main Street. The store displays a tidy collection of new releases, the usual collection of journals and cards and other sundry items on shelves and spinner racks, and a generous section devoted to regional books about Montana. In the more shadowy area toward the back of the store, though, where the air is redolent with the musty scent of old used books, I've already located one treasure: a gloriously battered set of the initial twelve Conan the Barbarian mass-market paperbacks—the ones with all the glorious Frank Frazetta art—that I first encountered and devoured, much to my English teacher's dismay, around forty years before. I glimpse the other treasure, arguably of greater value than the Conan books, in the glass display case under the cash register when I prepare to make my purchase, and my breath catches in my throat.

The book is *Frenchtown Valley Footprints,* a relatively slim, coffee table–sized hardcover produced by the Frenchtown Historical Society and published by Missoula's Mountain Press Publishing in 1976. It's got a yellowish cover featuring a sepia-toned photograph of the Catholic church in Frenchtown shot from a short distance away, along with the homes and buildings surrounding it. The title is rendered in large block text. I'm overjoyed to find the book, and I immediately add it to my pile for purchase. I've been searching for a copy after my mom's copy, which I couldn't have cared less about when she bought it in 1976, couldn't be located. I know there will be details between the covers that I need to know. Yes, it's about Frenchtown, but to me it's also about Missoula, or at least the idea of what Missoula encompasses.

Even though I didn't live inside its city limits until I returned to Montana as an adult, Missoula has always been my heart center. Having grown up on its fringes—places like Huson or Frenchtown—it was always easier to answer "Missoula" when people asked where I'm from. It's a place many people have heard of, whereas those other places . . . not so much. Despite this connection today, whenever I'm asked for a bio, I list my home as Frenchtown, even though the address is in Missoula. This may make the confused reader scratch their head, but it's simple to me. First, the kids in my neighborhood shuffle aboard a school bus that hauls them to Frenchtown. And second, I like the idea of being a Frenchtown writer. It just sounds cooler, and that's good enough for me.

I suspect Missoula was my dad's heart center. Mom's too. In 1962, when my twenty-two-year-old dad was honorably discharged from the navy and went looking for work, he found it in

Missoula. He joined a long tradition of Indians—nonreservation Indians, mostly, commonly called "urban" Indians—living and working here. He never lived anywhere else but in its vicinity, didn't even travel far away from it often. He loved it here. It's a beautiful place to live.

Missoula, which is sometimes called "the hub of five valleys," sits in a key geographical confluence of five mountain ranges: the Reservation Divide, the Bitterroots, the Rattlesnakes, the Sapphires, and the Garnets. The Clark Fork River, which runs through the center of the valley, is joined at the eastern end by the Blackfoot River and to the west by the Bitterroot.

I often like to squint my eyes and imagine the valley before all the settlement. No interstate, no Mullan Road, no Frontage Road. No traffic, no airport, no sprawl of houses and light industrial complexes and gravel pits and acres stacked with busted-up pallets. Just a broad valley of grass and creeks, with cart trails connecting north to south (Highway 93, if you remember) and tracing the meandering path of the river east to west (like I-90, for the most part).

Indians have been here for about as long as possible, considering it was all underwater as recently as thirteen thousand years or so ago. Glacial Lake Missoula, created by an ice dam farther west, filled the entire valley. When it burst for the final time, the magnificent flooding through the northwest to the Pacific Ocean created much of the familiar rugged landscapes we enjoy today, like that of Columbia Gorge in Washington and Oregon, between here and the coast. Mount Sentinel, on the eastern edge of Missoula and facing west across the entire valley, is identifiable by a large *M* made of white stone. It's a popular hiking location for excellent views of the city, especially the UM campus and downtown, if you don't mind huffing and puffing a bit. There's also a trailside marker just beyond the *M* that indicates the highest water level of that stupendous lake. It's a little sobering to imagine the entire region submerged and then, in a calamitous rush, flushing toward the sea.

Sources like *Frenchtown Valley Footprints* and others tell us that artifacts found in the area—tools like pestles and scrapers and mauls, and arrowheads—put Indians here as far back as three to five thousand years ago. I don't hear so much about them now, but as a youth I was often jealous of local kids who brought in arrowheads someone in their family found. There was also wildlife of all shapes and sizes here, which there still is, as many inattentive drivers discover with the fronts of their cars.

People have inhabited the valley, yes, but there aren't "official" records of it until the mid-1800s. Meriwether Lewis, who separated from William Clark and the main body of their historic, continent-spanning mission with a small party, didn't turn west after he left Travelers' Rest near the heart of what today is the town of Lolo in 1806 and traversed the Missoula Valley on his way back to Missouri. He and his men camped at Grant Creek on the northwest edge of modern-day Missoula, then continued eastward through the future downtown and from there just a short jaunt to the Blackfoot River and adventures north, like running afoul of the Blackfeet and getting shot in the ass by one of his own men. Lewis and Clark encountered almost a dozen separate parties of fur trappers headed west as they made their way home to St. Louis. If any of those intrepid men passed through my stomping grounds, and they surely did, they didn't mention it.

We don't get specific reference to the Frenchtown area for another four decades after the Corps of Discovery left it. This mention is connected to the area now known as Evaro Hill, which is the steep climb out of the valley on Highway 93 headed north to the Flathead. In this tale, the area earns the name the "Coriacan Defile."

It's one of my favorite stories, mentioned in a couple places and rendered most succinctly in *Frenchtown Valley Footprints*, which says, "Sometime in the late 1840s Coriaka, a Hawaiian, was a member of Neil McArthur's party of the Hudson's Bay Company, which had been trading with the Indians camped around Frenchtown. Coriaka went on ahead into the canyon and was ambushed and killed by Blackfeet Indians."

A Hawaiian guy working for the Hudson's Bay Company in the wilds of Montana is killed and gets a defile—a name for a long, narrow pass through hills or mountains—named after him? It's kind of weird to think it's the Hawaiian guy who gets sent ahead to scout, but who knows what they were thinking? There's an old trick where everyone in a group puts a finger beside their nose, and the last person to notice has to do whatever odious task is on offer. I somehow imagine a scene just like that playing out around the evening campfire. Coriaka loses, then suffers for it, but lives on in history in ways no one else in the party does. That isn't such a bad trade.

What grabs me is the tiny mention of "the Indians camped around Frenchtown." I grew up prowling the woods and fields "like an Indian," playing cowboys and Indians, all in a world of fantasy not so different from the world depicted in those Conan books. But the matter-of-fact nature of reporting on "Indians camped around Frenchtown" pierced my heart. Of course Indians lived here; I knew it all along. Everyone knows it, right? Indians *still* live here. Ask anyone who knows, and Montana is firmly Indian country. But to what extent? For all the ways the state of Montana exploits Indians for marketing purposes—postcards, T-shirts, and cheap gift store swag like plastic bows and arrows and rubber tomahawks—there aren't that many of us living here. It didn't take much poking around on the internet to turn up some relevant demographics.

Montana is the fourth-largest state in the country, and census records indicate that the state has only just recently passed the one million mark in total population, making it the forty-fourth most populated state. Given the wide-open spaces here, we're spread out; only 6.86 people per square mile. That means only Alaska and Wyoming are more sparsely populated. When I refer to people in Butte or Helena as my "neighbors," since they're a mere two-hour drive away (depending on how howling the weather is), I'm only being mildly facetious. For us out here, a drive over fifty miles to see someone or do something on a whim is no big deal; many folks elsewhere can't get their heads around that. An hour drive in Southern California, one of the three states larger than Montana, is a short trip extended by traffic. In Montana, an hour drive is consistently seventy or eighty miles, give or take.

Montana is one of the palest states in America, too, with a white-only population of 89 percent. (Maine is the whitest, at over 94 percent.) Despite that, our roughly 7 percent Native population is one of the country's largest; only Alaska, Oklahoma, New Mexico, and South Dakota have more. Of those Indians in Montana, numbering just shy of seventy thousand, around 63 percent live off reservation. (We have seven reservations scattered around the state.) After whites and Indians, Hispanic and Latino people are next, comprising 4.5 percent of our population. Other races are so sparse as to be almost absent, with Asian and Black Americans coming in at 1 percent and 0.6 percent respectively.

Missoula, my heart center, the second-largest city in Montana (Billings is first) and generally considered one of its more diverse, is nonetheless every bit as white as the rest of the state. Current population estimates have it around seventy-five thousand residents. Of these, 89 percent are white and 2 percent are American Indian and Alaska Natives. That weird "two or more" demographic comes in at 3 percent of the population.

In the early sixties, the population of Missoula was a little more than a third the size it is now. Census data from 1960 puts the city's total population at 27,090. Hard to say how many Indians lived in Missoula when Mom and Dad got together, but they were certainly a more common sight than they are now. At least that's how my mom remembers it, as she explained to me over breakfast that morning.

"It was always a thing when we were growing up," Mom says. "Quite a few Indians would come down from Arlee in buses. It sounds terrible I know, but people would say, 'Oh, the Indians must have gotten their Indian money and they're in town to spend it.' We just assumed. We didn't know better."

People still don't know better. One of the long-running false narratives about the relationship between the federal government and Indians is that the feds—in this case the Bureau of Indian Affairs, or BIA—give individual Indians money just because they're Indians. This isn't the case. There's no such thing as "Indian money"; there never has been. There have been lawsuits in the past that generated some checks for people, sure. The Indian Claims Commission was set up in 1946 to resolve such claims and, for example, led directly to the Pembina Judgment Fund Distribution Act of 1982, which earned some Turtle Mountain / Little Shell / Pembina folks checks related to what was called the Ten-Cent Treaty (more on that later). That was a one-time thing . . . unless we can somehow manage to get compensated for the millions of acres of unceded land we're technically still owed, but that's a battle for another day.

A second common assumption is that all tribes simply need to throw up a casino and start printing money. That's another false narrative. Something like only 15 percent of tribes who have casinos (most don't) are successful with them. There are a few that are hugely lucrative, but that's only because they're near population centers where they have lots of nontribal people visiting and spending money. There aren't a lot of those population centers along the Montana Hi-Line, or anywhere in Montana, for that matter. The Confederated Salish and Kootenai Tribes (CSKT) built the new state-of-the-art Gray Wolf Peak Casino just north of Missoula, named after a prominent land form there. In my experience it's a nice place to have a steak dinner in a big room with hardly anyone else in it.

Montana Indians generally don't control any other resources that would allow for extra money that could theoretically be divided up among members as "per capita" payments, as they're called. My friends among the CSKT get money largely due to their control of a dam on the Flathead River, but it isn't much. Nor does that money come from the federal government. My Blackfeet friends own up to having gotten "something like fifty dollars for something a few years ago, I don't remember," but no one's getting rich off that. No one's going to make a special trip to Missoula over that either.

Yet the narrative continues.

"If he was enrolled, how much money would he get?" Mom tells me people would ask her about Dad, even right up until he died. But he wanted no part of it. I'm ambivalent, though I'm not shy about taking money when it's offered. In 2016, just before my wife and I were set to take a road trip to Oregon and back that we could almost afford, a check arrived for me out of the blue from the government. It was a little over $800. There was little documentation, but it had something to do with "Indian trust" and "lawsuit." I didn't think much about it, I just deposited it before it could disappear in a puff of smoke. I wish now I'd paid closer attention, but I'm certain it was my share of the Ten-Cent Treaty payouts. It also came just as I was considering the possibility of enrolling with the Little Shell Tribe, and I suspect it's the only "Indian money" I'll ever get.

~

In 1978 my parents bought a home, a single-wide trailer with a built-on addition, on ten acres in one of the most beautiful places I could ever imagine living. The land was on the banks of Six Mile Creek, about eight miles west and a little north of where we lived in Frenchtown proper. The prominent peak of the previously mentioned Ch-paa-qn, which I've summited several times over the years, loomed overhead. Technically we were back in the Huson zip code, but we kept our Frenchtown post office box, so to me it was still Frenchtown. It wasn't until well after I left that any of the homes in the area received "proper" physical addresses, mainly due to the rise of delivery services like FedEx and UPS.

This was the home I grew the rest of the way up in. Where I had my own room with walls I could cover with magazine photos of KISS, where I went to sleep at night with their music blaring in my headphones. Where my friends and I gathered to play *Dungeons and Dragons* on winter afternoons so cold we used a hot-air popcorn popper to heat the room at intervals. Where my family buried several beloved pets. Where my sisters, one after the other, graduated high school before me and left. The home I eventually left too. My folks lived there, though they swapped the house out for a new one in the late nineties, until Dad died in 2014. Mom sold it a year later and moved to East Missoula, to the Hellgate Canyon. Sometimes, sitting at her dinner table or on her back porch, I wonder: Who sat here and camped and enjoyed a meal in this very spot, before us?

CHAPTER 3

2011

PLAINS, MONTANA

IT'S MAY 1, 2011. A CATHOLIC PRIEST stands at the head of a freshly dug grave in a cemetery on a windswept hillside in Plains, Montana. The rolling hills behind him—mostly bare, with patches of green and a few scattered pines—sprawl to the north, and the mountains just beyond are still capped white with snow. The sky is thick with dramatic, iron-gray clouds; it isn't cold, but it isn't exactly warm either. The priest seems tiny and insignificant against the landscape. He wears a navy nylon windbreaker and dark pants and shoes and clutches a large bible against his chest with folded arms. He's balding with thin, gray hair and a broad, pale forehead, and his chin is covered in a short, neatly trimmed beard. His glasses have turned dark in the pale sunshine. The priest is waiting for the casket to arrive. I'm waiting too.

I'm here in Plains—along with my mother, father, and Julia, my wife—for the first time since I was here nearly fifteen years earlier for the my grandfather's funeral. This funeral is for my grandmother Ruby, who passed a few days earlier, ten days after her ninety-fourth birthday. I haven't seen her since that day in 1996 either, though in the intervening years I've moved back to Montana, left again—this time to Ohio for three years—then returned a second time. As my life evolved, hers wound down, her final years spent in an assisted living facility far north of Plains—almost to Canada—in Libby, Montana, where she suffered dementia. We never really knew each other, and her presence in my life is faded beyond a handful of early childhood recollections. She lives in my memory though as the only person in my family who seemed willing to talk about our Indigeneity.

Before long, a black hearse pulls up. A pine casket is rolled out the back and six men, three to a side, solemnly carry it to the grave site. I know none of these people. My father should be among them, but his health is such that he sits in the passenger seat of his car and watches from a distance, his wide, clean-shaven face crumpled with a sadness I've never seen before. His hair is cut short and mostly gray, and his jowls (heavy from the medications he takes) hang from the sides of his face. He's in his seventy-first year.

My dad's demeanor contains none of the levity he showed when my grandfather died. That isn't the only difference between the funerals either. For one thing, the crowd to mark my grandmother's passing is far, far smaller and, with only a couple exceptions, largely devoid of Indian faces. The priest, the church, the people gathered to witness the proceedings, all seem exhausted. It's depressing and I'm eager to leave, even though I feel a deep obligation to stand with my father in this moment. When the graveside service ends, we part ways. He doesn't express anything of his sadness, just thanks me for coming. Then he and my mom go their way, and Julia and I go ours.

~

At the time of my grandmother's 2011 funeral, I've been back in the Missoula area for six years, this time, it seems, for good. When I returned to Washington after my grandfather passed in 1996, I was only there about a year before moving back to

Montana. My rock 'n' roll dreams were all dried up, and I'd grown weary of a commute that consumed three hours of my day when it should've only taken one. My then marriage—my first—had faltered, but we'd reconciled, or seemed to have, and the move to Montana seemed like a good way to recalibrate ourselves. My son was four then. I took a job in Ronan, Montana, in the heart of the Flathead reservation. To my mind, this is one of the most beautiful places on earth, a stretch of landscape called the Mission Valley that we would drive through when I was a child whenever my family visited my grandparents during the period they lived in Somers, Montana, just beyond the reservation boundary to the north and on the shores of Flathead Lake.

Encountering the valley, named for the Mission Mountains that comprise the reservation's eastern boundary, is a breathtaking experience on all but the cloudiest of days. Traversing north on Highway 93, one passes the Bison Range to the left—the long slopes painted bright yellow with arrowleaf balsamroot in spring—as the highway climbs a long, steep hill. At the top, the vista opens on the broad, sweeping valley, with the snowcapped crags of the Missions jutting ten thousand feet straight up from the valley floor to the right and stretching north as far as the eye can see. To see the sun rise from behind them or paint their faces in gold with the fading light of a long summer day is to be reminded we are just tiny pieces in the magnificent entirety of creation. I've made this drive countless times over the years, and the experience never fails to blow me away.

The Ronan gig entailed working in information technology. I didn't know anything about IT but was a quick learner. I'd largely gotten the job because I'd gone to school and played Little League with the guy running the department back in Frenchtown. This was pre–ubiquitous internet; I can remember hearing the dial-up modem stashed in the closet screech and squawk and ping and whine every time one of us checked our email, which was often. It was also a reasonably fun time to be in IT because we were untethered in unknown territory, figuring stuff out, solving problems, and trying to stay a step ahead of whatever needed to work today versus what was about to fail tomorrow. Looking back, considering the growth environment we were in, I think we did solid work.

The job was with a manufacturer of power tool accessories that had started in a local inventor-turned-entrepreneur's garage and grown from—at the time I started—just under three hundred employees to over a thousand, with a sprawling campus of large new buildings full of state-of-the-art machines. At the height of its growth, the company reached far beyond its grasp. Caught up in the rush of seeming success and desperate for cash to keep it all afloat, the company went public and almost immediately crashed into bankruptcy and restructuring. That rise and fall, at least during my time there, occurred over five years.

When all the air began hissing out, leadership started unleashing a round of layoffs on the dwindling workforce every few weeks. I survived several of those, but then my services were determined to no longer be necessary on December 7, 2001. I remember driving south to Missoula on Highway 93 on a cold, sunny day, listening to U2's "Beautiful Day" at high volume. And it was a beautiful day! The peaks of the Missions glared white with fresh snow, the sky a heartbreaking blue unbroken by clouds. For all the stress of suddenly being out of work, I was in remarkably decent spirits. The last year or so in that uncertain work environment had been stressful. The friend who'd hired me had already left, and every round of layoffs led to more coworkers who barely hid their resentment whenever I encountered them at the gas station or in the grocery store.

I wasn't any different when my time came though. In the weeks that followed my layoff, I got calls from people still working there asking things like, "What is this password?" and "How do we make such and such work?" It was with no small amount of self-righteous glee that I just sort of shrugged. Possibly not my best moment, but it felt really good.

In the final days of my tenure in Ronan, I was fortunate to receive a job offer from one of our vendors. The downside was they were located just east of the Indiana border in Ohio. I took the offer anyway, and in February 2002 I packed up a U-Haul trailer and headed thirty hours east, all the way to Sidney, Ohio. I became, for lack of a better title, a "manufacturing consultant." I helped manufacturing companies with data collection as it related to accounting for inventory, labor collection, etc. I traveled, at times extensively, around the United States, with some international travel to Canada, Mexico, and even the Czech Republic just weeks before they entered the European Union. Seeing places I wouldn't have otherwise had opportunity to visit was interesting enough, but I didn't enjoy the work and it was in no way fulfilling. It provided a relatively good living, incomewise, beyond what I might've ever expected, and it was easy to be comfortable with, if simultaneously miserable.

I lived in Ohio for around three years, then moved back to Missoula in 2005. I kept the gig and worked remotely. Over that stretch, my first marriage finally collapsed. Meanwhile I met Julia—I had a side hustle writing record reviews in exchange for free CDs for an underground heavy music site, and Julia and I became friends when her band's demo crossed my path. Julia ultimately moved from Tucson, Arizona, to join me in Missoula in 2006. We married a few months after, though we didn't tell anyone for several more months. My son lived most of the time with us in our crowded, rambunctious household that combined us three humans with a menagerie of a half-dozen pets, and a basement full of hobo spiders. Once we mostly dealt with the spiders, a small room in that basement became a jam room where we put together a little family band called Tater Pig, named after a type of fair food that features a greasy sausage nestled inside a baked potato. My son, Sid, played drums, I was on bass, and Julia played guitar and banjo.

This was a good stretch, even if the job was starting to wear on me significantly, and the US economic troubles of 2008 caught us in the wide ripples that affected just about everyone but the people who initiated the crash. In early 2013 we ultimately short-sold the house we were clinging to in Missoula proper and moved almost all the way out to my old stomping grounds in Frenchtown, where we still live today. By the end of 2015 I'd had enough of my job and the politics of my employers, and with Julia urging me on, I quit that gig to go all in as a writer.

Three or four quick paragraphs might not seem like much when it comes to documenting the better part of two decades, but not much in those years is relevant to the story I'm telling. It was a span of my life that, while it certainly connects my past to where I sit writing today, might be captured in a quick thirty-second montage were they to make a movie of it. I was a different person then, struggling to make a kind of life work for me that had no chance of doing so. It's only now that I can look at it with the clarity of hindsight and recognize how toxic it all was.

My time working in Ronan for those five years beginning in the late nineties, living on the reservation, deserves some spotlight. Those years were more formative to my life now than I realized until I started prodding my memories for this book. When I first relocated from Washington to Missoula, then got the Ronan job and moved fifty-odd miles north, I was excited. It was a totally new environment, and I was eager to live, for the first time, among Indians. The reality of that, however, came with some rude awakenings.

For starters, settlers outnumber tribal people to the tune of something like five to one. How is that even possible, one might wonder, given it's an Indian reservation? Aren't reservations for Indians? Without veering too deeply into the reservation's history (I'll touch on this a little more later in the book), I often say that if you want to see the worst of the dealings between the United States government and Indigenous people, study the interactions with the CSKT people beginning with the Hellgate Treaty of 1855, which created the Flathead reservation, and all the lies and double-crossings that came in its wake. I'll also point out that the CSKT people have had their lands stolen more than once. It began in 1855 with the aforementioned treaty, where they lost their land to the south and were removed into the reservation boundaries that exist today. But the feds didn't stop there.

What has become known as the "Allotment and Assimilation Era" began in the late 1800s, following the formation of Indian reservations. Again, more to come later, but renewed efforts to carve chunks of land away from Indian people (beginning with the Dawes Act of 1887) began to take hold on the Flathead reservation in the early 1900s. That turned collectively held tribal land into private land, much of which ultimately, and quickly, ended up in non-Native hands. On the immediate heels of allotment came the expansion of the Homestead Act in 1909. That cracked the reservation wide open to settlers. A disgusting pamphlet from that period called "Uncle Sam Will Give You a Home in the Flathead Indian Reservation"—you may find it online in PDF form, like I did one night while sitting at my desk in a dark room clicking from one rabbit hole into the next—spells out exactly how one may pursue that land. And for the next couple decades, vigorously pursue it homesteaders did. Those ramifications are still not so much reverberating across the reservation as they're booming like cannons.

Driving on the reservation today, whenever I see a billboard with some grinning settler realtor advertising land for sale—and there are many—I see that theft playing out over and over again. That's one example. Another is the rhetoric of non-Native folks who own land there claiming they're "guests" of the CSKT. Guests? Did the tribe call to invite you? Was it a letter, or email? Just because you ended up with some land that was stolen from them, via either a direct connection to an original homesteader or a transfer of still-stolen land to a different set of hands, it doesn't make it right. You aren't a guest. You're an unwelcome settler on land that never should've been yours, encroached on by the vicious influence of settler colonialism. You're an occupier on occupied land, because that's what the reservation is: occupied land. Yes, the CSKT government maintains some sovereignty, but not nearly enough. Nor can they afford to buy all that land back, because now it's real estate and market driven, and expensive beyond their reach. It makes me crazy.

The majority of people I worked with in Ronan—essentially all of them on the admin side—were settlers. The shop floor included some Native folks from the community, but still, it was largely a settler population. Settlers owned all the businesses in town, the ones I knew of anyway, except for, presumably, the one drab cinder block–built "Indian bar" I was warned to avoid. The tribe operated many successful businesses and services, they just didn't overlap with my life because I wasn't part of the tribe, that community. Nor was I any more a guest there than any other person; I was keenly aware of that even then, and it troubled me.

Moreover, as a white-passing Native guy, I occasionally found myself in the middle of conversations that would slide into Indian bashing. Often these discussions were various expressions of indignation that settler residents of the reservation couldn't vote in tribal elections. I wasn't shy about pointing out that I, too, was Indian, and folks should curb their tongues accordingly, when the bashing started. Then I would say that if any of them didn't like the rules, they were free to leave. It's one of the rare occasions in the United States where one can make the spurious "go back to where you came from then!" argument and actually have it mean something.

There were other challenges. The house I lived in was next to an open field. At all hours, teenagers walking back and forth from the schools and downtown Ronan cut through the field and essentially through the edge of my yard to reach a housing development largely occupied by Native families. During that time, occasional mild vandalism occurred. My house was broken into once (a Nintendo 64, half a leftover pizza, and a six-pack of beer were all that was stolen), and one morning I went outside to find two tires on the hooptie brown Dodge minivan I drove had been ventilated, apparently with a pocketknife. After this second event, I approached a group of passing teens the next time I had an opportunity. I told them I didn't mind them using my yard as a shortcut, but I also hoped they'd spread the word not to fuck with my stuff, because I certainly didn't intend to fuck with them. Nothing untoward happened after that, whether by coincidence or, as I hoped, by word of mouth.

I can't say these experiences didn't bother me; they did. But they didn't affect my nascent consciousness about what it was like to be an Indian in the twenty-first century United States. If anything I felt more solidarity with them than I did with my neighbors and coworkers. Other events occurred during my time there, tragic events. I remember a news story of a couple teenage girls who were found dead of either alcohol poisoning or exposure—likely one contributing to the other—in a van. Another young man we had interviewed for a position in our department was found a couple years later, dead in his vehicle on a back road. He, too, had died of a combination of alcohol and cold weather. These are just a couple of the tragedies I remember; there were certainly more. These tales of sorrow repeat over and over every year.

It was during my time in Ronan and my early efforts to fit in with the Native people I identified with more and more that I began reading Native writers like James Welch, Louise Erdrich, Joy Harjo, and Sherman Alexie. I also read Vine Deloria Jr.'s *God Is Red* and then, after finishing it, started again from the beginning. The works of these Indigenous writers breathed on the smoldering coals of my Native identity, and they only burned hotter as subsequent years unfolded.

I also reconnected to playing music in Ronan. A guy I worked with got wind that I had rock experience and approached me about joining him and a couple other guys in a band called Nobody's Heroes, a moniker swiped from the title of a 1980 record by an Irish punk rock band called Stiff Little Fingers. That was a fun group to play in. When we recorded a demo in Missoula, the studio was co-owned by two guys: Jimmy Rolle and Hank Donovan. Within a year or so Jimmy and I were playing in a band together called Lazerwolfs. When I moved to Ohio, we kept the band going; I'd fly home to Missoula every couple months and we would rehearse and even play a show or two. We held it together as a long-distance relationship until my return, and we still play together today, twenty-plus years later, in a band called American Falcon. Our friend Hank is killing it as the guy behind Rattlesnake Cable Company, making a living building all manner of guitar and speaker cables. Meanwhile Jimmy and I still await our rock-related "big break." It could happen any moment . . .

For all the challenges, at least there were Indians in Ronan and the surrounding area; the tribe had a strong, visible presence. This wasn't the case when I arrived in Ohio in February 2002, my life largely a shambles, the house I'd bought returned to the bank because who the hell could buy it when most of the boom in the area had drained away in the wake of all those layoffs?

All over that region of Ohio were places and landmarks bearing Indian names that didn't have any Indians. It disturbed me deeply. I was already familiar with the cringeworthy "frontier" writing of James Fenimore Cooper, foundational as my youthful experience with his *The Last of the Mohicans* was, and there were plenty more writers like him to uncover. While living in Sidney, the small town where my new employer was based, I read some of the historical fiction of Ohio writer (by way of Buffalo, New York) Allan W. Eckert. His Winning of America series carried titles like *The Frontiersmen* and *The Wilderness War*. As adventure stories set in the vicinity of my life "in exile," as I called it, they were fun in the same way as Robert E. Howard's Conan books. But to the growing hunger of my Indigenous consciousness, they fell far short of works from people like Harjo, Welch, Erdrich, and Deloria. As is all too common, Eckert's work, and those of his ilk, represents a settler historian playing fast and loose with the history, perspectives, and traumas of Indian people while uplifting the prowess of brave settler trailblazers, and I didn't care for it.

As grim as life under occupation for Indian people is out west, I find it far preferable to what I encountered in the Midwest. There's plenty to debate about reservations, but at least in the west they're centers of tribal life and community. Look at any US map of reservation land and you'll see they're all but nonexistent east of the Mississippi River. It saddens me to know there are Indians in places like Ohio, or the parts of Indiana, Kentucky, and Pennsylvania I regularly visited, disconnected by vast distances from anything recognizable as "Indian country," trying to reconcile who they are against what they see outside their window and all around them.

I would never claim to be an expert on the inner nuances of these regions, but in my experience, a grim "dark secrets behind white picket fences" vibe hid among the perfect lawns in many of the small communities. Scurrilous politicians like to dog whistle the region as being home to "real Americans" for good reason. My years there were uncomfortable, and I was eager to get away. I came home to Montana radicalized by the Bush wars and the politics of my coworkers, who gloated over everything he did, shared grainy videos of soldiers killing terrorists, and spoke seriously of how we should just "nuke" Iraq. It was an oppressive fog to live in, and I didn't do well with it. I reflected on the history of the United States and its dealings with Native people and came to understand that identifying a "terrorist" is largely defined by what side of the fight you're on.

I was also staggered by the erasure of Indians not just in Ohio but, in most of the places I traveled to, in almost every part of the country. If I ever doubted that Indians had been pushed to corners of the country, where they wouldn't be seen or heard, I certainly didn't now, because of all the places my work took me, it was almost never to those fringes. It was an enormous relief to be back under the big skies of my native, and Native, landscape.

CHAPTER 4

2013

MISSOULA, MONTANA

My committed journey to becoming Little Shell and making vigorous claim of my Indigenous identity begins on October 12, 2013. It's day three of the fourteenth annual Montana Festival of the Book in Missoula, Montana. Sherman Alexie—at the time arguably the most famous Indian writer in the country—performed to a sold-out audience at the Wilma to kick off the festival a couple nights earlier. And scheduled at the Roxy Theater is the debut of the film adaptation of Blackfeet writer James Welch's classic *Winter in the Blood.* Soaking up these events and the energy around them, Indians are much on my mind.

A presentation called "Overcoming a Western Legacy" is scheduled for two thirty at the Holiday Inn, the venue for most of the readings and panels. This presentation, in Ballroom D, leaps from the pages of the festival program and catches my eye; it will be presented by Nicholas Vrooman, a historian from Helena who's at the festival in support of his new book, *"The Whole Country Was . . . 'One Robe'": The Little Shell Tribe's America.*

I've heard of the Little Shell, but my knowledge is shallow. There was a recent article about the tribe in a regional magazine called *Montana Quarterly.* The article is titled "Waiting for the

Day." Its subtitle—"Montana's landless Little Shell Chippewa are emerging from 130 years of neglect and poverty, and they're dreaming big—even if the US government continues to deny their existence"—is an eye-opener for me, and I read the article intently. I've come to recognize that my family likely has roots with the tribe, but despite some interest, I haven't explored the possibility much. For all my talk of wanting to know, I've felt strangely resistant to the pursuit. After all the years of wondering, what if it turns out my family isn't Indian after all?

The name "La Tray" is all over the state. As I've said, my dad denies our relation to any of them, but the large turnout for my grandfather's funeral more than a decade earlier suggests otherwise. I hear of other La Trays even around Missoula; during a short stint of apartment living when I first moved back to Missoula in 2005, I had a La Tray as a neighbor. Julia held down a desk at a temporary employment agency for a short time. La Trays crossed her radar as well; one even sent her documents related to the family. When Julia passed them on to me, I ignored them. At the time, with all my doubts and uncertainty, I guess I just wasn't ready to know for sure. This time turns out to be different.

A book fair is set up in the spacious open area just down a flight of stairs from the Holiday Inn lobby. It's a noisy hubbub of people in knots of conversation or browsing offerings from various regional literary magazines and publishers. Long white plastic folding tables are laden with books written by festival participants. Besides names like Alexie and Welch, there's Andrew Sean Greer, Jamie Ford, Karen Joy Fowler, Claire Vaye Watkins, James Lee Burke, Robert Wrigley, and many others.

It takes some looking, but I find Vrooman's book. It's an oversized paperback, thick and heavy, like a university textbook. The cover is a reproduction of a painting by Paul Kane, an Irish-born Canadian who spent much of the mid-1800s depicting First

Nations people of the Northwest whom he encountered in his travels. This painting, titled "Half Breed Encampment," depicts Plains Métis of the Pembina River region, circa 1846. It shows an Indian woman beside a cooking fire, with rows of tipis extending into the distance behind her. Cattle and horses surround, and there are several two-wheeled wooden carts.

I pick the book up and flip through it with my thumb. Dense, small print fills the pages, as well as many grainy black-and-white photographs and color reproductions of paintings. I'm a little breathless. I turn to the index and quickly find a list of references to La Tray. There are eight. Next I look for Doney, my grandmother's family name. There are twenty-three references. I can hardly contain myself. I buy the book. There's no way I'm missing this session.

Ballroom D is a dull-hued and poorly lit conference room unrecognizable from its ilk in any other aging hotel anywhere in the country. There are long tables covered in white cloth, with glasses arranged around sweating decanters of water set at intervals on their surface. I'm one of maybe thirty people in the room. I find a spot near the back, pull out the metal folding chair tucked underneath, and sit down, alternating between bouncing my right knee and twiddling my thumbs. I feel an unexpected mix of excitement and anxiety.

Nicholas Vrooman is at the front of the room talking and laughing with a couple people in the last minutes before his presentation starts. He has a fringe of short gray hair around a mostly bald head. He wears glasses that can't hide pale blue, mischievous eyes, and he smiles and laughs regularly through slightly jagged teeth. He's a little taller than average, robust, and wears brown jeans, cowboy boots, and a pale button-down shirt, its long sleeves rolled just above his elbows and a ballpoint pen thrust into the breast pocket. Over the shirt he wears a cream vest embroidered at the edges of the lapels and left breast pocket in alternating bands of red, black, and turquoise. A flower—red with orange, black, and turquoise petals—is embroidered in the center of the pocket. In script below the flower are the words, "Metis '96."

"The foundational issue in the creation of the American nation," Vrooman begins, "is the dispossession of Aboriginal peoples of the land, and the genocide that occurred in that ongoing event, that actually remains a current issue."

I'm immediately captivated. No droning academic, Vrooman is an enthusiastic speaker. His voice, even without a microphone, booms loudly in the small conference room as he works through his presentation. There's a fire hose of information, and it comes so fast I can hardly keep up with my note-taking. Finally I give up, pour myself a glass of water, and just listen. There will be time to collect dates and names later. For now, I just want to absorb whatever I can.

Twenty minutes or so later, I feel like Nicholas Vrooman has altered the course of my life. I've learned more, and with greater certainty, about where I come from than I've known my entire life prior. His presentation concluded, several people approach Vrooman as he makes his way from the conference room, smiling and shaking hands. I sit, stunned, trying to absorb what I've just heard, feeling wave after wave of conflicting emotions. Elation. Fear. Excitement. Nervousness. As he approaches, I finally stand and move toward Vrooman. Face-to-face in the first of what will be many encounters, I tell him my name, how I'm now certain my family is tied to the Little Shell, and that I've been wanting to write about it but didn't know where to start. This last bit, the writing about it, is possibly the first time I've admitted the desire aloud.

Nicholas Vrooman laughs and smiles, and says that with a name like La Tray, I'm definitely Little Shell. Then he signs my book: "For Chris. Track it down. It's yours. All best, Nicholas Vrooman."

~

When I first met Nicholas Vrooman, he asked where I was from. I said Frenchtown. Almost offhandedly, he told me that was a Red River resettlement zone, too, like so many other communities around the state. It wasn't until deeper into my research journey that it really settled on me what he actually meant. It's part of why locating a copy of *Frenchtown Valley Footprints* was such a big deal to me. Frenchtown has been around a long time, longer than I realized.

Don't just take it from me, though. Writing in the October 1867 edition of *Harper's New Monthly*, in an article called "Rides Through Montana," no less illustrious a person than Irish nationalist, American Civil War hero, and an early territorial governor of Montana himself, Thomas Meagher, wrote of Frenchtown as "the oldest settlement in Montana, the first having been built there in 1857 by Mr. Moses Reeves."

Though spirited, the statement isn't true. Montana is a big place, and a busy one for at least a couple decades before Meagher got his ill-fated gig. (He would disappear under mysterious circumstances in Fort Benton less than a year later.) He did get the approximate date of its settlement correct, though. Historians like to argue, but one thing those who study the region can agree on is that Moses, or Moises, or Mose Reeves was one of the first settlers. Along with his father-in-law, Louis Brown, an older man named Baptiste Ducharme, and their families, Reeves settled the area somewhere between 1857 and 1859.

In *Frenchtown Valley Footprints* there's a photograph of a list of Frenchtown inhabitants, per the September 14, 1860, census. Of the more than twenty people listed—mostly the combined families of Brown, Reeves, and Ducharme (listed here as Deseim due to the language difficulties, translation, and illiteracy common to the time and location)—only two are listed as being of "White" race: Louis Brown and Moses Reeves. One person—Brown's wife, Emily—is listed as "Red." All the rest are "HB," or half-breed. Brown and Reeves are almost certainly "HB" men themselves, passing themselves off as white "French Canadians."

Claiming white ancestry if you could "pass" as white began early for Indigenous people and continues to this day. I have no record of my father ever identifying as anything but white. Now, with so many different shades of people marrying and having children and trying on and abandoning identities, it's that much more difficult to "prove" Indigenous heritage for those of us trying to, especially in a nation with such a narrow idea of what a Native person should look like. My dad never wanted to be viewed as Indian. I'm the opposite.

~

Vrooman's book exists because in 2010, the Montana legislature allocated funds to each of the state's tribes to produce a written history. The Little Shell, whom the state of Montana recognized in 2006 under Chairman John Sinclair, asked Vrooman if he would write their book. Vrooman, who was already doing work on the Little Shell's behalf to support their pursuit of federal recognition, was happy to oblige. The result of that request is the magnificent *"The Whole Country Was . . . 'One Robe'": The Little Shell Tribe's America*. I know this because Vrooman told us as much during that fateful 2013 presentation. The creation of this book is a key element in the inevitable securing of recognition for the Little Shell. Today, as I write in 2022, the book is long out of print and sells for upward of $1,000 online.

The vast majority of what I know about the Little Shell I owe to Nicholas Vrooman. I've picked up more bits and pieces in talking to other tribal members, visiting with other historians and scholars—armchair and professional—and reading books, but I stand on Vrooman's shoulders when I share what I know.

My initiation in the history of the Little Shell begins at the 2013 Holiday Inn event. Vrooman describes how various treaties and interactions with the United States government led to the creation of the landless Indians of Montana. But we're talking about negotiations like those initiated by appointed Washington Territory governor Isaac Stevens, whose journey west in 1853 paved the way for the railroad expansion. How settler colonialism forced Indigenous people to scatter across the high plains all the way to the northern Rocky Mountain Front and beyond in an effort to preserve a culture connected to dwindling bison herds. And finally the unconscionable Cree Deportation Act of 1896, where the United States tried to capitalize on calling any Indians not on American reservations "Canadian refugees" from the North-West Rebellion that exploded in Saskatchewan in 1885.

This is all history most of us have never heard before, and I sit with my notebook open in front of me, the pen forgotten. Every time the word "Chippewa" booms from Vrooman's mouth, a little charge goes off in my chest. These are the Chippewa people my grandma spoke of. My family. All those references in the index of *One Robe*. Elements of an "Indian problem" the US government attempted to solve through genocide.

The effort failed, but not without ramifications, namely a few thousand homeless and starving Indians nobody knew what to do with. The creation in 1916 of the Rocky Boy's reservation of Chippewa Cree people in north-central Montana was supposed to address the situation, but even that wasn't enough. There were too many people who had been pushed off their traditional homelands and not enough land the United States was willing to return to them. Essentially, all the people left out when Rocky Boy's was established are the Little Shell Tribe of Chippewa Indians today.

I've been to Rocky Boy's reservation on a couple occasions. It's beautiful, with broad rolling hills drained by creeks out of canyons nestled into the Bears Paw Mountains. If you pass the most accessible reservation entrance at the town of Box Elder just off Highway 87 headed north toward Havre, you have no idea what natural glories lie tucked away in the interior. I wish everyone who needed to fit there over a hundred years ago. How might my life had played out differently if we had? If I'd been born into that tribe? If my father and his father had? Who can say?

The Little Shell are related to all the displaced people who ultimately found homes at Rocky Boy's and on other reservations, a group of people who are directly related to the integrated history of the northern plains, but through a cross between miscommunication, misunderstanding, negligence—and not enough money—were left out of settling. As landless Indians living on the fringes, they became like houseless people in modern America. They were on the margins of society, buffeted by events largely beyond their control, and ultimately forgotten and ignored.

This "integrated history" plays out literally today, particularly in family names. You'll find names like Doney, Azure, and LaFromboise enrolled on just about every tribal roll in the state. Others too. Even before getting left out at Rocky Boy's, our people made homes and new relationships on other Montana reservations. I haven't encountered any La Trays enrolled with other tribes yet, but that doesn't mean there aren't any.

While the Little Shell—a formal name in use only since 1978, when the federal government finally established a path for unrecognized tribes to gain federal recognition—refer to themselves as "Chippewa" Indians, it's almost a misnomer. Chippewa is generally understood to be an alternate pronunciation of "Ojibwe" that resulted from European tongues mangling the word. But it's used interchangeably now by Indians and settlers alike to refer to a segment of the Anishinaabe people of North America. Consider the Anishinaabe as a vast umbrella sheltering a number of different individual tribes related by culture and language; besides the Ojibwe, other Anishinaabe tribes include the Potawatomi, Odawa, Nipissing, Mississaugas, and Algonquin people. In Canada, the Anishinaabe are the second-largest population among the First Nations people, while in the United States, they comprise the fifth.*

The makeup of the Little Shell Tribe is much more complex than the name might suggest. Chippewa is a good place to start when identifying the people, but the tribe is really a polyethnic amalgamation of what occurred culturally on the northern plains over three centuries, beginning with the seventeenth.

Westward expansion by European settlers backed by colonial institutions put enormous pressure on Indian survival. In response, Indians, as Vrooman described, "relocated, dislocated, intermarried, allied, and became new peoples." This intermingling included not just other native tribes, but the first wave of French explorers and fur traders, some Scots and Welsh among them, who pushed west of the Great Lakes region in the 1730s. Marriages happened, children happened, and generations of intermarriage among those children happened. Over time an entire mixed-race culture and ethnicity developed across Western Canada and the northern plains of what would become the United States. The resulting people became known as the Métis, from a French word for a person of mixed ancestry. The Métis were explorers themselves, working in the fur trapping and trading industry. Some took up farming and raised cattle, while others still followed the buffalo herds. By the 1850s, the Métis were a fully developed Indigenous society, with towns featuring a mix of established buildings and shops side by

---

* Important note here: Don't ever try to tell a Chippewa person they "aren't really" Chippewa but "actually" Ojibwe, especially if you're non-Native yourself. It's an offense punishable by a dead-eye stare at best, a punch in the face at worst, both equally justifiable.

side with lodges and tents; townsfolk living shoulder to shoulder with relatives who preferred to live more traditionally.

Over the last half of the nineteenth century, the Métis people tried and tried to establish themselves, only to be attacked, forced out, or otherwise displaced until there was nowhere else to go. This is a lost history few know. It's a history of my people. And whatever my father knew of it—and some of it he had to—he didn't share.

CHAPTER 5

2022

FRENCHTOWN, MONTANA

IN THE CLOSING PAGES of his timeless masterwork *Montana: High, Wide, and Handsome*, published in 1943, Great Falls historian Joseph Kinsey Howard writes of how one might go about defining what true Montana culture is. "It is a truism, of course," he writes, "that the degree of man's culture may be measured by the efficiency of his integration with his environment." That Montana culture, he figures, must then "effect a synthesis of all those which have gone before."

I love Howard's efforts toward defining this Montana culture, even if a lot of it is Western mythmaking at its highest level. These days, Montana is overrun with "all hat, no cattle" cowboys from other states driving $70,000 pickups to the local steak house, or to elected office bought and paid for out of their own wallets. Which, if you dig a little deeper into Montana state history, isn't so different from how it's always been.

Howard, who wasn't oblivious to that reality even in his day, grounds his idea of the state's defining traits in Montana's Native people—the Pikuni, the Cree, the Kootenai, the Salish, who "left Montanans a tradition of outdoor living, a regard for stamina and courage."

Next in line for establishing Howard's Montana culture are "the ill-starred Métis, whose nation was a vision or a mirage, a brief flame against the sky, projected from the brain of a mystic genius, Louis Riel. They were the voyageurs, the trappers, the great hunters; they were the ardent, fearless men . . . they helped to introduce Catholicism."

I knew of Howard's Montana book for years before I bothered to dig into it. It's a classic of regional history and on the shelf of just about any bookstore that sells Montana-focused titles. I grabbed it off the shelf of Fact & Fiction in Missoula only after being exposed, via Nicholas Vrooman again, to his other book, *Strange Empire: A Narrative of the Northwest*, which came out after his death.

Howard was only forty-five when he died of a heart attack in 1951. But he spent a number of years—and Guggenheim fellowships in 1947 and 1948—writing *Strange Empire.* That book, with its subtitle *The story of Louis Riel, the Métis people, and their struggle for a homeland on the plains of the United States-Canada border*, remains the go-to text for learning about the Métis, and I highly recommend it. Nicholas Vrooman is part of our story because of this Howard book; more than once I heard him tell the story of how, as a teenager living in upstate New York, he received it as a gift from his father and was transfixed. Vrooman wrote the introduction to the most recent edition of *Strange Empire.* Which might inspire the reader, at least a non-Canadian one, to wonder right out the gate: Who are the Métis?

There are many complexities to the events that led to the creation of the Métis as a distinct, postcontact Indigenous people, and I'm going to keep it as simple as I can. But there's an important point to make related to Joseph Kinsey Howard's assessment. The Métis aren't "ill-starred." We haven't gone anywhere and we're still here, stronger than ever, both in Canada and the United States.

The Métis story begins with the North American fur trade, at least as it relates to the Great Lakes region, and the establishment of the Hudson's Bay Company, or HBC. The HBC was incorporated by English royal charter in 1670, but it was originally pitched to them by two French guys, Pierre-Esprit Radisson and Médard des Groseilliers. Sometime in the 1650s, Radisson and des Groseilliers heard there were bountiful resources to the north and west of where all the fur trading action was happening at the time around Lake Superior. They originally approached the local French governor, but he wasn't having it, so the two looked elsewhere for sponsorship. They found it in the English prince Rupert, and the resulting chartered land became known, in his honor, as "Rupert's Land."

This was a vast territory that encompassed all the geography—1.5 million square miles—drained by every spring, stream, and river into Hudson Bay, a huge saltwater body named for English explorer Henry Hudson in the early 1600s. The bay itself encompasses 470,000 square miles and provides a water route to the Atlantic Ocean and beyond. Rupert's Land not only included a huge chunk of present-day Canada, but also extended south into the United States. The HBC authorities enjoyed complete control, and Rupert's Land essentially operated as a country all its own, though there were certainly periods where other players, like their sizable rival, the North West Company, complicated matters. Nonetheless, in the first forty years or so, the HBC established a half-dozen trading posts in key regions and then started counting their money. Imagine all the Walmarts in your community operating not just as the local supplier of nearly everything, but also essentially governing the region too. That's not so different from how this arrangement worked.

One important trader and explorer the HBC employed was a man named Henry Kelsey. In the summer of 1691, he left York Factory on the Hudson Bay loaded with trade goods. This was his second such venture, and his intention was to push farther than he had the previous year. Kelsey, who respected, traveled with, and got on well with Indigenous people, is believed to be the first European to come at the Great Plains from the north. He's also believed to be the first white guy to visit present-day Saskatchewan, possibly even as far west as Alberta. When he returned to York Factory the following year, he reported massive herds of buffalo, grizzly bears, and, most important, beaver. He also brought with him a contingent of Cree and Assiniboine Indians ready to do business for the first time with the HBC.

Ultimately the French wanted in on this action too. They sent a fur trapper and trader named Pierre La Vérendrye to the region to have a look-see. He journeyed from Canada in 1738 with his four sons and about fifty regular French soldiers. This company passed through the Turtle Mountains of present-day Canada and North Dakota and stopped at a Mandan village just shy of the Missouri River in December 1738. They couldn't push farther that spring, but two years later two of the La Vérendrye sons did, potentially as far as Wyoming. They're believed to be the first Europeans north of New Mexico to lay eyes on the eastern face of the Rocky Mountain Front.

It's entirely possible, even likely, that other adventurers and fur traders journeyed to North Dakota and points farther west from time to time between Kelsey's and the La Vérendryes' expeditions, but most free trappers and traders were illiterate. The La Vérendryes kept journals, though, so history gives them all the credit. Regardless, there are few records of anyone else in the area for more than another half century, when David Thompson arrives with his Métis guide, Jacques "Jocko" Finlay. Today's Jocko Valley—and its mountains and river—north of Missoula on the Flathead reservation are all named for Finlay. You'll see the name Finlay scattered all over the area, too, both as place names and family names.

Learning this detail—about "the Jocko," as I've always known it, and all the Finlay references—from books and online rabbit holes has entirely rewired my perception of where I live. Prior to all my sleuthing I never gave it more thought than any other Montanan who's bought into the notion that Lewis and Clark were the first. The larger picture concerning European exploration in the region wasn't anything I learned in school either.

With Kelsey and his men representing the English colonizers along the Saskatchewan/Montana border in the early 1690s, and then the La Vérendrye father and sons and their men less than five decades later representing the French, continent-shaping interactions began to take place in the form of mixed-race, mixed-culture children.

These children are among the first Métis. The word "métis" is French for mixed, or mixed-blood. When we see it capitalized, as throughout this book, it refers to the people who comprise the mixing of all these groups and cultures specific to this part of the continent: Indigenous women—mostly Ojibwe and Cree, and also some Assiniboine—and European men, primarily French (La Vérendrye's soldiers among the first). Some English and Scottish too.

"Thus there emerged," writes historian Verne Dusenberry, in one of my favorite explanations of Métis origins, "along the Red River particularly, a group of people who were neither Indian nor white; neither Chippewa nor Cree nor French, but a mixture of all three."

This vicinity, this Red River Valley on either side of the US/Canada border, is the region I'm writing from. Not because that's where "real" Métis come from—that's not for me to say—but because my people, my family, and my Little Shell relatives are generally recognized as having originated from there. There's a larger discussion going on in Canada even now as to who may truly call themselves Métis. I'm not entering into that with this book; no one from either side of the Medicine Line (the US/Canada border) will deny Red River Métis are who they say they are.

~

Beginning in the mid-1700s, this culture established itself. More marriages happened, and more children happened. Generations of intermarriage among these children, and with other Europeans and other Indians, also happened, and along the way the Métis people became something specifically their own.

This relationship between European and Indigenous people created a unique dichotomy of mutual need. First, the original "assimilation" that happened on this continent wasn't a matter of Indigenous people needing to blend in with their settler "conquerors." It was the other way around: the first Europeans to arrive in North America needed to assimilate into an Indigenous way of doing things or die. These first-arriving settler men simply weren't up to the task of surviving in a harsh and unfamiliar landscape without Indigenous help.

Meanwhile, Indians undoubtedly knew what was going on to the east with trade between settlers and Indigenous people, and were prepared for it. Looking forward to it, even. The Europeans had materials to offer that the Indians came to rely on. Conversely, as European traders set up posts, they weren't the ones venturing into the wild hinterlands to find fur-bearing animals. They relied on the Indians to bring those goods to them.

The resulting exchange wasn't just that of trade goods, but also culture. Both sides influenced the other in almost every aspect of living, just as such interactions do today. We like to think we're significantly different from our forebears of a few generations past, but we aren't. I'm certainly not. One day the Patagonia catalog arrives in my mailbox, and I'm thinking about how I might present myself accordingly (like almost every other Missoulian, it seems); the next day it's Filson, and I'm forced to decide whether or not I want to look ready for a spur-of-the-moment lumberjack competition. We're continually remaking ourselves through new fads and influences, and the people in the Red River Valley two hundred or more years ago were no different.

One of the most important, and often overlooked, elements of this exchange hinges on the complexities of marriage between European men and Indigenous women and how they shaped the emerging culture. Given the importance of women in the cultures of the Indigenous tribes most involved in this region and the ultimate creation of the Métis, the resulting identity couldn't have happened otherwise. These were unions not so different to marriages of alliance that had been happening in Europe for generations, with women as the focal point.

What makes métis/Métis then? When it comes to genetics, everyone was pretty much the same. But it was the way communities and individuals expressed themselves that created the unique cultural designations. Descendants of the first Métis set up their own communities and developed their own way of life. This Métis lifestyle blended the best of both worlds from their mixed European and Indigenous heritage.

Let's start with language. The Métis developed one of their own, called "Michif." Sometimes you'll see the people themselves referred to as Michif, which used to confuse the hell out of me. The word comes with various spellings, too, like "Mitchif." (The addition of the "t" makes me cringe.) This inconsistency is a common occurrence when dealing with records from this period.*

---

* It's even worse when tracing family names. For example, my own name, "La Tray," is from "Latreille" and is still used as such, mostly by relatives in Canada. I've thought of reverting back to that spelling with my own name, if only because I think it looks cooler.

Michif began as a trade language so that people from varying backgrounds could communicate. Based on French and a scattering of Gaelic nouns, with verbs from largely Ojibwe or Cree languages, it was a tongue people could use in mixed company and be able to reasonably communicate. It wasn't uncommon for Métis traders to speak as many as a half dozen of the different regional languages, which also made them valuable as interpreters.

Besides language, another critical blending of these multiple worlds appeared in clothing and fashion. As more Europeans arrived in North America, a new "global society" emerged, with the Métis among the first to express themselves as their tastes directed them. The result was a European/Indigenous fashion mash-up in every way imaginable.

My community is well sprinkled with Patagonia logos, as I mentioned, and lots of Carhartts, puffy vests, and beards. There are women dressed in athleisure from the mall like they plan to stop at the gym at any moment, and dudes in fly-fishing uniforms just in case a trout rises up in the Costco parking lot. Now and then there's the goth kid, or aging punk rocker, or Amish-looking family in the mix. All different expressions of anything from faith to fashion, but still all part of the same community. With new influences come new ways to express ourselves. Though the details may vary, I'm certain your community is no different.

Clothing was one of the most obvious outward expressions of the blending of European and Indigenous culture that the Métis were notable for. The women did the sewing, not to mention the tanning and preparation of hides. Beginning from a base of traditional materials—think moose hide or deerskin—they evolved to using cloth acquired through trade with the Europeans. A man might own a vest, for example, made by his wife from elk hide and then later, when he needed another one, she might make the same thing from velvet. Imagine the sigh of relief this woman might express when she didn't have to wrestle with (and brain tan) a dead animal just to make her man pretty enough to be seen in public.

It wasn't just the clothing materials that evolved, it was the styles and cuts too. Vests, pants, leggings, jackets, hats, moccasins, gloves, pouches, and bags . . . anything one could need. Additionally, derived from generations of Indigenous practice, just about everything was decorated with gorgeous bead and porcupine quillwork, often in flower patterns, such that the Métis became known by some as "the Flower Beadwork People." The floral designs were inspired by the Europeans, then combined with traditional Indigenous images, often in patterns specific to certain families. (This is similar to how tartan evolved from region-specific to identifying individual Scottish clans and families.)

Métis women mostly wore simple, high-necked dresses with puffy sleeves, or skirts with ribbons sewn onto them. Both were heavily influenced by European fashion and typically made with velvet, cotton, and wool. They wore shawls, often over their heads, and much of their garb—especially their moccasins—was embroidered with beads as well.

There are two items of clothing most recognizable as Métis fashion. The first is a long coat called a capote. These coats were a direct response to frigid north country winters, and trade around them was brisk. Often equipped with hoods, capotes were worn as outerwear over layers of clothing. When we see them depicted in art, particularly in the work of Western artists like Charles M. Russell and Frederic Remington, we often see the "blanket coat" version in which a Hudson's Bay Company point blanket is used. These blanket coat capotes are white, with the bands of indigo, yellow, red, and green horizontally striping them. The Métis also used leather and hide capotes, decorated of course, or wool capotes of a solid color, like blue or white.

William H. Keating wrote in his journal about a group of Métis hunters he encountered in the Red River Valley in 1823: "All of them have a blue capote with a hood, which they use only in bad weather; the capote is secured round their waist by a military sash; they wear a shirt of calico or painted muslin, moccassins [sic] and leather leggings fastened round the leg by garters ornamented with beads, etc. The Bois brulés [another name in reference to the Métis] often dispense with a hat; when they have one, it is generally variegated in the Indian manner, with feathers, gilt lace, and other tawdry ornaments."

A second defining item is a sash. It's worn in all weather, mostly by men, although women are known to wear them, too, especially today. The Métis adopted what was called the "L'Assomption" sash (also known as a "ceinture fléchée"), named for the Quebec town where they were initially produced. These sashes were ubiquitous among the Métis, and served multiple purposes.

Poking around on the internet one night, I found a wonderful article about the Métis sash. In it, Métis scholar Teresa Byrne is quoted as saying, "When I do my teachings on a sash, I explain that it's almost like a Batman utility belt." The men mostly wore this item around their stomachs because "most men died of hernias, so it became a weight belt."

Keeping the coat tied and preventing ghastly, painful death from lifting heavy objects were only a couple of the sash's uses. For example, the thread from the fringed edge of the sash could be used for patching things. Items—a knife, maybe a pipe and some tobacco, or some snacks—could be carried in it. Sweaty or filthy from trying to get a cart through a muddy washout? Wipe your face off on your sash. Toddler keeps running off? Tie him to a tree with your sash. One might use the sash as an emergency saddle blanket or, since life on the prairies was dangerous, prevent bleeding out by using the sash as a tourniquet.

The sashes we see today are the result of an evolution in bright colors. In the beginning, they were solid colors, and often symbolized the wearer's employer—say, red for HBC employees, or blue for those toiling under the yoke of the North West Company.

Eventually the Métis began making their own sashes, and from there started adding more colors, either as family designations or to be more decorative. In many cases, thread colors in a sash designate special meanings: green for growth and prosperity, perhaps, or blue and white to represent the Métis flag. Finally, the colors might be entirely personal to the wearer. As everything else in Métis fashion, the sash became more than a practical garment; it was, and remains, a means of personal expression.

Ultimately, whenever we see images from this period and region, whether in paintings, illustrations, or even early photographs, we have to be careful in considering what we're looking at. All these options for dress were constantly changing. For example, as the years passed, it was common for new fashions from cities like Edinburgh, Scotland, or Paris, France, to arrive in North America within the same year. These changes were then reflected in how people in North American chose to self-identify. Nicholas Vrooman once described to me an image of three men. One is dressed head to toe in a Victorian-era outfit—vest, topcoat, a rakish hat. Another is dressed in the Indigenous fashion of the day: deerskin breeches and shirt, with some beads and certainly moccasins. The third man wears a bright combination of the two. The realization is, these three men didn't necessarily represent three different cultures. It's entirely possible they were brothers, siblings, each self-identifying through their choice of dress how they wanted to present themselves to the world, just like we do with friends and family today.

Imagine the riot of color and style heralding the arrival of a group of Métis people, especially dressed to celebrate. What a scene that must've been, and continues to be, whenever there's cause to gather.

People don't celebrate without music, and that's a final piece of the Métis cultural puzzle. The Métis have always been a joyful people and never needed much excuse to throw a party. This included multiday celebrations over New Year's, or even just evening gatherings in a cabin or community space where all the furniture could be pushed to the side to make room for a dance floor. The usual suspects provided the rhythm—clapping, stomping, hand drums, and whatever metal utensils might be battered together to make sounds. But there was no more important instrument to Métis musical identity than the fiddle.

Hardly a more important instrument to the writing of this book either, if you must know. The soundtrack to *The Last of the Mohicans* is always in heavy rotation when I write. Both novel and film are set in 1757, and while neither is particularly known for historical accuracy, there are fiddle-based stretches of the movie's musical score that never fail to set my bottom lip to quivering.

The fiddle was first introduced to North America in the hands of the French and Scots and quickly became a key element in Métis expression. They learned to make their own, generally from birch and maple, because to buy or trade for them was too expensive. It's a jaunty instrument in skillful hands, and light and easy to transport for people regularly on the move. The music employed with these fiddles was usually upbeat and spirited to accompany high-energy moves on the dance floor. This dancing is "jig dancing."

Métis jig dancing evolved from eighteenth-century folk dancing traditions out of England and Scotland. It's typified by speedy, complicated footwork while the upper body remains composed. The faster the music, the more intricate the steps. It's an exhausting and exhilarating form of expression, and Métis people reveled in it. Not only was this fiddle playing and dancing a means of individual creativity, but it also brought people from widespread cultures together, connecting over a celebration of complete joy. A unique form of the dance that emerged was "the Red River Jig," which blended all these multinational influences.

I like to think of the Red River Valley and the communities that spread west as something akin to the bar scene in *Star Wars*, with many different people in numerous styles of dress, all babbling away in different languages, laughing and carrying on and giving one another side-eye. And then someone starts sawing on a fiddle . . .

~

It was with all this style and burgeoning culture that the first large groups of related families moved from their homes in the Red River Valley and Turtle Mountains onto the North Dakota plains. There was work to be done, and the bison were still there, if already beginning to dwindle. These early expeditions hauled back tons of goods to trading posts still connected to the rest of the world via rivers headed east and north. Buffalo hides and robes became critical to the trade, but it all really began with pemmican.

Pemmican was a food staple throughout the area, the trade of which at times was bitterly contested. It was made of dried meat—in this case buffalo—kind of like jerky, but mixed with whatever berries were available and held together by tallow, or animal fat. It was much sought-after because it provided a caloric hit well beyond its carrying weight. For many Métis, it was also their main source of income.

Both the North West Company and the Hudson's Bay Company wanted exclusive access to Red River Métis pemmican to such an extent that conflicts—known as the "Pemmican Wars"—over it caused a not insignificant amount of spilled blood and general mayhem starting around 1811. These altercations didn't subside until the two fur companies merged under the HBC charter in 1821.

Another root cause of these conflicts over pemmican was, unsurprisingly, a land grab. In 1812 the HBC "gave" a guy called Lord Selkirk 116,000 acres at the confluence of the Red and Assiniboine Rivers in the Red River Valley as a means of allowing him to lure more settlers to the region. The Métis were in obvious opposition to the idea because they already lived there and had for decades . . . longer if measured by the Indigenous side of their parentage, who were there first. By European perspective, and HBC charter, the people already there didn't own "legal title" to the land and were essentially squatters. This colonial influence raised the temperature on all the people in the region's interactions significantly.

By the 1820s, Red River Métis families traveled all the way to the Rocky Mountain Front and back twice a year to hunt buffalo and return with trade goods. As the last herds congregated in the Milk River region, the Métis simply moved there, establishing small settlements and homesteads. They were skilled buffalo hunters and, just as important, shrewd traders and entrepreneurs.

In 1815 a contingent of folks from Pembina and the Turtle Mountains also ventured south to what's now Missouri and Iowa. They brought back a herd of cattle and began breeding them as oxen for pulling their carts, which horses had previously pulled. This bursts another bubble of accepted truth about the northern plains and its cattle culture: the Anglo narrative of the Texas cowboy (as in Larry McMurtry's 1986 Pulitzer Prize–winning novel, *Lonesome Dove*) and the cattle drives up to Miles City are indeed fantastic, but the truth is that Métis were ranching cattle on the northern plains, including Montana, a long time before the Texas cowboys arrived. These Métis herds were well established by the 1840s.

The first major cattle operation in the Northern Rockies was started by a Métis family. Johnny Grant and his half brother, Richard, traveled from Canada in 1845 to join their father, Richard Grant, at Fort Hall. Fort Hall was the southernmost post of the HBC, located in Idaho, just north of Pocatello, and located today on the Fort Hall reservation, home to the Shoshone-Bannock Tribes. Richard Grant was Métis, and he ran the show at Fort Hall. This was a bustling community of predominantly Red River Métis people. From here, fur expeditions into the north—places like the Flathead, and as far west as Spokane, Washington—launched. The post also served to assist travelers headed west on the Oregon Trail.

When Johnny Grant joined his father, he started trading those westward travelers for their worn-out stock. He would pasture them, nurse them back to health, and turn them into strong animals again. After a few years of this, Grant relocated to the Deer Lodge Valley in Montana in 1850s, which quickly became a Red River Métis resettlement zone.

By 1860, the Grant operation was massive, with several thousand head of cattle. The base of operations was near today's Montana town of Deer Lodge, with a large main ranch house built in the fashion of an HBC "Chief Factor" house. The fur-trade era was largely over, but gold had been discovered a few years earlier at nearby Gold Creek (by Francois "Benetsee" Finlay, the Métis son of Jocko Finlay), and the area was booming with prospectors. Johnny Grant's cattle operations kept the mining camps well fed with beef all the way until 1866.

After the Civil War though, and its influx of what were essentially refugees from the Southern states arriving with distasteful views of Indians and "half-breeds," Grant decided it was too risky to stay. He sold the operation to his primary distributor, Conrad Kohrs. The remains of the operation is now a US National Historic Site called the Grant-Kohrs Ranch. The factor house remains. When visitors embark from the parking lot to tour the place, the first sign encountered along the way bears the same Paul Kane image that graces the cover of Vrooman's *One Robe* book, the one with the cattle and Red River carts. However, the sign makes no mention of Métis people.

This is a perfect example of what I've come to describe as an "Easter egg." A keen eye for these has been crucial to my research, and looking for them makes a fun sort of game. Métis contributions to the region have been largely erased by historians, who thought the Métis weren't Indian enough to be mentioned with the savages, but also not white enough to get credited for anything innovative or historically crucial. But the Métis are hiding in plain sight: sashes on characters from paintings by C. M. Russell and others, for example. And depictions of Red River carts popping up in the unlikeliest of places . . . unless you know how likely their presence actually is.

Johnny Grant wrote about moving his people back to the Red River Valley once and for all in 1867. When he "started for Red River quite a number of people came with me from Montana. Some were going to the States and others to the Red River. There were sixty-two wagons and twelve carts with about five hundred head of horses, two hundred of which were mine. There were one hundred and six men besides the women and children. I fed about sixty of the men and furnished most of them with horses and some with rifles. . . . I was the leader of the party, the men being divided into squads of ten with a captain over each squad."

Along the way, some of these Métis family groups split off to join family in other places, like the communities along the Front Range near towns like Choteau and Dupuyer. Over the years they spread to towns like Babb and Augusta, and many ultimately joined the Hill 57 community in Great Falls. These towns with their "Moccasin Flats" and "Breed Town" neighborhoods, spread across the landscape like island communities, comprise a term I've stolen, once again, from Nicholas Vrooman: the Métis Archipelago.

This dispersal across Montana is significant, so much so that in this part of the country, any historical references to "French Trappers" and "French Canadians" usually mean Métis. (Easter egg!) This speaks to one primary truth: it didn't take long before Indigenous Métis people, because of racist attitudes, would claim to be white if they could get away with it, which they did for generations.

Today the Métis are one of three recognized Aboriginal peoples in Canada, along with First Nations and Inuit people. Adam Gaudry, writing for *The Canadian Encyclopedia* that I found online, says, "While the Canadian government politically marginalized the Métis after 1885, they have since been recognized as an Aboriginal people with rights enshrined in the Constitution of Canada and more clearly defined in a series of Supreme Court of Canada decisions."

The 1885 marginalization resulted from the North-West Rebellion of 1885, when Louis Riel led a failed uprising in search of Métis independence from Canada and was subsequently hanged for treason. Riel's story, and the details of that conflict, have been written about extensively elsewhere—like in Howard's *Strange Empire*—so I won't speak much of it in these pages. The subsequent establishment and recognition of the Métis Nation as it exists in modern Canada is also beyond the scope of this book. But the Canadian Métis are our relatives; we are the same people.

We didn't cross the border. The border crossed us.

CHAPTER 6

2014

SIX MILE, MONTANA

I WAKE A LITTLE AFTER SIX in the morning on Thursday, October 30, 2014, and reach for the vibrating phone on my nightstand. The caller ID tells me it's my parents. My heart skips and stutters. It's one of those moments of panic that accompanies hearing from loved ones at odd hours, when the absolute worst thing is the first thing one expects. It's my mom; she's been trying to reach me for an hour, but my ringer is off.

It's a worst thing: "Dad died," she says.

The morning becomes a fog. I share the news with Julia. We get up and quickly prepare to make the twenty-minute drive to my folks' place. I send a message to my employer and give them the lowdown, tell them I don't know when I'll be back.

Soon Julia and I are on the way to where my parents live, maybe fifteen miles distant. The final stretch is four miles into the Six Mile, a road and a place to say you're from that was named after a creek. The road meanders into the forested hills north of the blink-and-you'll-miss-it town of Huson, which sits off I-90 some twenty-odd miles west of Missoula. Houses and driveways line the way as we pass. It's dark and wet and muddy, and I take it slow because of wildlife. Turkeys, raccoons, skunk, deer, elk—it could be anything. I pass a ponderosa pine where, just a couple years prior and in the same season, I photographed a mountain lion perched in its branches.

This area, with its horse and sheep pastures and myriad wildlife, is a picture-pretty example of Mountain West bucolic, especially in spring, when all is green and bursting with fresh life. The namesake creek, utterly clear and icy cold even in the depths of summer, twists through my parents' backyard. They've lived in this spot since we moved there in 1978. When the whole family was there—mom, dad, and my older sisters, Nikki and Mitzi—it was a single-wide trailer with an addition built on. I had a bedroom way in the back to myself, and my sisters shared what was originally two small bedrooms whose intervening wall was removed. My folks had a room in the addition, situated just off the living room. It made for cramped quarters by today's standards, but I have fond memories of the place. There was a big garden and a revolving cast of animals. Once us kids were all gone, my folks hauled off the original trailer and replaced it with a large, brand-new, manufactured home. The animal rotation continued—goats, sheep, cattle, horses. And always dogs and cats.

This larger home feels cramped this morning of my father's death, like most of the oxygen has already been breathed up. Every perception is compressed. Mitzi, who lives just up the road, is already here. She's sitting at the kitchen table with my mom and the coroner, an older man I've never seen before. I greet them; there are some tears, but so far I'm holding it together pretty well. I don't crack until I go into the bedroom, where my dad is still in bed. He died peacefully in his sleep. Mom says later she kind of heard him breathe in, cough, then that was that, and she couldn't wake him up. Now, though, I stand and touch his foot through the blankets. I can see him in the darkness a little, his head back, mouth slightly open, hands folded at his chest, and I don't turn on the light. My sister urges me to—"He looks beautiful," she says—but I can't. I just . . . can't. It's then that the tears come, when it really hits that what has allegedly happened actually has. I choke on sobs for a couple minutes, alone with my dad, my right hand still clutching his foot, then rejoin my family to wait for the funeral home people to take him away.

~

My dad's name is Sidney Robert La Tray. He was born in Lewistown, Montana, on November 10, 1940. We've met his parents already, also in the vicinity of their deaths: Leo Stanley La Tray and Ruby Katherine (Doney) La Tray. During his childhood, dad's family lived in the towns of Lewistown, Anaconda, and Hamilton, all in Montana.

Dad abandoned high school in Hamilton and enlisted in the United States Navy in 1958. He was a diesel engine inspector aboard the USS Acme (MSO-508), a minesweeper ship tasked with removing mines installed in the Pacific Ocean to prevent the safe passage of ships. He received his honorable discharge on February 18, 1962. Dad always spoke favorably of his time in the service, whether telling stories of the islands he visited—his ship was active in East Asia and on the Pacific coast—or the discipline the navy taught him for taking on the world once he left. When I was in high school, he made it pretty obvious he thought my best option was to sign up as well, but I never had any interest in it. He never discouraged them, but I can't imagine he thought much of my dreams of pursuing rock 'n' roll stardom.

I know very little else of my father. He essentially never spoke of his childhood and rarely shared specifics of his time in the navy. He had no close friends I know of. He wasn't particularly close with his family, and not at all with his extended family, which is extensive despite his denial of its reality.

There's this story in my family, almost apocryphal, about my father. I heard it on more than one occasion from Dad himself. I've also heard it from my oldest sister, who, during her few years working at the same mill, heard it from men who allegedly witnessed the event. I have no reason to believe it isn't true.

Dad is a young man at the time, not yet thirty, a few years removed from his navy discharge. It's early in his career at the mill in Frenchtown. Dad is leaning on a railing, on break perhaps. His foreman approaches, slaps him on the shoulder, and says, "How's it going, chief?"

An innocuous enough statement to our ears, but to my father, in that era—in any era—the comment was akin to squirting lighter fluid on a heap of red-hot coals. Enraged, Dad whirls on the man. A chase ensues from one end of the mill to the other. While machines belch and roar, the men lumber up and down metal stairways, steel-toed boots clanging along wall-hugging catwalks, until finally Dad catches the man. My young father is lean and mean, a confident six-foot tall and pushing 170 pounds.

"I grabbed that sonofabitch by the throat," Dad says in closing the story, through gritted teeth, "and I told him, 'Don't you ever fucking talk to me again.' And you know what? He didn't."

I tell this story because it's a snapshot of my father's life as best I know it. He was often kind and gentle; he loved animals, and he never raised a hand against anyone in my family that I can recall or heard of, certainly never to me. Yet he harbored a simmering rage that would erupt terribly at times, especially when aided by alcohol. He met any perceived slight with an unreasonable, knee-jerk belligerence. Many of his stories, and much of his advice to me, centered on physical confrontation.

"If you ever get in a fight," he told me more than once, "you've gotta hurt 'em. Don't think about fighting fair. You grab 'em by the hair, you do whatever you need to do to hurt 'em as bad as you can as fast as you can. Make sure they never want to fuck with you again."

Thankfully I never had to practice that advice, but I often wondered where it came from. Dad was a complicated man, and there were whiffs of stories I heard of his younger days that I tried to pry out of him with varying degrees of success. As I got older, had more conversations with my dad, and assembled the odd pieces of insight gathered here and there, it started to paint a picture of a life that was certainly far more brutal than mine has ever been. Growing up Indian in non-Indian towns certainly exposed him to conflicts that shaped his outlook, not to mention the abusive experience he suffered at his father's hands. His relationship with my mom—a marriage of fifty-plus years—was volatile, and his relationships with my sisters were, at times, rocky. I had my minor disagreements with him here and there, but I never questioned that he loved us all.

The mill where he essentially spent his life closed for good on December 31, 2009, forcing Dad's retirement. He didn't want to quit working, even though he was more than old enough to retire, and resented it. Much of his identity came from that mill, where he was respected and had an excellent reputation as a foreman himself. When the place shut down, Dad became even more of a homebody and didn't travel beyond the northwest (not that he ever really did), though he loved to drive all over Western Montana, Idaho, and Washington. An endless stream of tinkering projects on various cars, trucks, and tractors kept him out in his garage as often as not. Some of those projects he completed, but not many. Most of them never left the yard and driveway turnaround, turning into rusty heaps—or "storage units," as we liked to call them—waiting for eventual disposal.

Dad's passing wasn't unexpected. He'd suffered various maladies for years. When I moved back to Montana from Ohio in

2005 it was clear he was ill, and I urged my mom to get him in to see someone. She'd tried, but he wasn't having it. His physical state deteriorated in slow motion. Living close to him, it wasn't as noticeable for her, or him, but his condition was immediately apparent to me. Thankfully he relented and went to see a doctor.

A string of health crises ensued: His heart was failing. He had a kidney removed. A couple years before his death, he had a stroke and had only recently regained the use of his right hand. Through it all, he remained a heavy drinker.

When I think of the years he worked at the mill, it seems to me he stayed just long enough to get so sick he wouldn't have much of a life afterward. His health would decline, then he'd bounce back, sometimes miraculously, and he and I often discussed the things we would do when he "got better." At the end, though, I'm certain he was ready to go, and went willingly. Less than two weeks from his seventy-fourth birthday, it was a small miracle he'd lived as long as he had.

~

We sit around the kitchen table. There's some chatter, even a little laughter. My mom is doing pretty well, but when the funeral home people arrive, she turns away because she doesn't want to see him "that way." They work quickly, and I catch a glimpse: Dad's form wrapped in dark plastic, as they negotiate the gurney out through the front door.

A short time later, the phone rings. It's my dad's older brother, Leo Gilbert La Tray, whom we've always known as Uncle Gib. Except I don't know him; he wouldn't recognize me if he saw me and, out of context, I wouldn't recognize him either. He's calling to tell my dad he's just learned that their sister, Sharon, died several days earlier. Instead, Uncle Gib learns that of his immediate family, all are dead but him.

I'm trying to reach my son, Sid. Sidney Robert La Tray II, to be exact. He's twenty-one at the time of Dad's passing. I call and call to give him the news, but he isn't answering. Instead he calls me some hours later. He learned of his grandfather's death on Facebook; Nikki, living in Iowa, posted of his passing. That's one of the hardest moments of this entire ordeal, not being able to tell my son myself that his grandfather has died, having him get the news over fucking social media instead. It still hurts deeply today.

In these initial moments, I don't know what's to come. I know my dad never wanted a funeral, and that he'll be cremated. But I don't know that we'll never get together as a family in any kind of ritual to honor his life; I know now as I write that me, my mom, and my two sisters won't even be in the same room together for another four years, during the event to celebrate the release of my first book in 2018. I don't know that my mom will attempt to keep the place where she and my father lived for so many years, but it's just too big, too remote, and requires too much maintenance for her to manage on her own. She sells the place, gets a new one of her own closer to town and, quite possibly, is happier than she's ever been.

Other things about my father's passing still haunt me. I know Dad loved us, but he wasn't always the easiest person to get along with. As his health deteriorated, he became more volatile and unpredictable. We were never estranged, but our relationship stretched to breaking on several occasions in his later years.

When I came back from Ohio and worked as a remote employee, Dad respected the work I did, even if he didn't really understand what I did when I was away. He respected the work all us kids did. He was a "work ethic" guy. Show up on time, don't call in, do a good job. If nothing else, my dad raised three hard-working children.

But he never seemed to get that if I wasn't on the road, it didn't mean I wasn't working. When I moved back to Missoula, I set up an "office" in a spare bedroom in my home. The way things were configured, a customer could call the number in Ohio for support, and it would be routed to the extension on my desk in Missoula. I could then do remote support over the phone; I could even log in to a customer's system through my laptop to troubleshoot problems. It's common now, but when I first came back, it seemed like a kind of sorcery. Finally, if I wasn't practicing this web-based, long-distance, arcane drudgery, I was writing work instructions and technical specifications for our programmers, which I would then test and later install.

Dad assumed my time was free if I wasn't out of town. This caused a lot of frustration, for both of us. He made a habit of calling and asking for my help with one thing or another: attach the mower to his tractor, or come help haul some hay, anything like that. I did my best to assure him I was always happy and available to help; I just needed a day or two notice, if at all possible, unless it was an emergency. But I rarely got notice, and it was never an emergency. Dad would call, ask if I could help with something, and when I responded, "Sure, when?" the answer was often, "How about now?" If I couldn't help, he would get angry, as if I wasn't willing to help, and all but hang up on me. It made me crazy. I recognize now that, in many ways, he probably just wanted to see me, to spend some time with me, and his seeming anger was maybe frustration that things weren't going the way he wanted. At least that's what I tell myself.

The last time I ever spoke to him was one such occasion. On the weekend before his death, we made a plan for me to come and help split and stack some firewood. It was something I did several times, a project I came to enjoy. It was a family effort. I would split the wood, and my mom would help by gathering up the pieces and stacking them along the fence opposite their front door. Dad would sit in a plastic chair, or lean on the fence, and "supervise." It was generally enjoyable; it allowed us to spend time outside together, and it felt good to perform physical labor in the wake of all the ass time my day job required. If and when he got surly for one reason or another, it was easier to blow off. Afterward we'd drink a beer, if time and moods allowed for it.

The last morning we planned to get together, in the final half of October, Dad called. It was gray and a little drizzly outside. Not the best weather, but certainly not the worst considering the season. Dad suggested we postpone, because it was supposed to rain harder that afternoon. I was happy to oblige. I don't know what else I thought I would prefer to do instead to justify the relief at the change of plans, but I was relieved. I was liberated, free to pursue whatever. I assured him it was fine, that maybe we could get to it during the week or the following weekend. "I'll see you soon," I said.

"I hope so, Bert," he said, using my childhood nickname. "I hope so."

We hung up.

We never spoke again.

~

Thinking of that woodpile reminds me that one of my fondest memories of my parents' house, both when I lived there and after I moved away, is of the wood stove. Burning wood is its own special kind of heat, and I love and miss it. I've written many times about the winter cold of my bedroom, which was at the opposite end of the house from where the stove was in the house I largely grew up in. But being in the living room *with* the stove was another story. The sliding glass door to the covered porch was always open as an invitation to the cold air; that porch is also where an imposing wall of firewood was stacked. There was also a big plastic thermometer hanging at the roof level of the outside porch opposite the glass door. Often when I pick up my phone to check the weather app, I hear my dad inquiring of anyone close to the window, "What's the temp?"

It was the same story when my folks replaced that house with this new one years after I left, and how the sliding glass door just left of the stove, which led out to the deck, was almost always open to cold, fresh air, minus the thermometer.

But in either case, that stove, because it was so warm and centralized, became the hearth where everyone gathered during the dark, cold season. My favorite season, in fact, even with its melancholy. Family, pets, everyone in the same room, if not stretched out in front of the stove itself. Not to mention the communal effort of gathering the wood, splitting and stacking the wood, filling the woodbox inside, throwing more wood on the fire. So different from just twisting a knob on a thermostat, isn't it? What a pathetic little gesture, yet then like magic every room in the house is roughly the same temperature, but no one is gathering around a heat source, and there's no tub of stew or pot roast simmering on top of the same source making everything cozy—or even just a pot of water to defend against dry air. Another case where convenience isn't progress, to my mind.

Wherever my parents live contained that family hearth, even after we all went our separate ways, and my dad, for all of us, for better or worse, was central to it. His recliner forms a perfect triangle in the living room with the stove and the open sliding glass door. After my dad's body is removed from the house, I stand in the living room, my back to the stove, and look at my dad's chair. Beside it is a small table stacked with newspapers, crossword puzzles, and a book. I recognize the yellow cover immediately. It's a copy of *The Lone Ranger and Tonto Fistfight in Heaven*, by Sherman Alexie.

I'm immediately reminded of the moment, some months previous, when Dad asked if I ever heard of this Indian writer named Sherman who wrote a book about the Lone Ranger. I was astounded for a couple reasons. First, my dad wasn't a book guy, and here he was asking about one. And second, he was asking about an *Indian* writer. I don't know where or how he'd encountered it, and I didn't ask. I told him that of course I'd heard of it and offered to give him my copy. He told me he would like that. If he ever so much as cracked it open, I don't know, but I'm happy to see it here anyway.

Days pass. The folks in Ohio send me a bouquet of flowers, and I'm back on the clock almost immediately. Life goes back to a certain kind of normal. For some of us it takes longer; for some of us it's a daily reckoning with the new reality. There's an enormous shift inside that occurs that never shifts back, and it's difficult. How can it not be? Working on this book while reckoning with the change has been one of the largest hurdles in the entire process. As each piece of knowledge about who we are and where we come from is uncovered, I wonder, *Did Dad know this?* and he's not around to ask. Being from a "close-mouthed" culture, a description of our people I'll hear over and over in the coming years, it's entirely possible he didn't know much. But I'll never know the extent of his knowledge of our history, or be able to share it with him, and that makes me deeply, deeply sad. I know my dad was smart and keenly perceptive. He knew far, far more than he ever chose to share. I'm certain of it. He was just close-mouthed too.

I keep a text file, as I'm sure many people do, of quotes I encounter that I appreciate. This is one of them: "The worst part of mourning is realizing that at some point other people no longer care." My friend Mara told me that once. Her words stuck with me because she's absolutely correct. Aren't we all mourning something, all the time? Maybe if we paid better attention to that in our interactions we would be more compassionate toward one another; I don't know. It's difficult, mired as we are in our own dramas, to care much for others. But how can we not?

It takes several weeks before I have a true moment of mourning for my father's death, beyond the brief minutes in the room with his body. On a late night when I can't sleep, I decide to watch the movie *Smoke Signals*, a wonderful adaptation of Sherman Alexie's short story "This Is What It Means to Say Phoenix, Arizona" from the Lone Ranger and Tonto book. This film is one of my favorites, hilarious and sad and profound in so many ways.

In the closing scene, the character called Victor takes the can containing the ashes of his father and shakes them into the churning waters of the Spokane River, while in voice-over the other main character in the film, Thomas, recites the Dick Lourie poem "How Do We Forgive Our Fathers." It's a powerful poem. That moment, those words . . . it's too much. I break down and weep at my desk like never before. Wracking, shivering, snot-gushing sobs.

I sometimes wonder if my father's death was the catalyst I needed to get serious about writing this book. I had strands of it tangled in my fingers before he died, but I was hesitant, even fearful. What would he think? Regardless, with his passing I took up the project in earnest. I like to imagine he would appreciate it.

CHAPTER 7

2020

COUNCIL GROVE, MONTANA

It's a gray evening in late May 2020 just before twilight, on one of my favorite walking trails in the world. It's a loop just barely over a mile, and only that far if I keep to the outermost edge of its circuitous route and avoid various side paths and shortcuts back to the parking lot. The stretch I'm traversing on this occasion weaves through an expanse of robust ponderosa pines, several large enough to be more than a couple hundred years. They're magnificent beings, thick of limb, whose bark on hot summer days emits such a strong scent it's like walking through a cloud of vanilla. It's intoxicating.

This trail passes behind a towering, precipitously leaning old snag stripped entirely of bark; it's craggy, pitted, and pale and streaked in shades of tan and ocher, with jagged and broken limbs jutting out in every possible angle and direction. I call it the "condominium tree" because of all the bird species that live in it. Pileated woodpeckers have hammered holes up and down its length, their pale wood shavings in a permanent mound at the base of the tree. At any given time the occupants of these holes might include a northern saw-whet owl, American kestrels, and, in a large hole a third of the way down from the top, a nesting pair of great horned owls.

This year the owls have produced three owlets, and they're all arranged at various levels in a pine rising beside me. I'm here with maybe a half-dozen other walkers, out enjoying the early attempts of these young predators to learn to fly. The mother owl is in a different tree maybe fifty feet farther along the trail, seemingly paying little attention. It's a gift this place provides, the yearly opportunity to watch for the nesting to begin, then the first little faces with wide yellow eyes to poke out from the nest, then the first awkward forays into the world by the fluffy newcomers.

The owlets aren't doing much tonight. Mostly jerking and twisting their heads to see what's happening below while shifting their weight from one taloned foot to another. The other walkers point and chuckle for a few minutes, then continue on. I'm alone with the owls.

Then it happens. As if on cue, the three owlets stand upright and swivel their heads to the east. Instantly alert, the mother takes to the air and flashes across the sky, disappearing behind intervening treetops. Moments later, a gigantic bald eagle comes winging through the forest, as if following the very trail I stand transfixed in the middle of. She's not a dozen feet over my head. I can hear the swooshing as she slowly strokes the air with her wings. She's so big! Just above her and slightly to the side is the mother owl, trailing her as if in escort formation. She's making the strangest low, grunting whistles the likes of which I've never heard an owl make before. The two birds pass directly over me and disappear into the farther trees. The owlets are gyrating up and down, up and down. I would laugh if I weren't so dumbstruck.

The mother owl returns to her tree and perches as if nothing happened. The owlets settle back onto their perches. Slowly a single downy feather floats down from above, looping back and forth in the air as it descends. I hold up my hand and it settles into my palm.

I pause another moment, then continue on my way, astounded by what I've just witnessed.

~

Ever since I was young, one of my favorite things to do has been rambling around outdoors. Part of this is the result of being a child of the seventies in a household with essentially no television, living in a landscape nothing indoors could ever match. This place, where I witnessed the owls, is such a landscape. It's called Council Grove State Park. It's a few miles west of Missoula just off Mullan Road, on the banks of the Clark Fork River. There are large stands of old-growth ponderosa pines, gigantic cottonwoods, and open meadows. Its footprint encompasses 187 acres and is designated as a "primitive" state park, which means further development is prohibited. There's no visitor center and no on-site staff. There's a vault toilet and a few picnic tables and nothing else . . . except for a large monument that details the historical significance of the place.

Council Grove is where the infamous July 16, 1855, council between Superintendent of Indian Affairs and Territorial Governor of Washington Isaac Stevens and members of the Salish, Kootenai, and Pend d'Oreille Nations took place. This 1855 treaty, known as the Hellgate Treaty of 1855, created the Flathead reservation to the north, now home to the Confederated Salish and Kootenai Tribes. You can learn all this from a large weathered sign that discusses the events around the negotiation, located just a short stroll west into the park. This negotiation is key to as dark an episode as any in the history of relations between the United States and Indigenous people, one whose ramifications reverberate here every single day.

I bring all this up because I've fallen in love with the CSKT reservation, the land, and its people. It's the only reservation I've ever lived on, as I've mentioned, even though I'm not a citizen. In coming to know my history, though, I've also seen how deeply connected me and my people are to the CSKT people and every other tribe in the state. One of the common connections we share is in our dealings with Isaac Stevens. It's one worth spending time with.

~

In 1853, Isaac I. Stevens was headed west to take up his post as governor of the newly organized Washington Territory, which included Montana land west of the continental divide. Stevens, a West Point graduate with a distinguished record of military service, resigned his commission in March of that year to take charge of the expedition. His mission included the mapping and surveying of land for a railroad route that would connect Chicago with Seattle via Minneapolis. A large part of this process was identifying which Indian tribes were located where, and attempting to secure safe passage for the future railroad and the settlers who would come after.

Settlers were already beginning to stream into and through the region and create conflict with resident tribes. The United States made its first efforts to organize which tribes went where through the 1851 Treaty of Fort Laramie, recognizing the Indigenous people mostly south of where Stevens was traveling. This territory stretched from southwest North Dakota south all the way to the North Platte River in Nebraska, then west to Wyoming and back north into the very southeast corner of Montana.

The Fort Laramie Treaty didn't so much take land for the Americans (that came later) as allocate territory to the eight participating tribes. These tribes included the Sioux, Cheyenne, Crow, Arapaho, Assiniboine, Mandan, Hidatsa, and Arikara. Besides recognizing the traditional lands of the various Indians (the determination of which was rife with contention among them, particularly over the Black Hills), the treaty sought to establish peace among the Indians, provide safe passage to settlers passing through (which included the building of roads and forts), and, in return for coming to the negotiating table, allocate about $2.5 million to the tribes over fifty years. Suffice it to say, agreements didn't hold up.

For Stevens and his railroad-related responsibilities, negotiating peace between the Blackfeet and the allied tribes, which included the Nez Perce, Salish, and Pend d'Oreille (all tribes left out of the 1851 Treaty of Fort Laramie, but who, like the Pembina Chippewa, certainly had representatives there and knew what went down) was a critical piece of his expedition. His railroad surveying duties also determined who the players were, then he went back later to negotiate the treaties.

The results included the Hellgate Treaty of 1855 in July and, in October, the Blackfoot Treaty, referred to as the Lame Bull Treaty by First Nations people and the Judith River Treaty by Montana's Blackfeet. Article 1 of the treaty states simply that, "Peace, friendship and amity shall hereafter exist between the United States and the aforesaid nations and tribes of Indians, parties to this treaty, and the same shall be perpetual."

Much like the one at Wyoming's Fort Laramie, the Stevens treaty outlines boundaries, shared hunting grounds, and who's allowed to go where. It demands peaceful relations among the signatory tribes, as well as peace toward other tribes, except when acting in self-defense. It also states that none of these tribes will be allowed to establish any permanent structures within the agreed-on territories. Meanwhile, as stated in Article 8, the tribes consent and agree that

> the United States may, within the countries respectively occupied and claimed by them, construct roads of every description; establish lines of telegraph and military posts; use materials of every description found in the Indian

> country; build houses for agencies, missions, schools, farms, shops, mills, stations, and for any other purpose for which they may be required, and permanently occupy as much land as may be necessary for the various purposes above enumerated, including the use of wood for fuel and land for grazing, and that the navigation of all lakes and streams shall be forever free to citizens of the United States.

This is where the connection to my people, among them those whose descendants would become the Little Shell Chippewa, come in. While the Blackfoot Treaty is pretty much a checklist for implementing settler colonialism, what's notably missing in the documentation is any mention of concessions or arrangements made with the local Cree, Assiniboine, Chippewa, or Métis people, except, as stated in Article 2 relating to the Cree and Assiniboine, as potential adversaries. The reason for this is these tribes were to the north of where Stevens mapped the railroad. He was most concerned with the Indian nations directly in his path. To his mind, the Native people not mentioned, whose territory was almost exclusively north of the Missouri River, would be dealt with via additional treaty arrangements negotiated later.

Later never came.

On April 12, 1861, not long after Abraham Lincoln's inauguration as president of the United States, secessionist forces attacked South Carolina's Fort Sumter. The Civil War was on, and it raged bloodily until April 1865. Isaac Stevens left Washington Territory in 1857. He fought for the Union during the war and was killed at the Battle of Chantilly on September 1, 1862.

When the smoke cleared and the country began staggering back to its feet, one of the first things the renewed United States government decided was they were finished trying to draft treaties and make peace with Indian tribes. This practice had been going on since

1778. In the ensuing century, over five hundred treaties had been entered into, and broken, by the rising colonial power. In 1871, the US government ceased viewing tribes as independent nations they could contract by treaty, so they stopped even bothering to try. The time was ripe for a gruesome campaign of genocide, the extent of which most Americans are utterly unaware, against just about anything that lived in what would become the American West.

Over the next three decades, as war raged across the region and the bison herds were eradicated, treaty land was "renegotiated" or, in most cases, stolen outright. Six of the seven reservations in Montana—the Blackfeet, the Flathead, the Crow, the Northern Cheyenne, Fort Belknap, and Fort Peck—representing twelve tribes were established during this time, all except the Chippewa Cree reservation at Rocky Boy's, which didn't come until the second decade of the twentieth century.

~

Much of this seems like ancient history to many people, the "olden days" as we used to call them as kids when we chased each other around with toy pistols and rifles. The reality is that it's a living, ongoing history that deeply affects the lives of many people every day.

For example, writing this, I reflect on how often news of the day carries references to the Fort Laramie Treaty 170 years later. It usually involves tribes and tribal members exercising hunting rights the treaty guarantees, and the resulting backlash when modern American ideas about land and land ownership are superseded by treaty negotiations a few generations past. These treaty documents aren't dead either, they live on in the lives of the descendents of those people, who did their best to protect future generations by participating in their creation.

Council Grove is just a couple miles from where I live. I go there almost daily to wander the trails and watch for birds and other wildlife. I acquired whatever skills I've attained as an amateur naturalist there. It's a place of beauty as well as a scene of tragedy. There are many gigantic ponderosa pines with massive cones that were certainly there to observe the negotiations.

I know its history because I've made the effort to learn, and what I know are just surface details. Mostly the knowledge comes from books and online resources like articles and videos. At some point I think I'll make a deeper exploration of this history in an effort to honor the land I live on.

I often tell people that if you only have time to study one interaction between the American government and Indigenous people, the 1855 Hellgate Treaty and the horrible blow it dealt to the Salish people is as good as any. It's not a difficult story to track down.

This negotiation, contentious and perfectly illustrative of the worst of bad faith negotiations between the federal government and Indian nations, is key to the region's future as it relates to the relationship between the United States and the Indigenous people of the area. The ultimate result of this contested treaty, which was ratified in 1859, included the removal of the tribes to today's reservation. It took a long time to unfold, though; the final bitter result is the forced march in 1891 of the remaining Salish under the leadership of Chief Charlo, broken and starving, out of the Bitterroot Valley, across the Clark Fork at Missoula, and north to the reservation.

It's a trail of blood and tears. So many tribes have a similar tale. Including mine.

Of all the geographical locations I'll talk about throughout this book, none is more important to my personal history, at least as an adult, than Council Grove. This is a recent unfolding though, because in all my years growing up in the region, I don't recall ever visiting the place. Not for recreation, and not as part of a school field trip, which seems unconscionable given how important it is to what might be the penultimate historical event defining the region. This is also a good example of whitewashed, sweep it under the rug American history: I don't have any recollection of learning about the Salish and their history at all in the twelve years of education I received less than ten miles from this very spot. I've had to learn it on my own, reading books and clicking around online. It's all out there; one just needs to seek it out. Not enough people do.

I moved into the region in February 2013 after crawling out from under too much house in Missoula proper. Julia and I, with four dogs and two cats, settled into a manufactured home in a subdivision about a dozen miles west of the city. (We like to call it a "trailer park" when in reality it isn't one, managed by "Lahey," but that isn't the name of the manager. If you know, you know.) At the time I still worked for my Ohio employer and traveled extensively. I was sinking into depression as the strains of the work took their toll. I was indulging in probably my worst habit: food. I ate horribly on the road and then doubled down when I came home. My girth, which had been reasonable just a couple years earlier, ballooned. I have a photograph of myself seated at my mom and dad's kitchen table—the one we gathered around while waiting for the hearse the morning my dad died—when I'm at the peak of my size. My dad took it with his phone a few months before he left us. When I look at it now, I see me at arguably the height of my unhappiness. It's not so much being fat; I was always one of the largest kids in my class, and took all the ridicule and shaming that went along with that. It's mostly that at that size, I see someone—me—who's not living the active life that makes him the happiest. There were a couple bouts of tendonitis in my knee, a consequence, I suspect, of diet, weight, and stress that left me hobbled, frustrated, and gurgling with self-loathing.

Our pets had been with us for the better part of a decade by the time we moved, and we knew once we started losing them, there would likely be a quick and grim succession to follow. And there was; we just didn't know how quickly it would come, and that it would include members of our human family too. We lost our first dog, a legendarily crabby eighteen-year-old Jack Russell terrier named Orly, in June of that first year, less than four months after we moved. Slightly more than a year later, in the fall of 2014, my grandmother Doris died, and my dad followed less than a month later. Then we lost another dog—Velcro, also a Jack Russell—to a malign tumor three days after my dad. Bernard, the big dog (an alleged golden retriever / German shepherd mix whose true origins were always in dispute), died a couple months later, just two days shy of New Year's Day 2015. We found ourselves with one dog—Darla, another Jack Russell*—and two cats, Kitten and Puny, pets I'd taken from Ronan to Ohio and back to Missoula again.

This was also the year I "discovered" Council Grove. Julia and I had taken the dogs there on a number of prior occasions. I have a handful of cherished photographs from an outing there with the remaining canine trio just a couple months before two of them crossed over. But it wasn't my place yet, not until we were down to just Darla.

I've written extensively about my time with Darla the Adventure Dog and how, in my grief over my father's passing, I began taking her on regular outings to Council Grove. My first book, *One-Sentence Journal*, is in many ways about our relationship and how her companionship, enjoyed in this beautiful place of wild water and birds and old-growth pines, pulled me back from the brink of despair. Our near daily outings, broken only by my trips out of town for work, gave me back my life in many

* What can I say? Julia has a thing for Jack Russell terriers, and I admit to having grown a certain fondness for the little buttrats too.

ways. It certainly reconnected me to the outside world, something that was slipping away from me in my depression. Most of that happened at Council Grove.

My father's death was largely the catalyst for that reckoning, and Darla was the vehicle. When Dad died, I reflected on his life. He'd worked so many years at the mill, and for what? He gave his life to that place, and by the time its shutdown forced him into retirement in 2010, his health was so compromised—not so much by mill conditions, but who can say for sure?—he didn't have much of a life for the four years he lived after. I looked at my health, which was clearly on a downward turn, and the years I had ahead of me. How did I want to live them? Did I want to stay in service to employers that could toss me aside at a whim whenever it suited them? I'd already experienced that once. I said no and resolved to make a change.

I began a yoga practice the day before my father died. My second class ever was literally hours after he was taken away, and I spent much of the time prone on my mat, fighting back tears. But I kept up the practice. I also began my regular Council Grove excursions with Darla, and made time for longer hikes whenever I could manage it. I also began planning my employment future, or lack thereof. Julia and I hung a whiteboard on the wall next to our front door with all the items we would need to square away for me to leave my current job. We titled it "Freedom 17," because the plan was for me to leave in two years.

I only made it through 2015. A minor disagreement with my employers pushed me over the edge, and I said fuck it. I'd had enough. It wasn't so much the going places that bothered me, though I'd certainly had my fill of airports and aircraft and shuttles and the mindless litany of inconveniences I had no control over as a business travel drone. My work had me in industries I not only wanted nothing to do with helping succeed, but actively wanted to see fail. Think oil pipelines, fracking operations—industries propped up by the planned obsolesce of useless products that found their way to store shelves after months at sea crammed into containers on ships that leaked fuel from shore to shore, continent to continent. That stress, as much as the food choices and inactivity, was killing me. So ready or not, when the year rolled over into 2016, I was unemployed.

My plan was to be a writer. I was already a freelancer of sorts; I was writing regularly for the *Independent*, Missoula's late, great alt weekly, and had published articles here and there in a couple other publications.

It's hard to realize now that at this point, I was already more than two years removed from my encounter with Nicholas Vrooman and his *One Robe* book, though ideas about pursuing my ancestry still churned in my head, especially during those saunters under the watchful eyes of those old ponderosas.

In another year, they would begin to take shape in earnest.

CHAPTER 8

2017

GREAT FALLS, MONTANA

IT'S A MUGGY DAY ALONG the Rocky Mountain Front in early July when I set foot for the first time in the council chambers of my people. A nondescript office building in Great Falls, Montana, is the tribal headquarters of the Little Shell Chippewa tribe. By now I'm pretty confident I'm Little Shell. The purpose of my visit is the first step in attempting to prove it.

The first certain encounter I ever have with a Little Shell member occurs when I walk through that door in Great Falls. At the time of our meeting in 2017, Terri LaRocque has worked for the Little Shell for three years. She's tall, close to my six feet, and seems around my middle age. She has brown, lightly freckled skin and dark eyes. Her hair, with a few streaks of gray, is cut in a short bob. She's wearing a white T-shirt that displays the silhouette of a buffalo, and the words "Little Shell Tribe Wellness Program." She's attentive to my questions and smiles frequently.

Terri was born in Lewistown, same as my dad, though several decades later. When I tell her my name and my suspicions about where I come from, she laughs. "With a name like La Tray," she says, "you're definitely Native!" Her uncle is a La Tray, Frank La

Tray. Whether we're kin or not, I don't know. I assume so, as I've come to with all La Tray encounters.

I tell Terri how I've come to be here, how I grew up in a family that denied our familial history. She tells me she understands. The story of my father and his unwillingness to embrace his Native heritage is familiar to her. "There are many people of a certain era that will deny it," Terri says. "I don't know if it is racism, or if they were feeling disenfranchised in some other ways. But I hear about it a lot."

Terri's story is different. "I've always known that I was Native," she says. "But I was in high school when I finally got enrolled." Terri was headed to college and wanted help for school in the form of an application fee waiver, so she enrolled as a member of the tribe. What she received didn't amount to much—about ninety dollars, she says—but it helped. Besides the education, she was also after a sense of community she'd lacked growing up, when she attended five different high schools in towns with few or no Native communities. As a landless Indian she wanted to participate in Native clubs in college to have more of an experience of being around other Native people.

It's a sentiment I can relate to; a similar one led me to gather the information I needed to submit my own enrollment application. To reconnect. To belong to something. That's how I end up in Great Falls.

∽

My search begins online. Surely modern Indian tribes will have relatively modern web presences to communicate with their people, right? Some do; the Cherokee Nation, for example, the largest tribe in the nation based on number of enrolled members (over 450,000), has a fairly robust site with many links to resources, clever maps, and a scrolling display of current news items.

Searching for the Little Shell site, my first stop is a website maintained by the state of Montana. The Montana Governor's Office of Indian Affairs—"established in 1951 by the Montana legislature to facilitate effective tribal-state communications with special attention to the discussion and resolution of issues that Indian peoples face regarding their unique political status and as full citizens of the state of Montana"—maintains a website with links to information on all seven of the state's reservations, which serve twelve tribes. There are seven reservations in Montana. They include the Blackfeet reservation (Blackfeet Nation, Browning, Montana); the Flathead reservation (Confederated Salish, Pend d'Oreille, and Kootenai Tribes, Pablo, Montana); Fort Peck reservation (Assiniboine and Sioux Tribes, Poplar, Montana); the Crow reservation (Crow Nation, Crow Agency, Montana); the Northern Cheyenne reservation (Northern Cheyenne Tribe, Lame Deer, Montana); Fort Belknap reservation (Gros Ventre and Assiniboine Tribes, Fort Belknap Agency, Montana); and the Rocky Boy's reservation (Chippewa and Cree Tribes, Rocky Boy's Agency, Montana). Finally, there's the Little Shell Chippewa tribe, state recognized, headquartered in Great Falls. A consequence of having no federal recognition is that the Little Shell don't have a reservation either.

The state's website is fairly adequate in describing the Little Shell, if a few years behind and more pretty than informative. There's a short video about the tribe and contact information—address, phone number, etc. There's a link to the official website and a link to the "Constitution and By-Laws of the Little Shell Chippewa Indians of Montana" that, when clicked, is broken.

I click to the tribe's official website. The site opens on an "About" page that has a single paragraph about the tribe's history. Clicking "Culture" from the menu options provides three more paragraphs. The council members shown on the "Government" page are up to date, but on the "News and Events" page, information is sparse and nothing is dated, so I have no idea if it's current or not. There's a "Little Shell Member Update" option that links to a PDF of a letter from Gerald Grey, the tribal chairman, that's also undated, and appears to be at least a year or two old.

The lack of information is disappointing but understandable. Websites cost time and money. For a tribe that, as I've since learned, funded their operations essentially via bake sales and raffles up until fairly recently, there aren't a lot of resources to keep up a web presence. Volunteers perform all the work, and web presence probably isn't much of a priority. I want more, though. I want people who hear the words "Little Shell" to be able to get on the internet and learn something from the source. Sadly, the curious won't find much here. Appearance is everything online, and at this time the Little Shell website is far from adequate. It leaves me depressed.

My search isn't a complete bust, though. There's a menu option called "Forms." There I find links to four different PDF files, and the first is the one I want: the Little Shell enrollment application. Jackpot. If I can meet the following requirements, I'll be enrolled, presumably, in the Little Shell Tribe. There's a simple enrollment application form—name, address, etc. I need to submit that with a check for twenty dollars. I need a birth certificate to prove who my parents are; that's simple enough. Finally, I'm required to compile a family tree as far back as I can determine. Particularly, as far back as my great-great-grandparents. Not an easy task given that the entire paternal side of my family, besides an uncle I can't say I know—the Little Shell side—have passed on.

∽

For Christmas 2016, my mother gave me one of those DNA test kits from Ancestry.com. She'd sent one in for herself and was excited about the results, and wanted to know if I would be interested in learning what it had to say about my DNA. It seemed a good idea at the time, and I was eager to find out. Or I thought I was. Once I had the kit in hand—a little tube for collecting my saliva and a return mailer for sending it back to the lab for analysis—I didn't immediately proceed. I realized I was fearful of the results. What if it turned out there wasn't any "Indian" in me at all, that the stories I'd heard all my life were false? What would I do about the identity I'd created for myself then? Eventually I screwed up my courage and sent the tube in, then waited.

The test results were more a curiosity than anything else. Ancestry told me I'm "20 percent Native American" and 68 percent "Great Britain and Northwestern Europe." Curiously, it claimed I'm only 3 percent French, despite the areas with the most instances of my "closest DNA matches" being in the regions of "Saint Lawrence River French settlers," "Montreal and Detroit French settlers," and the "Québec Rouge River Valley French settlers." Those clustered spaces did more than any allocation of DNA percentages to make me feel I was on the right track.

An article from the *MIT Technology Review* titled "2017 Was the Year Consumer DNA Testing Blew Up" reports that more people took genetic ancestry tests in 2017 than in all previous years combined, exceeding 12 million people. The service I used, Ancestry, reports having tested "more than seven million people, including two million during the last four months of 2017. The company's customer rolls exceed those of all competitors combined."

In 2018 the industry kept rolling like a juggernaut. Again, "as many people purchased consumer DNA tests in 2018 as in all previous years combined," *MIT Technology Review* reported, with the total number exceeding 26 million as of February 2019. It's a huge consumer business, bolstered by staggering advertising budgets. DNA testing has been discussed at our highest levels of public discourse, particularly how the technology might be used in the future to connect people, mostly to the economy. Others howl about the willing surrender of such deeply personal, private information to corrupt capitalists and their databases.

Most relevant to my purposes at the time is the hornet's nest kicked over by 2016 Democratic presidential candidate Elizabeth Warren. She has long claimed Native descent through a distant Cherokee relative. Rising to the bait (I would argue stooping to it) of President Donald Trump, who never shied from referring to Warren with insipid racist remarks, the United States Senator from Massachusetts took a DNA test, which "proved" she has a splash of Native American DNA.

If her intention was to somehow gain Native support, the plan backfired. DNA is a hotly contested issue in the Native community, and it should be. Just because one has Native American DNA doesn't make one Indian is what the argument boils down to. To suggest Indian-ness based on a few strands of DNA from a distant relative is to ignore all the day-to-day ties that comprise an actual community, a belonging that one doesn't have just because they share similarities with people at a genetic level. Investigations around the incident uncovered instances of Warren checking the "Native American" box for race on various forms early in her education and career, which led to a chorus of accusations she did so only to take advantage of any benefits such racial status might incur. She's just one high-profile example of this too; it happens all the time, particularly in academia.

In her book *Native American DNA: Tribal Belonging and the False Promise of Genetic Science*, author Dr. Kim TallBear, an enrolled member of the Sisseton-Wahpeton Oyate tribe in South Dakota, describes how, "Genetic concepts further support the ownership of Native American history, bodies, molecules, and identities by whites." TallBear has devoted her career to the study of how technology and science (technoscience) have contributed to the ongoing colonization of Native people. She also studies how tribes themselves will govern in this growing, and constantly changing, world of high tech, and how it all relates to tribal sovereignty. It's a dangerously slick slope for everyone, not just Indian tribes. After all, the DNA sample of your average Métis person is quite a boiling pool of genetic representation when viewed through the lens of a platform like Ancestry.com.

I'm not without sympathy for Warren's situation, at least on the surface. Who knows the environment she grew up in and how her family was introduced to and interacted with their alleged Native heritage? Was she confused about her own identity? It's easy to look at her and say, "That woman is as white as any white woman." The same could be said about me in my ability to "pass" as a white man. It's also easy to be cynical and assume that any politician who has reached the heights Warren has constantly speaks out the side of their mouth or says what they think the listener wants to hear, if only to further their own ends. But I've been in similar situations myself. Faced with a form that forces me to check my race, I've struggled at times. My father chose "caucasian" on my birth certificate. I've chosen to identify as Indian whenever possible, as long as I can remember. He had his reasons, I have mine. I want to own what he chose not to.

Where my Ancestry test helped the most was in tracking down my relatives. Exploring the Ancestry.com website is a fascinating experience of descending into a familial rabbit hole, where hours can disappear in what seems like minutes. Then again, because I'm less familiar with rabbits, perhaps a better analogy would be exploring a prairie dog town, where mounds and holes scattered over a vast prairie landscape unexpectedly descend into myriad interlocking tunnels and side passages that can easily lead one astray and into a universe where time doesn't exist, let alone matter.

The Ancestry.com website layers a graphical user interface atop a genealogical database that must be mind boggling in size and complexity to the folks shackled to its maintenance. All the research anyone has ever done as it relates to one's ancestors—in my case the Doneys and the La Trays—are linked through their relationships, largely from people all over the country—the world, even!—who add whatever bits and pieces of family lore they can to the data. I've never considered myself particularly interested in genealogy, but for several nights in a row I was captivated. The database doesn't just track relationships—who married who, how many kids they had—but offers photographs, official census documents, and marriage licenses and birth and death notices . . . just about anything you might imagine. It's overwhelming and all but blew my mind. It was like going through an old family museum I didn't know existed, all from the discomfort of my low-budget desk chair at home.

I managed to avoid paralyzing distraction. To complete the Little Shell paperwork, I needed to trace only so far back as those great-great-grandparents to determine what my relationship was to the tribe, and I remained pretty focused on it. I suspect my task was simpler than it might be for others because I was only concerned with one side of my parentage, my father's. While equally important to who I am, my ancestors on my mother's side, all exclusively of European descent, would have no bearing on my enrollment as a Little Shell member, so I didn't have to provide that side of my heritage.

I knew my father and my grandparents going in. I keyed their names into the interface. I called my mom and got the names of my great-grandparents; she was pretty certain who my great-grandmothers were, but was a little less clear on who their husbands were. What she gave me was good enough. Even a half-dozen years ago there were clearly many La Tray and Doney people tracking their family history, because the information I needed came in a wave. Just typing in those five names I knew—Dad, Grandma and Grandpa, and both my great-grandmothers—got me where I needed to be. I scratched the names of people I'd never heard spoken of before onto the printed PDF form. Names I was certain my dad had to have known; people he had to have known, but never spoke of.

When I walked into the Little Shell headquarters on that afternoon in 2017, these three or four generations of people fleshing out my family tree were still just names on a piece of paper. Bits of information I was required to gather. I was curious about who they were, but against the bigger picture of who the Little Shell people were, it wasn't that big a deal to me. I never even went back to Ancestry for a couple years. Is that callous? Maybe. It's hard to know how one should feel about family connections when you've never had many, or to imagine such connections could be different from what you've experienced. I was after something bigger, or thought I was. In my ignorance at the time I didn't realize just how key the names on that family tree, and who they connected me to, would be to this entire journey.

It wasn't until two years later that a real interest in who my relatives were as people blossomed. During dinner with my cousin at her home in Great Falls, she handed me a business card for a woman named Sandra Kennedy. Kennedy previously worked with the enrollment office for the Little Shell and was responsible for significant contributions to the gathering of genealogical data. I never met her in person, but she graciously sent me a ten-page printout of my family tree from the Little Shell side of things. It's a broader family history than what I explored online, and through its breadth the connections of people, the "kinship ties," are more apparent. By then I was farther along in learning about the tribal people who predate being called "Little Shell," so the names gained greater significance. Where we came from, how we found ourselves landless, where we were born and ultimately traveled to—my family tree is an excellent snapshot of how related everyone who came from this landless Indian community really is. There's even a "LeRocque" in my ancestry (if spelled slightly different, which is typical; Doney appears at times as spelled but also as Lyonnais, Delauney, Lonais, and Delaunais—go figure), ensuring that Terri and I are related to some degree.

Still, if I hadn't been able to build that initial family tree of my father's side of my family over the course of just a few dedicated evenings of referencing and cross-referencing data from Ancestry.com's gigantic genealogical database, it's likely I wouldn't have written this book. The process was revelatory, perhaps more in retrospect than I realized at the time. I don't know that I could've built my family tree without it; certainly not nearly as quickly. I doubt I would've encountered Sandra Kennedy's business card and had the bigger picture revealed to me. Gathering this critical information so quickly was akin to crossing North America via jet airliner instead of an ox-drawn, two-wheeled cart.

Back in Great Falls, chatting with Terri as she reviews my forms, I express the challenges I faced in gathering them. I describe my angst over the possibility the Native identity I'd always claimed might turn out to be false. That maybe even the route I'd taken, leaning so hard against a DNA database to learn who my people are as opposed to living among them, might reveal me to be some sort of wannabe. She nods. I'm sure she's heard similar stories.

"It's too bad your dad isn't enrolled," she says, almost as an afterthought, "because then you would only need to be an eighth."

Ah, those fractions, so quick to the tongue in any discussion of tribes and their enrollments. Indian "blood": The real dark cloud roiling over Indian country. Something that doesn't exist, that's entirely a colonial fabrication, yet is the measurement that almost exclusively determines one's viability for tribal membership. Blood quantum.

CHAPTER 9

2017

BROWNING, PABLO, AND MISSOULA, MONTANA

WHAT IS "BLOOD QUANTUM" ANYWAY? At its simplest, Indian blood law (i.e., blood quantum or BQ) was passed to determine and regulate who's classified as Native American in the eyes of the United States government. After the Indian Reorganization Act of 1934, BQ was adopted at the urging of the federal government as the way most Indian tribes determine tribal eligibility as well. BQ sets a minimum percentage of "Indian blood" a person must have to be enrolled as a member of a given tribe. It's quasi-science at best, patchwork arithmetic at worst, and based on an entirely arbitrary set of determinations in its origin. It's also incredibly divisive in Indian country.

BQ is defined as percentage of so-called "full-blood" Indian a person might be, going back as far as possible among their ancestors. For instance, a person who has one parent who's a full-blood Indian and one who has no Indian ancestry has a blood quantum of 1/2. Most tribes set their requirement for enrollment at 1/4. But in a majority of Indian tribes it doesn't really mean Indian blood, it means blood of that specific tribe. Most tribes don't recognize other tribal blood relationships in determining the BQ number for someone enrolling within their tribe. In the scenario above, let's say the father was full-blood Salish and the mother was full-blood Blackfeet. When it comes time to determine BQ, any children the two have are still only going to have a BQ of 1/2 when it comes to enrolling with either tribe.

BQ is a product of what has become known as the "allotment era." The allotment era refers to the General Allotment Act, or the Dawes Act, adopted in 1887. The Dawes Act, enacted during a time when more settlers were heading west and demanding more land, was created with the singular purpose of wresting more of that land from Indian tribes who had already been pushed into the tiniest fragments of their previous ranges. Those fragments—Indian reservations—were unavailable to settlers. The purpose of the Dawes Act was largely to change that.

An amendment in 1906 (the Burke Act) allowed the secretary of the interior to determine an Indian as "competent." If an Indian was deemed competent, they could get a fee patent to their land (essentially a deed of ownership) and pursue a "civilized" life. The land, which started as an "allotment," would no longer be held in trust by the federal government as Indian (reservation) land and could also now be taxed or sold off like any other parcel of private land. As a result, many of these people and their tribes ultimately lost their land altogether, often due to an inability to pay taxes on land they'd never had to pay taxes on before to a government of a country they were still a couple decades away from being allowed to be citizens of. It was a government grift from the get-go. The result was thousands of homeless Indians and reservations carved into chunks of Indian land checkerboarded with larger and larger swathes of private, non-Indian-owned land.

One of the standards the feds began to use to determine competency—competency a cynical reference to the ability of an

Indian to be something other than a savage who needed to stay put on a reservation—was how much Indian blood an individual had. The less Indian blood an individual had—say, a quarter or less—the more likely they were deemed capable of integrating with civilized society. To determine baselines, then, the federal government scattered Indian agents across Indian country. They set up tents all over tribal territories and advertised for people to come in and be added to the census rolls.

Of course only a fraction of any given community showed up. The idea of lists of "who belongs" was totally antithetical to any sort of notion of what community meant to Indian tribes. The standards were set by settlers with no concept of how Indians traditionally identified themselves or determined tribal membership. Regardless of "blood," tribes had been expanding their ranks from outside the tribe for centuries, and those adopted members and their children were as welcome a part of the community as anyone. These new rules and lists the feds sought ignored such traditional practices.

Indian agents, often barely literate and certainly ignorant of tribal languages and customs, did whatever it took to get the job done and would just "make shit up if they had to."* In the eyes of the federal government, these original rolls, accurate or not, became the official membership rolls of tribal nations. It was an entirely fabricated process designed to generate some kind of documentation as a means to wrest even more land away from Indians. That's the root of BQ, just like all Indian policy up until that time. It was an effort to dispossess land and holdings because

* I owe my foundational knowledge about BQ and the Dawes Act to my friend Monte Mills, professor and codirector of the Margery Hunter Brown Indian Law Clinic at the Alexander Blewett III School of Law at the University of Montana, who described the highly technical "make shit up" process in a conversation we had in 2017

that was the intent of the allotment era: to destroy tribal culture and tribal governance.

Those census rolls, valuable as historical artifacts but essentially useless as any kind of meaningful document of a people, contain the names of tribal members that serve as the baseline for tribal membership today.

I didn't have knowledge or opinion of blood quantum, let alone a personal relationship to it, until I faced being judged by it. Of course I'd heard of the idea of "Indian blood" and been asked many times "how much Indian" I was whenever the subject of my Indigeneity came up. It still happens today, and often. When I was ignorant I, like just about everyone else, thought it was a legitimate thing, like a human could be of different measurable blood types based on where they come from. But we aren't. If we were, like giving blood at the clinic, you'd think people could go in for a couple pints of Blackfeet or whomever just to boost their BQ, right? But no, it's not like that. And to base the state's interpretation of who I am, let alone the modern iteration of my tribal ancestors, on such an arbitrary and divisive system is ludicrous.

But facts and fractions and numbers and dates of when evil legislation was passed as part of the ongoing efforts to erase Indian people make the most curious of us scratch our heads, if not lose interest entirely. I decided I needed to hear from modern people who faced the difficulties of such an inane process. So I turned to a handful of my friends.

"Blood quantum is only about who you choose to breed with," says Robert Hall of Browning, Montana, headquarters of the Blackfeet Nation. He tells me this as we sit outside in East Glacier on a bench near the eastern entrance to Glacier National Park. His hair is wild and poofy in the breeze, and he wears a Hogwarts T-shirt.

Robert is still a young man, a bit taller than average with dark hair and dark eyes, and one of the smartest and funniest people I know. Last I checked on Twitter, before it became X, he still had a large following, where he hilariously and succinctly lambasted every instance of anti-Indian ridiculousness that crossed his path—both from inside the Native community (where vicious lateral violence is the norm) and out.

Robert is currently the director of Blackfeet / Native American studies for Browning Public Schools. To get there he earned a BA in Native American studies, a BA in anthropology with an emphasis on linguistics, a certificate in language maintenance and rejuvenation, and a master of interdisciplinary studies through the University of Montana. His thesis was titled "Theories on the Pedagogy of ASLA (Accelerated Second Language Acquisition)." He has been formally recognized and honored for his advocacy and protection of the Blackfoot language.

Both of Robert's parents are enrolled Blackfeet yet he isn't. The Blackfeet adopted blood quantum in October 1962, and any child born after that time requires a BQ of no less than 1/4 to be enrolled. Robert's father, born before that date and part of a family that has lived in the area for more than a hundred years, has a BQ of less than 1/4 but remains enrolled. After running the math between Robert's mother and father, Robert arrives at a fraction of 15/64, 1/64 shy of what he needs to be considered Blackfeet by the tribal council. It's a travesty.

Robert's biggest gripe about his exclusion is that he's denied the right to vote in tribal elections—the right to help guide the future of his people. They're his people regardless of his enrollment status: He speaks and teaches the language. He knows the culture as well as anyone. He's lived on the reservation his entire life. Yet he isn't considered truly Blackfeet by a set of rules the Blackfeet tribe continues to let override their sovereignty in protecting their people's long-term survival.

"Every single movement that has moved the world forward socially has been through a vote," Robert says. "Nonenrolled people don't have this opportunity. To undermine the power of a vote is to undermine sovereignty. Black activists have spoken about 'the sacred right to vote.' And I believe in that."

These BQ requirements, which essentially force Indian people to have children only with people "of their kind," are an interesting contrast to a controversy on the opposite side of Glacier National Park from the Blackfeet reservation. The small city of Whitefish is the former part-time home of neo-Nazi activist Richard Spencer, whose greatest claim to fame might be getting punched in the face on live TV while attending Donald Trump's 2017 inauguration.

"Richard Spencer gets coldcocked on TV and people cheer because he's a white supremacist," Robert says, "but if I do that to someone here on the rez who's pro–blood quantum, I'm an asshole."

Where is the difference between white supremacists advocating for whites not to mix with other races when Native tribes, at the urging of the federal government, essentially force the same thing on their members?

"There is no new full-blood being introduced into our gene pool, ever," Robert says. "Not unless we find out there's Indians on Mars or some shit."

~

What does BQ look like from the perspective of someone engaged in the government of their tribe? Or from the perspective of a mother? To get this answer I drive less than an hour north of my home near Frenchtown, to the Flathead reservation and the CSKT headquarters in Pablo. I've arranged, via an email and a couple phone calls, to meet with my friend Shelly Fyant. At the time of our conversation, Shelly is a member of the tribal council. In two years she'll actually be voted chairwoman of the tribe.

Shelly invites me into the CSKT council chamber for our discussion. In the pale, natural light from skylights above, padded chairs, each with a computer monitor facing it, are arrayed behind a heavy, raised wooden desk that forms a half circle in front of a smaller facing table. Above the chairs are two taxidermized buffalo heads and oversized black-and-white portraits of former tribal chiefs Charlo, Alexander, and Big Knife.

Shelly has personal experience in how BQ rules split families. The CSKT has amended their enrollment requirements several times. Prior to 1953, any Native blood from any tribe was counted when considering an applicant for enrollment, so long as the combination added up to one quarter blood. After 1953, though, only Salish or Kootenai blood would be considered. Mixed-tribe families found themselves with children before 1953 who were enrolled, but children born after that new cutoff date whose BQ number fell below 1/4 due to a parent not having Salish or Kootenai blood could not be. This fracture creates a domino effect of subsequent generations being denied access to whatever benefits their family has earned from being in a particular place, sometimes for many prior generations.

"The whole concept of enrollment and how we do it is just a colonized way of thinking," Shelly says in a quiet voice. "They [the federal government] had it in mind for us to eventually wash out and dissolve into mainstream society. But we wholeheartedly adopted it, and continue to adopt it."

Shelly is soft-spoken and fierce. She's tall and graceful, with long, gorgeous hair. As I write in 2022, she's no longer an elected member of the CSKT government, but she remains active in Indigenous social justice, particularly as it relates to tribal food sovereignty. Shelly has been married twice and has children from both marriages. She has two sons who, despite being raised Salish and being Salish in culture and lifestyle, are enrolled into tribes on their paternal side that they've never been a part of. They're contributing members of the Salish community but aren't allowed to be "legally" part of it. The same can be said for Shelly's mother, who has lived on the reservation and participated in its culture for decades, yet can't be adopted into the tribe because she isn't Native.

"In traditional society and as part of our culture we always adopted other people from outside the tribe into our own tribe," Shelly says, "if only to keep us all from being inbred. So to try to keep anything 'pure' Salish or 'pure' Kootenai, it doesn't make sense traditionally, if you want to go back far enough."

And "back far enough" isn't even all that far. Just a couple generations, in fact.

Why care about being enrolled anyway, given all its hassle? There are a number of reasons people think being a card-carrying member of a tribe—or a "papered" Indian—is an advantage. Money is a big one. I'm constantly surprised by how many people believe that being an enrolled Indian living on a reservation is some kind of free ride on the backs of American taxpayers, or that all Indians are rolling in the fruits of casino wealth. That there's some financial reason for someone to seek tribal enrollment even if they aren't Native.

To explore this question I didn't even have to leave Missoula. I sought my friends Migz and April, and we meet in their little upstairs apartment just off the "Hip Strip" area of town south of the Higgins Avenue bridge. They're in their final days living in Missoula, about to head out for work elsewhere.

"The idea that there is this monetary thing to being an Indian, or being enrolled, is incredibly false," says my friend Migizi Pensoneau.

Migizi, or "Migz," is a writer and filmmaker who earned an MFA from the Institute of American Indian Arts in Santa Fe. Since the day we met in Missoula in 2017 he has gained producing, writing, and acting credits in such excellent Indigenous television shows as *Reservation Dogs*, *Barkskins*, and *Rutherford Falls*. Migz is an enrolled member of the Ponca Tribe of Oklahoma, though he has spent hardly any time there. Instead, he grew up in Minnesota among his mother's Ojibwe people.

His partner, April Youpee-Roll, elaborates. "It's true that there are some very wealthy casino tribes that give out very generous per capita payments to their members," she says. "But there are also some very pernicious myths about all Indians, like free college, or this idea that we're all sort of living on the federal dole, and in my experience that doesn't exist. At Fort Peck, we would get seventy-five dollars from the tribe's coffers at Christmas. And that's it."

April is an enrolled Dakota from the Fort Peck reservation. She grew up in Poplar, Montana, in the far northeastern corner of the state. Once she graduated high school, she earned a degree in sociology from Harvard University. After that, she went on to graduate from law school at the University of Montana in Missoula. Her first gig postgraduation is what's luring the couple out of Missoula. Today April is a litigation associate in a Los Angeles law firm. Her practice focuses on complex civil litigation and investigations, and she also maintains an active pro bono practice in American Indian law.

I love these people, and writing this chapter reminds me of how long it has been since I've seen either of them. We laughed a lot that day and took some photos when we finished chatting, but I don't realize at the time how long it will be before I see them again.

They're a hilarious contrast. April is small and bubbly while Migz is soft-spoken and towers over her. Both wear glasses and, like me, are kinda nerdy. Both are incredibly smart and erudite, too, as all of us higher-quality nerds are. The couple have traveled a long way since we sat in their tiny upstairs apartment in Missoula having this conversation. I admire and miss both of them immeasurably.

Their situation as potential parents isn't unusual. Because of the "bullshit math," as Migz describes it, if the two ever decide to have children, their children could only be enrolled (as the last possible generation because of their low BQ number) as Ponca, the related tribe least known to their parents.

"I grew up in a family who have a very civic and politically oriented idea of who we are," April says. "So for me, it was always about that; it was about being a member of a community. It was never about race. Even now I don't consider myself racially anything. But it bums me out that if I have a kid I can't enroll that kid at Fort Peck. My family was born, lived, died, and was buried there. We are very tied to this one place. And I will always be part of it."

As a member of the Indigenous comedy troupe the 1491s, Migz starred with Dallas Goldtooth and Ryan RedCorn in a hilarious 2011 skit called "Blood Quantum Leap." You can find it on YouTube. In the skit, Migz argues against BQ, while Goldtooth—who many will recognize from *Reservation Dogs*, where he plays the horse-mounted warrior "Spirit"—argues for it.

"It matters about as much as your beautiful little hair length," Migz tells Goldtooth, who's shaving while clad in only a towel. Goldtooth disagrees and proudly says he looks forward to his children being full-bloods, his butt crack in full display above his towel as he turns back to the mirror to continue shaving. "You're only going to bed down with full-blood ladies?" Migz calls to him, then mutters under his breath, "All right. Inbred."

Proponents of blood quantum rules say they're necessary to protect tribal resources. To make certain existing members can be cared for. That they're critical to protect Indian blood and culture. Effectively managing and caring for people will always be the greatest challenge to maintaining a successful, sovereign nation, but all blood purity–related arguments are ridiculous. Indian blood law is an insidiously brilliant long game that, over time, will eliminate Indian tribes completely. Most tribes buy into them with irrational stubbornness and the worst kind of willful ignorance. These arbitrary blood percentages will reduce enrollment more and more; the gene pool of available, viable mates between members will continue to shrink; and finally, ultimately, tribes will cease to exist.

There are ways to make a more open enrollment work. I would happily take a test to prove I understand the history of the Little Shell, that I know the culture of the tribe, to be considered for enrollment. Why should tribal enrollment be any different from how other sovereign nations welcome people from other lands and cultures into their community? To ignore other approaches to preserving tribal culture and identity is shortsighted and ends only in sorrow. Especially if tribes continue to consider these questions only in a view acceptable to—rather, dictated by—the settler colonial power structure still trying to eradicate them.

"We need to think carefully about how we resolve these questions," Shelly Fyant says. "Is it for my family alone, and what's good for me now? Or is it for all the generations yet to come? To me the real benefit of being enrolled is just being raised with the values and the culture and the spirit of our people. Blood has nothing to do with that. It is loving this land, this water, and these people. It is heart. It is spirit."

I've pondered these questions relentlessly. It's true that claiming relationship to some long-past ancestor doesn't make one "Indian." At the same time, growing up in a tribal community, like on a reservation, isn't the only thing that does either. In questioning my own identity it's something I come back to again and again: Where do I, and people like me, fit in as Indians?

In the years that have unfolded since clicking and scrolling that Ancestry database while building a family tree, I've come to learn many of the connections, the kinship networks, that tie us all together. Not just my people specifically, but how related all the tribes of this region are, through marriage and family relationships. Some of us grew up on reservations, but most of us didn't and may never live in the midst of a majority of our own people. That experience as urban or displaced Indians—"landless" Indians—making an effort to find our way home is every bit as much a part of the Indian experience under colonization as any other.

I agree with Shelly Fyant: blood has nothing to do with it. I'm committed to uncovering the culture of my people. I'm committed to learning as much of the language as I can. I've always loved this land, and I've always loved Indian people. The more I dig into it, the more I interact with my Indian relatives, the more it blooms in my heart. The more it blooms in my spirit. Focusing on this rhetoric over blood and race is a smoke screen to mask the slow roll of continued genocide.

CHAPTER 10

2017

ULM, MONTANA

THE SUN IS HOT ON MY FACE and the breeze is warm and smells of smoke. The air is hazy from any one of several wildfires burning in August 2017, to date the hottest summer on record in Montana. Fires are our new reality in the West, something I don't recall being as much of an issue when I was growing up. I remember the 1977 Pattee Canyon fire near Missoula that burned five homes and made everyone aware that living in the city was no certain defense from being torched by a runaway forest fire. I still see scars from that blaze, forty years removed, when I hike the area. I think of fire all the time now. I spend most of June through August, even September, dreading every thunderstorm.

All around me the world is brittle and dry. The plains spread out for hundreds of miles before me. The sky here, infinite and blue and curving from horizon to horizon, even with the smoky haze, is stupendous. It puts any notion of what I imagine "Big Sky Country" to be, living where I do in a valley ringed by mountains, to shame.

I'm standing on the edge of a cliff at the First Peoples Buffalo Jump State Park, maybe a dozen miles or so south and slightly west of Great Falls, and I'm sweating. To the west I can see the massive landform known as Square Butte, rising from the plain like a gigantic overturned stone box maybe a score of miles distant. It's not the only formation in Montana that bears the name, but it's probably the most notable due to its magnificent size and how it dominates the landscape for miles in every direction. As long as people have been here, over thousands of years, anyone standing where I am and turning their head to the right would see it. Other landforms are blue in the distance—more hills and buttes, the Rocky Mountain Front farthest away.

From the vantage point of the cliffs, the land stretching away in all directions is a unique type of beauty. Squares of farmland mostly, some greener than others. A large tractor moves in the distance. Far below, a white pickup leaves a rooster tail of dust as it speeds along one of the rural roads that crisscross the countryside. A squint and one can almost imagine what this view looked like a hundred, a thousand years ago, but even this bears only the faintest resemblance. Before the land was plowed and converted to agriculture, it would've been far more diverse. Plants and flowers would bloom in wild colors and, depending on where you were, the native grasses would wave in the breeze at heights most of us would consider unbelievable, passing through them akin to moving through a modern cornfield with towering stalks all but obscuring the sun.

The cliffs I'm standing on also served a purpose for procuring food. They extend maybe a half mile to each side of me. Their faces are jagged and rocky, with bushes and plants clinging to the edges and cracks of the rock. The ground below rises and falls so that the height of the feature varies, but there's nowhere I'm comfortable standing at the edge. Even climbing down carefully I'm not sure I could pull it off without ending up with a broken bone.

Depending on who you ask, this place—the Ulm Pishkun, named for the nearby town of Ulm, combined with "Pis'kun," a Blackfeet word that means "deep kettle of blood"—has been used for anywhere between fifteen hundred and five thousand years, at least up until horses were reintroduced to Indigenous plains culture around the eighteenth century or so. Buffalo are fast, ornery, and tough to kill. Before Indians became quick and mobile themselves via the horse, bringing them down was a daunting task. So they had to be creative.

Pretty much all the tribes in the area used this place. Archaeological investigation reveals campsites that indicate it was used heavily for centuries and that untold thousands of bison died here. The bone bed—a geological layer that includes bone fragments—runs an amazing thirteen feet deep from one end of the mile-long cliff face to the other. That's a lot of dead buffalo, and probably a horrific scene to participate in.

Imagine you're chosen to lead the bison over the cliff. You're young, strong, and the fastest person in your tribe or band. You probably begin miles away. Everyone, your entire tribe, maybe several combined, turns out in a big circle to separate a large number of the animals into a single group headed in a common direction. I can only imagine this must've taken some time and a fair amount of territory. Eventually you become the bait to focus the bison's attention, then you're out in front luring them on as their speed picks up. Imagine the dust and the sound of so many hooves pounding across the plains in your wake. Your friends and family—this is pack hunting after all, like wolves—are chasing along behind, waving blankets and hides to incite the panic.

Leading this stampede must've been equal parts terrifying and exhilarating. To fleet across the ground is a joy, and living at the bleeding edge like this, knowing a stumble could leave you pulped into the soil, must've been transcendent.

When the ground starts to slope you pick up speed, and you know the critical moment is here. This is the part that gets me. Somehow you would have to go over that rocky edge without launching into space, find a spot to tuck yourself into, then huddle there as masses of shaggy bodies come tumbling over the lip behind you. The chaos at the edge must've been terrible as the hurtling bison realize their peril, but the weight of momentum behind them doesn't allow them to escape.

What mayhem. What horror.

Broken bones. The screams of the dying. The whoops of your companions below who move among the animals, dispatching the injured. (This part had to be incredibly dangerous as well, right?)

Then the cookfires, and the butchering and the rich scent of roasting meat. Flies buzzing. Other wildlife gathering—birds, foxes, coyotes. Wolves and large grizzly bears circling, waiting for a turn at the feast. The ubiquitous smell of blood. It's everywhere, on everything.

Finally the celebration, and the honoring you would certainly receive for leading, for surviving, this important undertaking: Thousands of pounds of food. Bones for tools, hide for housing and clothing. All materials from an animal that only hours ago was tearing grass from the plain, chewing it, and swallowing.

I'm here for two reasons, one of which involves a different kind of celebration. It's August, and the Little Shell Tribe is holding their annual powwow here, closer to the park's visitor center, which is maybe a mile downhill from the buffalo jump cliffs. The tribe considers this area sacred, as do many of the neighboring tribes, the Blackfeet in particular. The shared use of this landscape, this resource, and the intermingling of Indigenous people that happened here, is a perfect example of precolonial life across this vast ocean of grass. Connection. Kinship. Not just between human tribes, but with the buffalo and everyone else who shared this landscape.

Besides curiosity about the powwow, my other reason for being here is more self-serving. The Little Shell Tribe holds quarterly meetings, and this one, for 2017's second quarter, is in a conference room at the visitor center just before the powwow festivities kick off. In these meetings the tribal council gets together in a public forum to share news, discuss new and old business, swear in new council members, the usual stuff. Updates on in-progress projects—mostly state-funded programs for things like tobacco awareness, health and wellness, and language preservation—are provided, and attending members are encouraged to ask questions. These meetings are about the only regular opportunities for the tribe to gather in any kind of scheduled capacity.

This is also, I'm told, when the tribal council approves enrollment applications based on recommendations from the enrollment office. My application—turned in during my encounter with Terri LaRocque a few weeks earlier—is pending, and I suspect today is the day I'll learn whether or not I qualify for tribal enrollment.

∽

Linda Watson is in charge of enrollment for the Little Shell Tribe at the time of my visit. She still is when I query her in 2019 for this book. I've questioned her relentlessly about how it all works, and Linda, a serene, grandmotherly woman with a quick smile who looks to be in her late sixties or so, has been endlessly patient with me. I've only spoken to her in person on a couple occasions; most of our interactions have occurred over the phone and email.

"I've only worked in the enrollment office for four years," Linda tells me when I query her in early 2019. "My sense is that enrollment applications have been slowly increasing."

The tribe averages fourteen to fifteen new applications monthly. A small percentage are denied for a variety of different reasons. Linda's office received 140 applications from January through October 2019 and carried 18 applications from late 2018 into 2019.

"We notice these past few months that whenever there's a media notice about the status of federal recognition efforts," Linda says, "we seem to get a flurry of new enrollment applications. We anticipate that when recognition actually is signed into law that there will probably be a significant increase in that number."

There's a fairly complex bureaucracy that goes on behind the scenes for every application for enrollment that gets submitted. If the application in question doesn't meet the initial requirements of a signed and dated form, a birth certificate listing both parents' names (or, if a father isn't listed, a notarized statement from the father acknowledging paternity), and the registration fee, it's already dead in the water.

Next, it's determined whether or not the applicant has a parent enrolled in the Little Shell Tribe. Per the Little Shell constitution any person possessing at least 1/4 Indian blood degree, including Pembina Chippewa, is eligible for enrollment, provided they aren't already enrolled in any other tribe. They must also be US citizens. If a child possessing 1/8 total blood degree has a parent enrolled in the Little Shell Tribe with at least 1/4 total blood degree, that child is eligible for enrollment.

If a parent isn't enrolled, as was my case when I applied, there are still options. If the applicant has direct, verifiable lineage to a person included on a historical US document that quantifies blood degree, they can still get in. The documents in question typically include the Roe Cloud Roll of 1937 (a list of unenrolled Indians in Montana that was prepared by Henry Roe Cloud for the Office of Indian Affairs), the 1892 McCumber Commission report (a list of eligible enrollees at the time of the infamous Ten-Cent Treaty), and very early Turtle Mountain Indian censuses.

Earlier US Census records, say 1910, 1920, etc., are, Linda tells me, "Not acceptable because the blood degree was entered to the form by a census taker who was entering his own opinion of blood degree from observing the person."

As I've already mentioned, blood degree, the whole blood quantum model, is a flawed nightmare. For example, in 2019 the tribal council of the Red Lake Band of Chippewa Indians in Minnesota voted to recalculate their blood quantum baseline. Essentially, every person who was an enrolled member of Red Lake Nation on November 10, 1958, the most recent instance of a blood baseline being established, would now be considered a full-blood, or 4/4 blood degree. This reset the fractions for anyone coming after as well.

An article from the *Bemidji Pioneer* about the change quotes Red Lake secretary Sam Strong, who initiated it, as saying, "Although it is a great first step, it is important to recognize that it is a first step and we need to continue to visit this enrollment issue until we can come to a consensus to end our current practice of mathematical genocide and move forward with a solution that will allow us to protect our nation forever."

It's a mighty and interesting move but also exemplifies how arbitrary these numbers are.

When it comes to Little Shell enrollment, blood degrees that include other tribes must include tribal verification from those tribes of CIB (Certified Indian Blood) for the person contributing that blood degree to the Little Shell applicant. This could be Salish, Blackfeet, Crow, or any other tribe. This can create complex calculations when parents have a spider's web of tribal relationships, which most do.

Finally, after all research is completed and entered into a file, a second person reviews the initial reviewer's calculations. Only then will a final determination be made.

If a person fails to meet the enrollment requirements, they will immediately be sent a letter of rejection that includes reasons for the determination. If requirements are met, the applicant is added to a quarterly enrollment list that is submitted to the tribal council for approval. Either way, it's a time-consuming process, but the enrollment office tries to make sure all applications are determined eligible or ineligible within thirty days of receipt.

Linda Watson believes there are a number of reasons people seek enrollment. Some hope there may be financial benefits, such as "per capita" payments (money divided up as "tribal property" among members when tribes have a particular resource, like casinos or natural resources that generate income, none of which the Little Shell currently have) or help with rental expenses. Some hope to claim Native American preference in job hiring opportunities. Others, like me, are after a sense of belonging to something larger. To be part of the wider American Indian community and to learn about the culture and history of one's ancestors.

Linda isn't particularly fond of blood quantum either, though her answer is guarded. Given her role with the tribe she's in a difficult position.

"Because I'm the one that has to do all the calculations," Linda says, "I'm bound by this set of rules, and I'm bound by the tribal constitution and what the constitution says is acceptable for enrollment. I have to tie that to official historical United States documents that quantify blood quantum, and I understand that I have to do it. But no other races have to show proof of blood quantum. So I have some negative feelings about it. I also want people who have lived here for generations to benefit from services, who have need of those services, and that has to be done through an official enrollment process."

∽

As a result of my curiosity and desire to find out if I'm enrolled, I experience my first quarterly meeting of the Little Shell Tribe of Chippewa Indians during that steamy 2017 afternoon. I'm in the presence of several people I'll come to know as this project unfolds: Chairman Gerald Gray, for example, and Kim McKeehan, who's sworn in as the council's newest member and will become one of my best friends; Duane Reid, whom we'll meet later; and finally, Nicholas Vrooman. I'm amazed he not only recognizes me but greets me by name and asks how my project is going, even though a couple years have passed since we last spoke.

The meeting is a dry affair. The conference room off the foyer of the visitor center is cramped, but there aren't many folks in attendance. Previous meeting minutes are covered, current budget status is reported, and a few other pieces of news are discussed. It feels rushed, and it is, because everyone wants to get it over with and head outside for the powwow. I'm distracted because I expect there will be some announcement of names of new enrollees, some kind of welcome. But that doesn't happen. Chairman Gray merely asks Linda Watson for an enrollment update and she announces some numbers. And that's it. No names, no fanfare.

The meeting adjourns. I stand, a little stunned and disappointed. Then I find Linda Watson and introduce myself. I tell her I submitted an application and wonder if maybe she can tell me if I was on the list of those accepted for enrollment. She asks me my name.

"La Tray," I say. "Chris La Tray."

"Yes, I remember your name," she says. "Your application was accepted. You can expect a letter in the next month."

I thank her, then walk to my car. In the open field beyond the parking lot next to a small RV, a small flock of ruffed grouse cluck about, scratching at the dirt and making short dashes that seem completely random. I smile at their antics, then burst into tears.

~

The news of my enrollment in the tribe, and all the thoughts swirling in my head on that smoky day in 2017, accompanied me on the slow hike up the winding trail from the visitor center that delivered me to the broad vista from the top of Ulm Pishkun. I've been identified in the family of this specific circle of tribal life interconnected with all the Indians who ever roamed across these cliffs, through generations of blood and kinship.

Atop the cliffs I can see people gathering for the powwow beneath a round framed arbor below. The structure provides shade, and the enclosed space in the middle, open to the sky, is for dancing. I feel a surge of emotion toward the tiny figures. We're all a little lost, most of us anyway, and we're coming together to reengage with who we are, what we've been. It's slow going—we are all just people after all, many of us buffeted by generations of trauma—but we make the effort. I make the effort, even when the urge to stand apart from it all is just as present as love. To see my people, Indian people, gathered at the base of this particular landform to celebrate, to dance and drum and be thrilled, to be living among friends and family, is beautiful.

I take a breath. I'm part of this, part of them. I wipe the sweat from my brow and take a quick look around me for snakes. Then I follow the trail down the slope, across time, through genocide and diaspora, and fear and death and now rebirth, to food, to companionship, and increasingly, to community.

CHAPTER 11

2021

HELENA, MONTANA

STANDING IN THE LOBBY of the Myrna Loy theater in Helena, Montana, in the wake of a wonderful Métis celebration featuring exuberant music and dance, I tell a colleague I'm setting out before dawn on a road trip to Minnesota. She makes a face and says, "Well, I hope you have a good audiobook or something to listen to."

"Why?" I say.

"Because North Dakota," she says.

I've traversed North Dakota by car from west to east and back several times (and countless times from the air) over the years for various reasons unrelated to writing this book. I find it beautiful in the same way all the Great Plains states are. The open sky, the broad expanses of grassland waving in the breeze . . . I don't know, I think it gets a bad rap. This time when I cross during an unseasonably warm October, I'm particularly moved by a context I've never carried with me before: the idea of it being a kind of homeland. Not the state so much as the sheer magnificence of the unforgiving landscape and how, for all the ideas people have of it being a wasteland, it has always supported abundant life. Driving, I stop and squint and imagine these plains crowded with immense herds of buffalo. Of elk, antelope, and wolves and grizzly bears. Rivers and creeks and all the birds that would gather there. A magnificently wild Missouri River, free of dams. And the people who crossed over and back across them for decades, even centuries. Sometimes afoot, sometimes on horses, and sometimes in enormous trains of squeaking and screeching Red River carts.

I must pause here and ask you to imagine the sound. On approach, it has been reported to have been audible anywhere from two to six miles distant. Some have suggested up to ten miles. It's a clamor hard to grasp when considering distance relayed as numbers rendered as words on a page. Think of that context as it relates to locations you're familiar with. Where I live, just shy of mile marker nine on Mullan Road leading west from Missoula, that would mean when the travelers hit Reserve Street—the main north-south road on the western edge of the city, where all the ugly and gross big box stores are—is about when I might be able to hear them first. But I wouldn't be certain.

Outside on the quietest days, with no jets taking off from the airport or turboprops warming up on the tarmac; no trains, no traffic on the interstate—circumstances extant only during the shutdown in the deepest depths of the COVID-19 pandemic—it's unimaginable that I could hear at that distance even the loudest jacked-up pickup revving its engine to roll coal on an unsuspecting Prius driver. Maybe I could from the stripped-down remains of the paper mill where my dad toiled for a lifetime, but that's only three miles away by car, perhaps less overland.

A terrible noise it must have been, then.

I'm talking about the sound generated by a packtrain of Red River carts squeaking and squealing their way across the open prairie—this North Dakota prairie, the Eastern Montana prairie—sometimes a few at a time, sometimes (say, during the height of Métis buffalo hunting power) by the hundreds.

"Almost every northern plains historical writer has attempted to describe the horrible screeching that a train of such carts made," historian Verne Dusenberry writes, "but probably none has been presented more graphically than [J. K. Howard's description]: 'It was as if a thousand finger nails were drawn across a thousand panes of glass.'"

Just imagine.

The most advanced technology on the northern plains in the early nineteenth century was a product of Métis ingenuity: a conveyance that came to be known as the Red River cart. There can be no discussion of the Métis or Little Shell people and their historic movement without a discussion of these carts. Many historians consider it to be the first example of wheel use by anyone in this part of so-called North America. Invented in 1801 by Métis traders operating out of Fort Henry in what's now Ontario, Canada, the carts allowed access into areas that river systems no longer did. By the early 1800s the fur trade, which was the economic backbone of the continent from the moment colonial powers first turned greedy eyes across the vastness of its forest and water systems, was already drying up due to overtrapping of fur-bearing animals, primarily beaver. Rivers and lakes had been the primary highways all along, but as trappers and traders moved westward onto the plains, they needed something different. The Red River cart was that something.

The Métis Resource Center reports that the October 1878 issue of *Harper's* magazine describes the carts thus:

> It is simply a light box with a pair of shafts, mounted on an axle connecting two enormous wheels. There is no concession made to the aversion of the human frame to sudden violent changes of level; there is no weakness of

> luxury about this vehicle. The wheels are broad in the felloes (rims), so as not to cut through the prairie sod. They are long in the spokes, so as to pass safely through fords and mud-holes. They are very much dished so that they can be strapped together and rawhide stretched over them to make a boat. The whole cart is made of wood; there is not a bit of metal about it, so that, if anything breaks, the material to repair it is easily found. The axles are never greased and they furnish an incessant answer to the old conundrum: "What makes more noise than a pig in a poke?"

The carts were indeed made entirely of wood—sturdy elm for the wheel hubs, flexible oak or white ash for the rims, bow, and tongue—and buffalo leather in strips, like rawhide, called "shaga-nappi," that tied the whole construction together. The actual box cart was suspended on poles between two wheels as tall as five or six feet in diameter. The wheels were wrapped with green buffalo leather that, when dried, became a very effective tire, tight and nearly impervious.

The secrets of the cart's construction were kept close; if you saw a Red River cart, you were seeing Métis. The box could be removed in winter and pulled as a sleigh, or floated across a river or stream crossing. The carts were easy to load and unload and could carry upward of nine hundred pounds. There was only one downside: the noise. Wheels turning on an axle, wood on wood with no grease, generated an unimaginable cacophony that could be heard long before the carts were seen. Even when grease was available these travelers opted not to use it, for a couple reasons. First, it could coagulate and make the wheel nearly impossible to turn. Second, the grease tended to get clogged with dust, rocks, and other prairie detritus and grind the moving parts to failure.

That doesn't mean wheels and axles didn't fail anyway over the long haul of so many miles. Of course they did. But the landscape the Métis typically traversed had no lack of raw material that with proper tools—a screw auger, a saw, an axe—couldn't be transformed into a ready supply of spare parts. Which is why, even when metal became available, the carts remained true to their original design.

The invention of the cart did many things for the Métis people. It expanded the fur export business into new territories unreachable by boat or canoe. Most important, it gave the Métis access to the dwindling buffalo herds and enabled entire families to travel in search of them. There were no roads in this part of the world, but the Red River carts were uniquely adapted to handle the rough, grassy terrain of the northern plains. Tied together like trains, they would travel in caravans with dozens, hundreds, or even more than a thousand carts, lurching and screeching across the landscape. Not to mention the livestock—dogs, oxen, horses, cattle—that accompanied every trip. Métis trails north and south, east and west, created cart tracks that ultimately formed the basis of many roads and highways in use today.

~

My trip back toward the Red River Valley isn't in a cart, thankfully. I'm in a rental car. I'm headed sixteen hours east, where I'll collapse in a room at the Seven Clans Casino in Thief River Falls, owned and operated by the Red Lake Band of Chippewa Indians. I'm joining a small delegation of Little Shell Tribe members—four of us including my cousin (and LST council member) Kim McKeehan and two other women, plus an attending entourage of two husbands and a couple grandchildren—who have made a similar trip all the way from Montana. A few months of organizational meetings online have led to this: we Little Shell are dignitaries from our "lost" tribe invited to participate in this commemoration of 158 years since the signing of the 1863 Treaty of Old Crossing. It's an honor, and my excitement to have been invited is overflowing. It's a first for us to be included, and though our delegation is small we are hopeful that in coming years our participation will be much larger. The roots of our tribal connection to this event are deep; more than 94 percent of our present membership can be traced back to signers of this treaty. I'm eager to visit the location where it all went down nearly 160 years ago.

~

The Red Lake River is wide and slow where it passes by the Old Crossing Treaty Park near Huot, Minnesota. The location was a popular stopping point for cart trains passing back and forth and trading goods between what's now Minneapolis all the way up to the Red River Colony. The park, established in 1933 on just under nine acres on the river's west bank, is beautiful, with manicured grass and an abundance of trees. I'm terrible at identification in my own landscape, and this part of Minnesota, with so many deciduous varieties, reminds me of my ignorance. I recognize cottonwoods and some gigantic oaks. There are also ash, I think, and possibly beech trees as well. I'm probably wrong. But it's October and the leaves are changing, and all the competing shades of green and red and gold and yellow are a buffet for my eyes. There are bulky gray clouds and a few spits of rain after a night of downpour, but then the sun breaks through and the day is gorgeous.

The slope down to the river is heavy with willows, but there's a decent span of muddy sand along the banks. Mushrooms press up through the broken soil. It's quiet; there aren't any busy highways close by, or don't seem to be anyway. I can hear the low gurgle of the river. If I squint and ignore the poles and sagging power lines, I can almost imagine the place looking not so different from what it did 158 years ago, even though it was. One thing that more than a century of area farming by white people hasn't changed though is the small hill that rises above the landscape just opposite this side of the river. It's there that Alexander Ramsey, a former governor of both Minnesota Territory and state, arranged his forces, which included, "290 army men, 340 mules, 180 horses, 55 big oxen and 90 vehicles and wagons." It was late September 1863 and he arrived with the intention to negotiate with the Indians, a Gatling gun—one of the most ferocious military weapons of its day—ominously in place to cover the entire site below.

What exactly is the 1863 Treaty of Old Crossing? David Treuer, an Ojibwe author from Leech Lake who likely had relatives here same as me, writes in his book *The Heartbeat of Wounded Knee*, "In 1863, the Red Lake Band and Pembina Band of Ojibwe were induced by Alexander Ramsey, governor of Minnesota, to sign a treaty ceding roughly eleven million acres of prime woodlands and prairie on either side of the Red River. The Treaty of Old Crossing promised them [the Indians] considerable annuities and the right to hunt, fish, and travel in the ceded area in exchange for what Ramsey described as the 'right of passage' for oxcarts and wagon trains headed west."

The gotcha here is this idea of "right of passage." This is what the assembled chiefs thought they were negotiating, what they were led to believe they were negotiating. But it wasn't. It was another land grab. Ramsey deliberately misrepresented the language of the treaty in an effort to yank all that beautiful land out from under the Ojibwe people who already lived there.

Fourteen days of lowball offers and arguments and grand speeches and threats and mistranslations across languages finally led to a confused agreement. On October 2, 1863, the Pembina and Red Lake Treaty—the Old Crossing Treaty—was signed. Six Indian chiefs and nine warriors signed it. Pembina chiefs Red Bear and Little Shell both signed the treaty. Of the handful of

Pembina warriors who signed it at least two of them represent direct ancestors of members of today's Little Shell Tribe.

The result? Eleven million acres of land ceded to the United States. The agreement included annual payments of $20,000, divided equally as per capita payments to enrolled tribal members, for twenty years; funds set aside for farming and education; money specifically for chiefs, and even houses built for them. Land, 160 acres, for "each male adult half-breed or mixed-blood who adopted the customs of civilized life or became a citizen of the United States and homesteaded the claim for five years."

The Indians understood that they could stay where they were, continue to use the territory as they always had, but would leave the settlers alone. That's what they agreed to. But it isn't what the document actually says.

Of course it doesn't end here. Once the treaty went to Washington for ratification, changes were made, some significant. This led to a revised treaty being signed in Washington on April 12, 1864. Little Shell didn't make the trip to DC and didn't sign the revised treaty (Red Bear did, however). He'd had enough with the doublespeak and betrayals of the United States government and determined to never negotiate again.

This is why, while many people refer to the McCumber Agreement of 1892—more to come on this—as the blow that left the Little Shell people landless, I set the true beginning thirty years earlier to this treaty, Old Crossing, in 1863, and Little Shell's refusal to sign the remade document. While the treaty itself had greater consequences to the Ojibwe people still in Minnesota, its ripple effects were the beginning of the end for the related Pembina Chippewa north and west of the Red River.

Sixteen hours in one shot is a long time to drive, and I spend most of it without the audiobook my friend recommended. I don't listen to podcasts or music. I spend most of the trip in my head reflecting on how I've come to be headed west with a trunkful of Little Shell swag to be handed out as powwow freebies. Reflecting and also turning over the plethora of questions I still need answered.

My mind takes me back to a warm spring day in downtown Helena, Montana, some years before. In the months and years that followed my accepted enrollment application I stepped up my interest in learning all I could about my tribe. I attended quarterly meetings and spent a small fortune on books for research purposes. I also began a steady correspondence with Nicholas Vrooman via email and the occasional phone call. I recall sitting with him in his second-floor office in an old building on the corner of Placer Avenue and historic Last Chance Gulch, my view the outer wall of the post office opposite the street my chair by the window faces.

I chuckle to myself when I recall how I asked him for a short answer to this question: Why are we called the "Little Shell" Chippewa people? I laugh because there isn't a short answer and even if there was, I don't think Vrooman would be capable of providing it. Yet I'm going to try.

We could as easily still be called Pembina Chippewa—named for the Ojibwe word for what we call the "high cranberry," a bitter little fruit from the honeysuckle family that grows in small, bright red clusters on thick, bushy shrubs—or Turtle Mountain Chippewa, or even Rocky Boy's Chippewa Cree, who are our close relatives. We're called "Little Shell" because of a *man* called Little Shell who lead these related people during a tumultuous time that, for all the decades stacked up before his arrival, truly began to unravel in the 1850s and rapidly fell apart in the wake of the Old Crossing Treaty of 1863, just as it did for all the related Indigenous people of the region.

His name was Ayabe-way-we-tung, which means "He Who Rests on His Way." He was the third hereditary chief of the Pembina Chippewa to be called Little Shell, so he's sometimes referred to as Little Shell III, but for my purposes, when I refer to Little Shell the *person*, it's this man.

Little Shell never led his people into great battles against the settlers in defense of his homelands in the way more recognizable Plains Indian leaders like Red Cloud, Sitting Bull, or Crazy Horse did. Nor was the Pembina peoples' forced exodus away from their homeland as dramatic as that of Chief Joseph and the Nez Perce. But it was no less harrowing; the same rifles that were aimed at Nez Perce women and children in 1877 under the charge of Nelson Miles were directed our way too. His name should be spoken with at least as much reverence as these other guys. Perhaps it's because in America we tend to exalt our historical figures as much by the body counts they achieved as anything else; I don't know. I contend Little Shell's efforts on behalf of his people are no less significant than these other leaders.

Discussing "Little Shell" the man can be confusing because there was a "Little Shell" who was hereditary chief of the Pembina Chippewa for a long time. As I read different sources and cogitated on timelines, I was often confused myself by who did what. It wasn't until the pre–Old Crossing celebration Zoom meetings and subsequent conversations with historians from Turtle Mountain and Red Lake that I finally sorted it out.

Little Shell, the man the tribe is named after, became hereditary chief of the Pembina Chippewa when his father, Weesh-e-damo, died around 1872. Weesh-e-damo (aka Little Shell II) was the tribe's leader starting in 1815, after his father, Aisance, the first of this Little Shell line, was killed in battle with the Dakota near what's now Devils Lake in Minnesota. Aisance's leadership began around 1770. So this Little Shell dynasty lasted over a hundred years with only one interruption: when Aisance was killed in 1813, his son, Weesh-e-damo, hadn't yet come of age. A leader named Black Duck—who ultimately became Weesh-e-damo's father-in-law—served as a regent of sorts for two years until Weesh-e-damo was old enough to lead the tribe. Black Duck was reputedly a great warrior and leader himself, serving his people from a camp at Turtle Mountain. He was also killed fighting the Dakota in 1824.

Sorting out the achievements and interactions between the Pembina people under Little Shell and the federal government can be confusing because of this hereditary name, especially since Ayabe-way-we-tung is the only "Little Shell" we have photographs of. All three men appear in various journals and records from the earliest days of the fur trade around the Red River Valley, under various names and spellings and interpretations. For example, I spent probably a year assuming it was Little Shell I who signed the Old Crossing Treaty based on something I'd read, but that's ludicrous if one does simple math against dates of birth. Then I concluded it was Little Shell III at Old Crossing, but even that's incorrect. It was Weesh-e-damo who was there, Little Shell II, "my" Little Shell's father. Also, starting with Little Shell II, the United States did everything they could to undermine his leadership because he wasn't particularly cooperative in getting screwed by them. So in an effort to stiff-arm any further confusion, I'll pick up the story when Ayabe-way-we-tung becomes Little Shell.

~

One of those North Dakota historians I mentioned who helped me figure all this out is Les LaFountain. LaFountain is a Turtle Mountain Chippewa tribal historian and former North Dakota state senator. He teaches at Turtle Mountain Community College in Belcourt, North Dakota, where the Turtle Mountain Chippewa are headquartered. I first made LaFountain's acquaintance via those online meetings to organize the Old Crossing Treaty event. He's probably a decade older than me but doesn't look it. His face is lined and his short hair is dark and streaked with silver. The smile he flashes from beneath an impressive mustache is wide and features a narrow gap between his front teeth.

LaFountain and I met in person for the first time at the Old Crossing event in Huot, Minnesota. We had wild rice soup together at a long table under a big pavilion, where we hit it off. We made plans on my return trip for me to stop and visit him again at the college. On the way I visited the North Dakota town of Pembina—at the time of the Old Crossing Treaty the most populous trading post in the region—where I ate a peanut butter sandwich for lunch while sitting on a dock jutting out onto the Red River. From there I drove to Belcourt and the Turtle Mountain reservation. I took a picture of the sign for Chief Little Shell Street. I secured a room at Sky Dancer Casino and Resort at the western edge of the reservation and got LaFountain on the phone to coordinate plans for our meeting.

When I arrive at the Turtle Mountain Community College just before noon on the following day, LaFountain greets me with a smile and a firm handshake. He wears a beautiful beaded turtle medallion around his neck. He gives me a tour of the institution and it's beautiful, surrounded by forest and hills. The Turtle Mountains—more rolling hills than what we in Montana might call mountains—are gorgeous in the fall light. We begin a deep discussion of who Little Shell really was, and what he represents to our people.

"Little Shell III is probably the most significant leader at Turtle Mountain," LaFountain says, pointing at a portrait of the Pembina chief, "and the reason for that is he was challenged at a time when the land base was being taken away or being threatened."

Consider the state of the world Little Shell became chief in. The Old Crossing Treaty was signed just under a decade earlier, an interaction his father walked away from in disgust, vowing never to make treaty with the Americans again. But encroachments on Chippewa land were gaining steam, and the region was crawling with homesteaders looking for land regardless of what any treaty said about who it belonged to.

This land the Pembina Chippewa occupied at the time, about ten million acres worth, had been established in an agreement signed in 1858 that came to be known as the Sweet Corn Treaty. The agreement was "forged between the chiefs and headmen of the [Pembina] band and the Sisseton and Yankton Dakota," and "sought to establish peace and to define hunting and territorial boundaries so that there was no cause for warfare and so that resources would be shared without animosity."

By the 1870s that language was meaningless. Agreement or not, settlers wanted the land, and the government was determined to see they got it.

Little Shell would spend the rest of his life trying to preserve a people and culture that was threatened on all sides. By 1872 the buffalo, and the centuries-old cultures that revolved around them, were largely gone. Many of the Turtle Mountain people who used to travel out of the region to hunt buffalo were still out and staying away longer. By the 1880s the buffalo were essentially eradicated. There was more and more pressure on Little Shell to turn this land over to the Americans, but he was steadfast in retaining the Turtle Mountains for his people.

"There was no reservation," LaFountain says of the still-unceded land. "He resisted the removal of the Turtle Mountain people from the Turtle Mountains. That was all the doings of Little Shell."

It should be noted that even as chief, Little Shell didn't enjoy the kind of "my way or the highway" leadership one might expect. So he wasn't just negotiating with settlers. He had to accommodate all the factions and concerns of his own people, a task that was certainly daunting as well. He couldn't force anyone to do anything; he had to lobby and convince and lead through wisdom. His influence depended entirely on his ability to suggest reasonable decisions and lead with integrity. This leadership included presiding over councils, making general day-to-day decisions related to his band, and mediating disputes. He represented his people when it came to interacting with the Americans or even with gatherings of other tribes.

This wasn't top-down leadership like we see in tribal governments today. There weren't any "Robert's Rules of Order" protocols in place like what I suffer through whenever I attend a tribal council meeting. That's a colonial form of leadership. The Pembina Chippewa didn't operate like that. In his role as chief, Little Shell had a number of subchiefs called "headmen" to advise and assist in leading the Pembina people and hearing their opinions and grievances. These included a number of leaders in the Métis community as well, who were a large part of the population. Little Shell even had a lawyer working on the tribe's behalf, Jean Baptiste "J. B." Bottineau, the Métis son of notable guide and fur trader Pierre Bottineau, who represented the interests of the people of Turtle Mountain until his death in Washington, DC, in 1911.

Yes, a lawyer. Because by now these negotiations were largely being waged by bureaucrats, not soldiers. Between the time Little Shell began his tenure as leader of the Pembina Chippewa and the McCumber Agreement of 1892, he and his representatives made several trips to DC to make a case for where they should be allowed to stay. Most of their efforts fell on deaf ears. If there's an upside to all this it's that these visits are largely where the photographs we have of Little Shell come from.

Little Shell's tenure can be described largely as one of resistance in an effort to preserve as much as he could for his people. He rejected early efforts to move the Pembina Chippewa to what's now the White Earth reservation in north-central Minnesota, created in 1867 and one of seven Chippewa/Ojibwe reservations in that state. He also rejected an attempt to move them to the Fort Berthold reservation, which, while on Pembina land, would've forced them from the Turtle Mountains and onto land to be shared with the three affiliated Sioux tribes of the Mandan, Hidatsa, and Arikara Nations.

Little Shell could see the writing on the wall as his people clashed with more and more settlers. He wanted a reservation but it had to include the Turtle Mountains. He finally got one in 1882. It was roughly 450,000 acres. Two years later, two executive orders by United States president Chester Arthur reduced the reservation by 90 percent, to 46,000 acres, where it remains today. Little Shell spent the rest of his life trying to restore the original boundaries. These tireless efforts directly resulted in the fateful McCumber Agreement in 1892, which Little Shell refused to cooperate with, that led ultimately to him and all his followers off reservation being disenrolled, creating the ludicrous situation of *any* Indigenous North Americans being described as "landless."

"This reservation really is here because of Little Shell," Les LaFountain says of the people who became the Turtle Mountain Chippewa. "We would not be here if not for Chief Little Shell."

We're Little Shell Chippewa because we are the people who were shut out, driven, essentially, into exile. When the US government established means for unrecognized Indians to gain federal recognition in 1978, the official "Little Shell" tribe came into existence as a unique entity splintered off from a larger people. During my time in Minnesota for the Old Crossing event, I spoke with several members from the Minnesota Ojibwe tribes—a couple even in positions of leadership—who told me they didn't even know we were out there.

~

When our lunch is over I give my friend Les LaFountain two bags of tobacco in exchange for his hospitality and knowledge. I drive around a little more after leaving and decide to spend another night at the Sky Dancer. In the morning I rise before dawn and walk maybe half a mile out onto the prairie. I want to get clear of the floodlights around the casino parking lot. It's cool, maybe fifty degrees, and a slight breeze is blowing. I climb up onto a hill that looks out over the dark, rolling landscape below and sit down. The moon is to the east, just a sliver, but the light of her reflection is so bright I can see her fullness even in shadow. Such fullness, and so beautiful. And the stars, oh, the stars, brighter than they ever are where I live.

I wish I could say it's quiet. The hulking, brightly lit casino is just yonder, and big buildings are noisy for all their immobility. A few cars pass on the highway below. I don't get to hear the rustle of any relatives who might be up and moving in the grass. I hope coyote might happen by, give me a sniff, a wink. I've not seen him since Montana several days ago.

If I could stand, arms wide in my best shaman's pose, and cast my vision out for miles and miles, across the plains to east, south, and west, and up north through the rolling hills and forests that comprise the Turtle Mountains, I would place my loving gaze on Chippewa land. But the reservation is small; at six by twelve miles, it encompasses a mere seventy-two square miles. It's all the United States allowed the Turtle Mountain people to keep after stealing everything else.

I spend the day driving back across land that was free for us to roam, all across North Dakota. There are more oil wells than people it seems. I reach the Montana border at the town of Plentywood, in the extreme upper-northeast corner of the state, in the waning moments of sunset. Darkness falls quickly, and driving at night I get a taste of what it might've been like before market hunters decimated indigenous animal populations; there's so much damn wildlife beside and on the highway that it's white-knuckle driving for hours until I find a place to stop for the night. I average a top speed of maybe forty to forty-five miles per hour. At one point I come to a full stop in the middle of the highway, my headlights shining on the still form of a slain porcupine. Here is a coyote beside the animal, laughing at me, and not that swift in retreating from my approach. Just beyond the reach of my high beams is a cluster of deer, at least a dozen or so, also watching me. By the time I find a room at the La Casa Motel in Glasgow I'm emotionally exhausted, and my voice is raw from yelling, "Stay off the fucking road!" out the window at all my unwary four-legged relatives.

It's still dark in the morning when I set out again, this time on the more travelled Highway 2 heading west. I plan to stop at Cree Crossing, near Malta. At the turnoff there's a brown sign—or "brown board" as I've since learned they are called—indicating a site of historical significance. I pull off and stop in front of a three-walled structure encasing two large rocks, both with faded petroglyphs carved into them. The sign indicates the larger rock is called "Sleeping Buffalo Rock" and it reads:

> Montana's native people revere this boulder that once perched high atop a wind-swept ridge overlooking the Cree Crossing on the Milk River. The ancient, weather-worn effigy resembled the leader of a herd of reclining buffalo in an outcrop of gray granite. Ancient markings define its horns, eyes, backbone, and ribs. Since late prehistoric times, native peoples of the Northern Plains have revered the Sleeping Buffalo's spiritual power. Oral traditions passed down among the Cree, Chippewa, Sioux, Assiniboine, and

Gros Ventre as well as the more distant Blackfeet, Crow, and Northern Cheyenne tell how the "herd" fooled buffalo-hunting parties. While each tribe has its own culture and beliefs, all Montana tribes share worldviews. A Chippewa-Cree elder explained, "These rocks are sacred, just like our old people." Locals claim the Sleeping Buffalo, relocated to Malta's City Park in 1932, was restless, changing position and bellowing in the night. The Sleeping Buffalo found this final resting place in 1967 where the smaller "Medicine Rock," also collected near Cree Crossing, rejoined it in 1987. These timeless objects continue to figure prominently in traditional ceremonies, linking the present with the past when the power of the prairie was the buffalo.

I follow a dirt road back off the highway for a couple miles past Nelson State Recreation Area to get to Cree Crossing. It's now an officially designated state wildlife management area. This location was a point where the Milk River could be safely crossed even during periods of higher water. Everybody who needed to ford the river used it, but it bears the name of my Cree-named relatives.

I arrive just at sunrise, an indescribable red glow stretching all across the eastern horizon. I park and walk out onto the bridge that spans the low, slow flow of the Milk River at the end of what has been a hot, dry summer. It's incredibly stirring; white-tailed deer start and rustle and retreat into the willows and cottonwoods on the southern bank. In the distance I hear magpies rasping out their greeting to the morning. In my mind's eye I imagine people queued up here, laughing and cursing, urging their animals and two-wheeled carts across the river. I take some photos and wipe tears from the corner of my eye.

This place, this prairie, this sweeping landscape I've crossed that was the territory of people so many now know so little of.

Chief Little Shell died in 1901 (or possibly 1903 according to some records), "unsuccessful in his quest to bring his Montana brethren into Turtle Mountain." A July 4, 1901, article on his death in the *Minneapolis Journal* said Little Shell was prominent in the "Indian troubles" of 1895 that could have led to "the sacrifice of many lives." Finally, it said, "The chief was eloquent and never could forgive his race for surrendering title to a foot of land or leaving it without making a fight."

Until my trip to Minnesota and my brief time at Turtle Mountain, I'd never felt a connection to Little Shell beyond the idea he was a man whose name our people chose to identify ourselves. But now I sense his presence as an individual, a person who faced more difficult choices than anyone should have to, all in service to his people. More than ever I feel a sense of pride and duty to live up to this name, Little Shell.

"Great leaders around the world," Les LaFountain told me, "we think of them as people who gave of themselves for the people. Little Shell was one of those individuals."

Ayabe-way-we-tung deserves far more recognition than he has received, and the days of him being largely ignored are, if I can help it, over.

CHAPTER 12

2018

GREAT FALLS, MONTANA

IF ANYWHERE ALONG THE EPIC TRAIL the Lewis and Clark expedition made between August 31, 1803, and September 23, 1806, from St. Louis, Missouri, to the Pacific Ocean and back resembles what they saw, it's stretches of landscape along the Missouri River through Montana. This region—much of which was designated the Upper Missouri River Breaks National Monument in 2001—is rough country. Craggy, windswept, hot in the summer and lethally cold in the winter, the Breaks own all the best parts of what we consider geographical badlands.

The Corps of Discovery had been on the river almost two years when, on June 13, 1805, Meriwether Lewis was allegedly the first white guy to lay eyes on what would become known as the Great Falls of the Missouri River. Lewis described the view of crashing water and spray towering into the prairie sky as "the grandest sight I ever beheld." But it wasn't just one big waterfall, it was a series of five, including rapids. It would take the expedition an entire month to portage all their gear eighteen miles around the area, pushing "crude cottonwood carts with rounded trunk slabs for wheels . . . across ground churned up by bison herds and filled with prickly pear cactus that cut into their feet."

I say Lewis was allegedly the first to see the falls because he was merely the first to write about them. It's entirely possible the Corps was preceded by other, less literate adventurers looking to make a buck. Regardless, others were hot on the expedition's heels into the region.

"First settlers along the Missouri were the half-breed trappers, who feared nothing on earth," writes Joseph Kinsey Howard. The upper Missouri was soon flooded with trappers, adventurers, and fortune seekers almost before Lewis and Clark had a chance to be home again and thrilled at the sight of a cow. Tough-as-buffalo-leather Métis were among the first to seek a living along this stretch of the Missouri, and the living was abundant.

The landscape teemed with wildlife, readily accessible to meat, hide, and fur hunters. Until the coming of the railroad, the Missouri River was also the route that provided best access to this part of the continent, and access was vigorously sought.

Indian people had been here for thousands of years, of course, and still were. The area, and the falls themselves, remained pristine, wild, unconquerable country for decades after the Corps of Discovery passed through. Then in 1880, an entrepreneur from Fort Benton visited the area because he'd read about the falls in Lewis's published journals and was fascinated. The man's name was Paris Gibson, a businessman who'd already succeeded and failed magnificently in the Minneapolis area before seeking fortunes anew, like so many other people, farther west. He looked upon all that crashing water and, besides beauty, saw dollar signs.

In 1883 Gibson, with a few financial helpers, "acquired" the land and laid out his dream city. With grand plans to turn it into "another Minneapolis," he called it "Great Falls." His best, most hopeful connection was with an old associate from Minnesota, James J. Hill. Hill was the president and primary stockholder of the Great Northern Railway, who told Gibson of his plans to push his railroad out west. Gibson knew that if he could get his city connected to the railroad, that would open up vast opportunities to markets all over the growing country. With mines in Butte and Helena blowing up, Hill agreed. He established the Montana Central Railroad, which came to town in 1887. Great Falls was incorporated on November 28, 1888, just over two weeks after the final connection was made linking Helena, Butte, and Great Falls north to Havre and from there, connection to the entire length of the Great Northern Line, what we call today the Hi-Line. Already boasting a population of over two thousand citizens, Great Falls doubled in size in just a couple more years.

Industry kept coming. The first dam on the Missouri at the falls started generating power in 1890 at a spot called Black Eagle, named from another Lewis journal entry because of a bird sighting he wrote of on a small island here. Over the coming decades, four more power-generating dams would follow, granting Great Falls its nickname the "Electric City" and obliterating any resemblance the falls had to what Captain Lewis saw.

The Black Eagle dam provided power to a 502-foot smelter stack built and operated by the Anaconda Copper Mining Co., or ACM. The ACM and others used the smelter to process ore from the copper mines in Butte. Operations began in 1893, where it proceeded to provide an abundance of working-class jobs . . . as well as unimaginable pollution to the local air and the waters of the Missouri. It was shut down in 1980 and the stack was demolished in 1982. The immediate 250-acre area around the operation was declared a Superfund site in 2011 due to elevated levels of many substances that will make people die. Today, the town of Black Eagle overlooks the Missouri River and Giant Springs State Park, which contains the Roe River, which, at only around two hundred feet long, is claimed by many to be the world's shortest.

When the Butte mines were raging, the Black Eagle smelter employed upward of 1,400 workers to purify material that was first torn out of the ground in Butte, initially processed in Anaconda, then sent up the rail line to Black Eagle. "The final product, refined copper, zinc, and other metals and minerals, was then distributed to manufacturing plants across the United States, or turned into copper wire and cable by another group of Black Eagle workers at a different part of the facility."

Black Eagle, which began as little more than a man camp of construction workers, quickly attracted many immigrants from Croatia and Italy who found themselves less than welcome in Butte. They settled in fine here along the Missouri, and "by the early twentieth century, although a number of other racial-ethnic groups peopled Black Eagle, Croatians and Italians so dominated the town that it was called Little Chi (for Chicago) or Little Milwaukee, after cities known for their large numbers of Southeastern Europeans."

Concurrently, as Great Falls grew to be the largest city in the region, it also attracted—or, more accurately, retained—a growing population of displaced or landless Indians at its fringes. The west side of the city, on what would come to be known as Hill 57, is where they congregated.

∽

I never had any connection to Great Falls before I started digging around in the Little Shell community. Over the years my rock band has played a handful of shows here; one at the fairgrounds, a few at a now-closed dive bar off Highway 87 headed toward Malmstrom Air Force Base, and another preposterously unattended free-for-all well over a decade ago outside at the Harley-Davidson dealer in early fall that was cancelled due to a hailstorm and noise complaints. The last time we were slated to play there, in 2019, we cancelled the morning of the show because we determined it wouldn't be safe to make the round trip due to a winter storm warning. The warning was prescient: the storm unloaded almost two feet of snow on the city by nightfall, essentially shutting it down. In mid-September.

From its headwaters far to the south, the Missouri River flows north through the heart of the city, absorbing the Sun River coming from the west along the way before curling off to the east and then northward toward Fort Benton. The bulk of the city sprawls eastward from that crook in a mostly reliable grid. There are plenty of tree-lined streets and park spaces—magnificent in spring and fall—and several lovely museums. The Charles M. Russell Museum is particularly beautiful, as much to see the display of Russell's Métis sash as his art, and though I get a little hot under the saddle over all the Lewis and Clark worship in this region, the Lewis and Clark National Historic Trail Interpretive Center, a beautiful museum built right into the cliffs above the Missouri river, is always an interesting visit.

I don't want to dump on it, but I have to admit Great Falls is a difficult city to love. I try to find reasons to warm up to it but it's a tough go. It's in a beautiful part of the state but the weather is unpredictable and often brutal. In most parts of downtown the city itself runs a little dilapidated and has a hard-luck vibe, and no one I know ever says good things about it. A friend once quipped that every time she's in Great Falls on a weekend the downtown at night is like a ghost town, except maybe one distant figure staggering down the middle of the street yelling things. It's a sad, not inaccurate description of my experience of the city too. All that long-gone industry once made it a strong union town. Now, like so many other parts of Montana, it's more a hotbed of far-right reactionary politics than ever before, and that hangs like a cloud over the entire city.

For all its troubles I maintain a soft spot for Great Falls and don't mind visiting. In fact, it was at a reading at Cassiopeia Books for *One-Sentence Journal* that I met and became friends with my first known Little Shell relative. Cassiopeia at the time was a little hole-in-the-wall shop just off the edge of the Great Falls downtown, in a ramshackle building shared with a store selling music gear. The owner was a young man named Andrew who, through diligence and loveliness, had cultivated a vibrant community of people who came out to support literature. My event was no exception. There had to be fifteen or twenty people squeezed into the little nook where events were held, seated on folding chairs while I took to the lectern at the front, and I really had no business drawing that many people at that point in my so-called career.

After my reading, a woman approached me who looked oddly familiar though I couldn't place her face. She wore a faded denim jacket and a skirt. She had straight, dark hair reaching to her shoulders, dark eyes in an open face, and a smile as warm as her hug. She introduced herself as Kim McKeehan, there with her husband, Kelly. She told me she'd seen an article about the event in the local paper and had come out to support a fellow Little Shell member.

When I asked Kim if she was Little Shell, too, she said, "Yes, I'm on the tribal council." That's when it all clicked: Kim was sworn in as a member of the tribal council at the same quarterly meeting where I learned my application for enrollment was accepted. The synchronicity felt momentous, and it was. Kim has since become one of my closest and most cherished friends. Similarly aged (though I have a few years on her), we occasionally rant to each other over the phone, share poetry via text messages, and email articles and event information about all manners Indigenous and spiritual. I've eaten meals in her kitchen and offered tobacco and shared prayers at the firepit in her backyard.

We're also blood relatives. Kim's connection to the LST is through her father's side, the Doney family—my grandma Ruby's people. With that shared ancestry we've determined we are some degree of cousin, but neither one of us has really dug into it to figure out exactly the path or degree. We just got close enough and that's that: we're cousins. Kim is, in every way, my kin.

Our paths in connecting to our Indigenous heritage aren't so different either.

~

"I knew I was Little Shell ever since I knew I was Indian," Kim says, bustling around her kitchen in 2019 and preparing a meal while I sit at her table recording the conversation. "I can't remember a time not knowing. My mom kept me aware of it. She kept me going to Native community things whenever I could."

Kim's father was in and out of Kim's life, and at various times she would find herself part of a large Indian community. But it never lasted. Kim lived with her mother, who wasn't Indian, so when her dad wasn't around those Native ties loosened.

"I didn't have a steady connection to my dad's family and no connection to other Little Shell people until I was forty years old," Kim says. "Of course I knew some of my family members a little bit, but mostly I was out to sea with the Little Shell community. I had to piece together Chippewa identity from what I could find."

Kim saw writer, activist, and two-time United States vice presidential candidate Winona LaDuke on the cover of a magazine. "Because she identified as Chippewa, she became a role model for me," Kim says. "That's all. She was sitting in a wicker chair that my eyes tricked me into believing was a big brown wing. A very celestial meaning! She's *Major Arcana,* man. I've actually met her several times now. I sat next to her for lunch the first time but couldn't say a thing! So I wrote my feelings in a card, all that she'd meant to me, and gave it to her assistant. I learned a lot by following her story."

Kim was enrolled with the LST by one of her father's sisters in 1990. For Kim, enrollment meant an opportunity for advanced education. She used the Indian fee waiver and got started at university that same year. She has since earned a BA in English literature, an MA in Native American studies, and a master of social work. Today she's a licensed clinical social worker.

During those years, Kim continued to make inroads to the LST community, but she says low self-esteem and fear kept her from really reaching out. She knew she had aunties in Great Falls, and knew they were involved in the tribe, but she wasn't sure how to connect to them.

"At one point in my travels across the state I visited with an auntie, and she knew exactly who I was," Kim says. "She took me to bingo or something and bragged around about me and I was like, 'Wow, this is really weird.'"

Slowly the stars began to align for Kim's direct involvement. While working on her master of arts in Native American studies in Bozeman, she drove to Great Falls to attend an LST quarterly meeting. Another summer she attended the Little Shell powwow. Later, Kim worked with the enrollment office to get a copy of her family tree.

"In 2017 I answered an ad to become part of the research team for the language program," Kim says. "I got hired by Gerald Gray Sr. to work on that project. I've been a part of it [the tribe] ever since, about as much as you can be involved."

Besides working full-time as a social worker, Kim has other duties related to her position as a council member. She serves as a health liaison for the Little Shell Tribe and is a member of the Montana Native American Suicide Task Force, American Indian

Health Leaders, the American Indigenous Research Association, and the Indigenous Research Initiative. It's a lot of work.

"Don't think I know what I'm doing when I'm doing this!" Kim says with a laugh. "I just know I need to do these things."

I share this sentiment with Kim: being enrolled means something intuitively, that it's part of that elusive "something bigger." Even then it takes work, as any relationship does. But the effort to reconnect is worth it, even through periods of frustration.

"It is my joy and my pleasure to be warm toward the Little Shell people," Kim says. It's why she lives in Great Falls.

~

As I've said, the people who became the Little Shell Tribe have been in the Great Falls area for generations. They were largely overlooked and willfully forgotten . . . until they weren't.

The massive smoke-belching smelter at Black Eagle dominated what was then the western edge of the Great Falls skyline for almost one hundred years. The work there was dangerous and hard, but the immigrant workforce was happy to have a place to create a community. By the time WWI broke out in Europe in 1914, the smelter had been operating for roughly a quarter century. On May 18, 1917, the United States federal government authorized the Selective Service Act of 1917. This act, "the draft," was instituted to raise troops through conscription to serve in the war. Many immigrant laborers were drafted, depleting their numbers, so the ACM turned to the next readily available workforce: the local landless Indians.

Barely a year earlier the Rocky Boy's Chippewa Cree reservation had been established by an act of Congress just north of Great Falls on September 7, 1916. The goal had been to provide a home to all the mixed-race Indians living in communities like Hill 57 and shuffle them off, out of sight and out of mind to the good white citizens of the city. Unfortunately, the land set aside at Rocky Boy's was too small to accommodate everyone, so many found their way back to the "Moccasin Flats" and "Breed Town" areas of cities like Great Falls and Havre. Some found work at the meat plant in Great Falls. Others got by as best they could, and others found work at the ACM smelter.

Indian community leaders determined who received those valuable ACM jobs too. These early Little Shell leaders began to manage their people "through Moccasin Flat communities in the form of access to jobs . . . and helped provide quality workers that got along well enough with other immigrant groups." The Indian community benefited, and so did ACM management.

For most of the Indians working, though, it didn't last. By the thirties copper prices were down, and as other immigrants returned from the war or migrated to the Black Eagle community, anti-Indian sentiment flourished. Historian Matthew L. Basso writes, "One Black Eagle worker's recollections hint at the all-too-familiar mechanism of accusation blended with stereotype used to remove Indian workers from the plant: 'The Indians, they stole too many things. In fact they cleaned out one of the welding shops for the Zinc plant. They had all the stuff, but [the Company] found it. Finally we just had to eliminate the Indians, that was all. I'll never forget it.'"

In a joint effort by employer and employee, the white immigrants burned all the riverside camps of landless Indians they could find and drove the people living there away. Most retreated back to the relative safety of Hill 57. A few Indians remained employed at the smelter—those perhaps who had managed to avoid living in camps or could "pass" as white—but the vast majority were out.

Great Falls has by now swallowed up almost all its little fringe communities such that, if you don't take time to learn about them, you'll never know of their significance. It's rare that a municipality puts up a sign that says, "Poor people were allowed to live here." Quite the opposite. Like every aspect of US history that's less than stellar, and there's a lot of it, the dominant culture does its best to bury anything that doesn't fit the intended narrative.

Hill 57, looming over the northwest edge of Great Falls with its base clustered largely now by residential homes, could've suffered that fate. It hasn't, at least not entirely. The Little Shell Tribe still openly occupies Hill 57 today. In 2012, the tribe used funds raised by selling land donated to the tribe in Kalispell to purchase 2.5 acres at the base of the hill, just off Stuckey Road. Later, the tribe was able to add another acre to the site and has added more since. Here is where the tribal cultural center was built. The choice to establish a presence here is determined and significant, because without Hill 57, there may not be a Little Shell Tribe.

Of course, there remains this question: What *is* Hill 57?

CHAPTER 13

2020

GREAT FALLS, MONTANA

IN LATE 1958 NBC DEBUTED A Sunday-afternoon program called *Kaleidoscope*. The show was to be a news magazine of sorts, airing a different story every week. Its second episode featured a segment called "The American Stranger." It's an interesting watch—the intrigued viewer may find it online easily enough—and fairly progressive for its time. It focuses largely on the United States government's policy of Indian termination, which spanned roughly two decades from the 1940s to the 1960s. "Termination" was an effort to undermine Indian sovereignty through the abolition of tribes and reservations completely. Termination was, as ever, a land and resources grab, and Indians would be assimilated into American culture whether they wanted to be or not. The effort largely failed, though it did create an untold degree of hassle, hardship, and expense for tribes who either found themselves terminated and had to fight to regain their status or had to struggle to fight the effort in the first place. In Montana, the CSKT reservation was marked for termination, but the tribe resisted and ultimately overcame the threat in 1954.

During the "The American Stranger," Montana political legend Lee Metcalf is interviewed from his office in Helena. At the time of the documentary Metcalf, who would go on to serve nearly two decades in the US Senate—the first from the state to have actually been born in Montana—is Montana's lone member of the US House of Representatives. Metcalf was opposed to termination. He says the BIA policy of termination is "calculated to sandbag the Indians into selling their land and other resources," that the ramifications of termination would be complete loss of tribal identity, tribal income, and make Indians a burden on the state "in and around the communities" where they had always lived.

It wasn't just an issue in Montana. Louise Erdrich's 2021 Pulitzer Prize–winning novel *The Night Watchman* is a fictional account of her own grandfather's efforts to stop termination of the Turtle Mountain reservation in North Dakota. Suffice it to say, wherever there were Indians, the government was still trying to terminate them.

"The American Stranger" uses several examples from communities around the country to show what Metcalf's assessment might look like, particularly, the landless Indians of Montana, the poor mixed-race people living on Hill 57 in Great Falls.

"Can't talk about Great Falls and the Little Shell without talking about Hill 57," says Duane Reid, the Little Shell tribal historic preservation officer. For Reid, and for many others in the Little Shell community, the landmark is synonymous with the tribe. I went to Duane Reid for answers because few know more about the place and its history than him. While pursuing a master of arts degree in Missoula he studied Hill 57 and wrote about it extensively.

Duane is a curious individual, which I love that about him. He's stocky bordering on stout, with light brown hair and stunning blue eyes. He speaks in an odd, high-pitched, singsong of a voice that's dropping some high-level science on you one moment, then a ribald, inappropriate-in-most-contexts joke the next. Like Kim McKeehan, I first encountered Duane at the fateful quarterly meeting of the Little Shell tribal council where I learned my application for enrollment was approved. Duane was there giving a presentation on many of the things we later discussed over the phone. Like many Little Shell members, Duane and his family make their home today on the CSKT reservation. An avid fisherman, Duane has promised to show me "all the good spots" on Flathead Lake, but I've yet to take him up on it.

Reid grew up in the mixed-race Native communities of Choteau and Havre in Montana. Reid's grandmother was Joseph Dussome's niece. Joseph Dussome is the subject of historian Verne Dusenberry's magnificent 1958 essay "Waiting for a Day That Never Comes: The Dispossessed Métis of Montana," which was published in the Montana Historical Society's magazine, *Montana: The Magazine of Western History*. Since the 1920s Dussome was directly involved in efforts to get land for his people. Dusenberry's essay remains possibly the best exploration of that era we might now call Little Shell history. Duane Reid's grandmother participated in Dussome's efforts to get the landless Indians of Montana recognized, and helped organize various dances and other social events to raise money for tribal delegates to travel to Washington, DC, to make their case for recognition. Hill 57 served as a central gathering place where people convened to plan how to move efforts forward.

"Growing up it was just something that all the elders talked about, and such a famous place," Reid says of Hill 57. "I would consider it to be like the capital of the Little Shell Tribe. You know, one of the main places that business and everything got run out of."

While he wasn't enrolled as a member of the LST until he became an adult, being among the people was very much part of Reid's life.

"You ever read the book *The Outsiders* or *Rumble Fish*?" he says with a laugh. He refers to the classic young adult novels written by S. E. Hinton that feature rival gangs of poor youth squaring off against gangs from wealthier families. "It was like that. We were always like our own people, and it was kind of fucked up. I remember being told to fight kids I had no problems with but like their dad or uncle was being prejudiced to our general community. It was like that; that's who you belonged to, that's who you spend your time with."

Reid grew up hearing much lore surrounding the use of Hill 57—from even before the 1920s when it came to be called that—and its importance to Indians. We know Indigenous people have been in the Missouri River area for thousands of years, using and sharing the region's boundless resources, like the buffalo jump at Ulm Pishkun, less than a day's journey away on foot. Or the Old North Trail, which has been used by Blackfeet people and others for thousands of years, that connects the far north with what is Mexico today. This path skirts the Rocky Mountain Front near modern towns like Bynum, Dupuyer, and Choteau, all locations in what we call the Métis Archipelago. It's no stretch to surmise that a landmark like Hill 57 would be part of these ancient migration paths.

"There's a lot of cosmology around [Hill 57]," says Reid, who holds an MA in anthropology and a BA in tribal historic preservation. "In my studies, with Hill 57 and Montana, [I believe] there's a good chance there was Chippewa culture in Montana for a couple thousand years. Archaeological research can prove this."

Reid speaks of migration stories passed from generation to generation, and priceless old birch-bark scrolls that reference, if one knows how to read them, geographic locations like Red Lake and Leech Lake, both Chippewa homeland communities in Minnesota that connect westward to rivers in North Dakota and Montana.

~

There's dispute over where Hill 57's modern name came from. Depending on who you ask, you might hear it's an aerial designation tied to the Great Falls Malmstrom Air Force Base, or that it's a kind of map quadrant description that was indicated for future use as a reservation. "The American Stranger" documentary claims that the landmark was named "from the maps used by army / air force pilots when they made a brief and spectacularly unsuccessful effort to carry the US mails."

The correct answer is its simplest. In 2019 I was in Billings for the High Plains Book Awards. *One-Sentence Journal* earned me the award for best first book and finalist nod for best book by an Indigenous writer. Renowned writer Thomas McGuane was also there for an award, and we got to chatting about future projects. I mentioned this book and he asked, "Is it true that Hill 57 in Great Falls is named for a guy selling pickles or something?" McGuane was right. That's how the landmark got its name.

The Hill 57 moniker results from a quasi-marketing scheme / art project by a pickle salesman named Art Hinck who, in the late 1920s, was trying to advertise his line of "Heinz 57 Varieties of canned goods, pickles, and condiments."

Hinck, originally from Minnesota, worked for the H. J. Heinz Co. in various parts of Montana before landing in Great Falls in 1918. Later, over the course of several months in the late 1920s, Hinck and his family combined picnic visits to the top of the hill with sign building. They piled and shaped rocks onto the face of the hill into two numbers eighty feet long and thirty-five feet wide. After hauling water up to whitewash them, the giant "57" could be seen for miles.

The sign is long gone, though there's a large "GF" near the same spot, which stands for Great Falls High School and is maintained by students. But the name has stuck, especially as it relates to the Indians living in the area. As the story goes, the landless refugees existed on the fringe of a larger settler community and were there because they had nowhere else to go. They quickly became known as the Hill 57 Indians.

~

"There were more than just Riel refugees [from the North-West Rebellion of 1885, as often alleged] living at Hill 57," Reid says. "There's a reason why people came to these places. Hill 57's use is much older than as an enclave for refugee Indians. People went there because it was a place where they'd already gathered."

Reid employs computer software to overlay aerial photos from as early as the late thirties on top of those from subsequent years to illustrate the evolving pattern of settlement on Hill 57. It shows change over time as well as where different building structures were and the comings and goings of early traffic.

"It's really neat, too, because you could actually see the old trails and roads that would lead down to the waterfall [the namesake of Great Falls, on the Missouri River]," Reid says. "The trails lead down to the river, and different other places coming and going to Hill 57. You can see that all of the infrastructure of a tribal nation was already there prior to the white settlements."

I've seen Reid's overlaying photographs on multiple occasions and I'm never less than fascinated. Indeed, as the city of Great Falls expands, the photographs reveal new square neighborhood tracts over the Indigenous trails, slowly erasing and replacing them. Today, while there are still open spaces and some signs of people having lived a somewhat rougher existence not so long ago if you know where to look, Hill 57 and its surrounding area looks like any other suburban area sprawl. The most overt evidence of the people who lived there in the early to mid-twentieth century are gone, replaced by quiet neighborhoods, traffic, and, at the hill's base, convenience stores and fast-food restaurants flashing neon signs.

~

There's nothing pretty about Hill 57. At around two thousand feet of elevation, it isn't even that tall, though you can pretty much see it from anywhere in the city. It's just a bald, treeless knob of sandstone, covered in rock and scrubby, ground-hugging plants. In today's world there really isn't any reason to so much as look twice at it.

But it's a landmark, and the importance of landmarks on a landscape can't be understated. It's easy for us in the modern world to lose touch with their significance, relying more and more every day on the beeps and exhortations of GPS devices that belittle our navigational choices in any number of voices. Most of my drives I spend arguing with that voice because it's just me and her and who else am I going to talk to? And what does she care if I veer half a block off course to get gas or use a restroom or whatever other reason I have to deviate from the route she's demanding?

When stars aren't visible to navigate by, any sizable bump in the horizon is going to matter to hunters looking for a particular spot to camp with good shelter and water access, or to travelers leading a train of squeaking carts across the wide-open prairie. These navigational landmarks often carried spiritual significance as well.

Duane Reid, Nicholas Vrooman, and others believe Hill 57 was part of a much larger network of trade routes that connected sacred sites and villages Indigenous people used for centuries. Hill 57 communities probably served as seasonal camps or even permanent habitation long before Europeans laid eyes on the region. In other words, Native people lived on and around Hill 57 long before they were exiled there or, more likely, chose to gather there in the face of encroachment. It's then that places like Hill 57 take on even greater significance.

This much at least is a familiar story to many: When the United States began expanding westward in earnest in the early 1800s, the grasping hands of empire wanted every bit of land and its resources. Wars were fought and blood was spilled. Indian tribes, inhabitants of the landscape for millennia, were herded onto reservations or killed. Despite the attempted genocide, tribes held on or hid right out in the open.

It wasn't until the early 1920s that Indians were considered, or allowed to become, American citizens. Even then, the United States continued its policy toward assimilating tribes out of existence and taking, once and for all, what few resources they had left. Tribes were moved farther from their traditional homelands, or squeezed into the tiniest corner of them. Children were taken and placed in boarding schools where they were forbidden to speak the languages of their parents. Those languages began to fade, dying out with their last remaining speakers. Cultures teetered on the brink of extinction as Indigenous people were largely forbidden to engage in traditional spiritual practices.

In the context of shared territory that existed precontact, landmarks like Hill 57 served as safe havens for people who risked deep harm if they were caught mixing with settler communities. Reservation Indians risked imprisonment or worse for leaving their reservations without permission. That doesn't mean they didn't risk it, especially if they needed specific, traditional rituals that couldn't happen under the watchful eyes of government agents assigned to the reservations. Even today, more than fifty Indian tribes are represented in the Great Falls population. They aren't there for its hospitality to their ancestors.

"Places like Hill 57 are where traditions were kept alive," Reid says. "When people talk about how sick people living up there were, it's also because that's where sick people would visit for healing. If you go looking just for poverty and sickness, that's what you're going to find."

It wasn't merely a location to go for healing either. People from all over gathered for religious ceremonies, for drumming and dancing and celebration, and for fellowship and a place to speak their own forbidden languages. There was constant movement from Hill 57 to settlements in the canyons of the Rocky Mountain Front Range near Choteau and on north and west to Heart Butte on the Blackfeet reservation (a community also featured in "The American Stranger"). From there people might move to Canada or east along the Hi-Line to Havre and settlements in the Milk River country, to the Judith Basin and south to Lewistown and its mixed-race enclave, or to any number of settlements in the Métis Archipelago—the Moccasin Flats communities—scattered across Montana. None of the movement were random. These were trade and travel routes established long before Europeans ever ventured into the North American wilderness. People traveled to visit family, or move to a place and stay awhile, or on to other opportunities as they presented themselves. There were even groups of Métis people who journeyed farther west to work in the orchards of Eastern Washington and stayed there.

This movement is particularly familiar to me because I've spent the last several years making similar trips for similar reasons: visits with friends and family, ceremony, and all the other reasons. Given the familiar faces I often see—including relatives from Canada down for the same reasons—it's obvious the tradition is alive and well. We modern folks are fortunate to be able to cover way more ground and faster.

It's not to say life on Hill 57 wasn't hard. It was. Poverty was severe and heartbreaking well into the middle of the twentieth century. The entire community shared a single water pump.

There was no electricity. Food and income were scarce. The local dump was scavenged for recyclables and useable household items. Families received leftover scraps from the slaughterhouse to make meals from. Those without jobs found work where they could. Conditions were bad enough to receive the attention of scholars and aid organizations. And television producers.

~

It wasn't until the American Indian Religious Freedom Act of 1978 provided that "it shall be the policy of the United States to protect and preserve for American Indians their inherent right of freedom to believe, express, and exercise the traditional religions of the American Indian, Eskimo, Aleut, and Native Hawaiians, including but not limited to access to sites, use and possession of sacred objects, and the freedom to worship through ceremonial and traditional rites" that Indians could move their practices, for the most part, into the open. As cultures and languages teeter on the brink of extinction, it remains to be seen if it came too late. For those that survived, it's because of people keeping their ways alive by going underground with them in locations like Hill 57.

By the seventies the population of Indians on Hill 57 had dwindled as people scattered to the growing cities of Montana and Idaho, where work could be found. A core population of Métis and Chippewa Cree people who comprise the Little Shell Tribe remained in the area, and still do. As efforts toward federal recognition intensified, the Little Shell maintained a base of operation in Great Falls. If not at Hill 57, then very near its shadow.

In 2013 the tribe built a two-story aluminum-sided building on the two-plus acres of land off Stuckey Road to serve as its cultural center, now called the Shawn Gilbert Event Center for the late son of former tribal chairman John Gilbert. It's where the tribe gathers for meetings and celebrations. It's hoped that one day it can be a focal point of more Little Shell activities centered on Hill 57, a place, despite its history of darker times, still sacred to the community.

"I was raised on stories of Hill 57 told by people like my uncles, my mother, and my grandmother," Duane Reid says. "It can literally be said that Hill 57 . . . molded me and is inseparable from my identity and my worldview."

∽

I can't claim anywhere near as personal a connection to Hill 57 as Duane Reid and others can. The first couple times I visited our cultural center, I didn't even realize it was at Hill 57. When I asked Nicholas Vrooman during a gathering there where the hill was in relation to where we were, he pointed, grinned, and said, "That's it right there." I was a little embarrassed.

One afternoon I drove out to the cultural center. It was closed and nobody was around. I walked to the back fence and turned my gaze up the slope of the hill. I imagined what it might've been like to live in the area in tar paper shacks, or in the remains of broken-down cars. When I left, rather than return to the highway and head for home I turned right and followed the looping dirt road that winds up and around to the top. I wasn't even sure the route would take me where I wanted it to. I really didn't even know where I wanted it to take me. It was a day in late summer, and the air was hot, and the unrelenting wind blew the dust from my passage west across dry, brown fields. I was thinking of an acquaintance who had grown up in Great Falls who asked me, "Why would anybody want to live up on top of an exposed rock like that anyway?"

Maybe what we now call Hill 57 wasn't ever supposed to serve as a place for our people to live. But when you're forced to make a stand, you don't always get to choose where. One person's grubby exposed rock is another's unassailable fortress, whether that be in a physical or spiritual sense. Our ancestors did what they had to for us to even be here, and clearly they knew what they were doing.

I visit Great Falls several times a year now. From where I live it's a six-hour round trip by car, and given the traffic and terrain the highway passes through one really can't shorten it by merely driving a little faster. I avoid the route entirely at night because of all the wildlife. I'm not talking about little critters like raccoons and badgers and foxes, though there are those too. I mean big animals like elk and moose and grizzly bears. At the ranger station in Lincoln, about halfway between Missoula and Great Falls, they have on display a taxidermized grizzly bear that was struck by a man driving a pickup just outside Ovando, a small town along the route. My dad and I drove to Lincoln and back one day just to have a look at it. As much as I love bears, I wouldn't want to come face-to-face with such an animal, particularly if either of us was feeling a little crabby.

The drive on Highway 200, up over 5,600-foot-high Rogers Pass and across the Continental Drive, is magnificent. Much of it on the west side parallels the storied Blackfoot River through rugged, pine-covered canyons and willow-crowded meadows until the highway begins to climb up and over, the course of the river in summer speckled with rafters and kayakers and folks slinging fly rods. The seasonally changing colors of the myriad cottonwood trees are as glorious to me as any photos I've seen of similar changes in the northeastern part of the United States. And then, descending down the east side of the Front Range and into the fringes of the rolling hills of the Great Plains is a sight to behold. Endless hills and canyons painted by shadows on either end of every day that isn't cloudy, small groups of pronghorn almost as likely to be seen as Black Angus cattle. I never get tired of this drive, not in any season, even the ones that make me sweat in my seat either from heat or white-knuckling the steering wheel as I guide my vehicle over treacherous snow and ice.

Suffice it to say, most of my Great Falls trips are overnighters. Whenever I'm in the city, I make a point to orient myself against Hill 57. I just like to know where I am and what I'm doing in relation to it. I think of this as being a kind of connection back across time and distance to how our ancestors found their bearings across the expanse of prairie.

The landmark's significance has certainly taken on a large part of my view of what it means to be Little Shell, if only through the stories of people closer to it. My worldview as an Indigenous person was shaped by attitudes related to Hill 57 and the shame that was imposed on people who live in poverty, and how that affected my father and his view of his family. How it affected so many people I've come to be acquainted with. I don't know if there were La Trays in the Hill 57 community, but there are La Trays in Great Falls now, and all across the Hi-Line. We're as culturally connected to that history as anyone in the tribe, whether my dad chose to accept it or not. That means something to me.

CHAPTER 14

2019

BRITISH COLUMBIA, CANADA

NORTHBOUND ON HIGHWAY 93 en route to Canada for a long weekend retreat in Banff—a place neither Julia nor I have ever visited—we stuff contraband into our mouths so we aren't accosted by stern border guards while attempting to cross. Only we're middle-aged so it isn't drugs, it's fruit: three or four nectarines and an apple we need to make scarce, all because more than one of Julia's friends urged her not to have any fruit in the car at the border or she might "get in trouble." So at the last moment, realizing we're minutes away from a potential international incident, Julia tears the rinds off the citrus and stuffs the evidence in the compartment between the front seats. Then we both jam the little sections into our faces.

Soon we're at the border crossing. The guard, a bit surly (a requirement for employment, I think), asks a few questions, looks at our passports, then allows us through. He doesn't even mention fruit, and I'm a little disappointed.

It's beautiful, this part of the continent, and British Columbia doesn't disappoint. We drive for miles—kilometers now, since Canada, like every other reasonable country in the world, uses the metric system—without seeing so much as another car. There are looming peaks around us, lush pine forests, and deep, green meadows. It's magnificent and invigorating.

That's when an unfamiliar alert lights up on the dashboard. We're making the trip in a new-to-us car, a secondhand blue 2006 Prius we received only a couple months earlier from Julia's father. I show Julia the ominous orange light and she digs into the glove compartment to find the user's manual, then looks up the indicator to see what it means. The results are inconclusive—maybe something related to the oil? I have a moment of panic, certain that somewhere along the line we dropped the oil pan on this high-tech, strangely unfamiliar vehicle and we're moments away from being stranded in a foreign country where our phones don't work. We pull off the highway as soon as we can into what looks like a convenience store but also isn't, as so many things in Canada are just slightly different from what we're accustomed to. It's an old bread box–shaped, whitewashed building with a couple drab hand-painted signs that, in Missoula, the city wouldn't be able to tear down fast enough to replace with some glass-and-neon abomination representing some awful regional chain establishment.

I get out of the car, pop the hood, and pull the dipstick to make sure we have oil. We do. Nothing appears amiss; maybe it's just a warning to tell us we're due for an oil change, not an indication that any sort of dire situation is imminent.

As I tinker under the hood and scratch my head, I can hear the voice of a young woman. I can't hear her clearly but peeking around the upraised hood I see her: a young Indigenous woman standing near the entrance of the little parking lot we pulled into, a backpack and a duffle bag at her feet, arguing into a cell phone. She stands still, then paces, then stands still again. I can't understand what she's saying but she's agitated.

I get in the car and report my conclusions about our vehicle to Julia. She agrees we don't seem in any immediate danger but should get the oil changed at first opportunity. Then she gestures toward the woman. "Did you catch any of that?" she asks.

"Some," I say. "But not really."

"Sounds like boyfriend problems," Julia says. I nod, and we sit looking at each other for a few moments. "Do you think we should see if she needs a ride?" Julia says.

"I think we probably should," I say. Julia nods, gets out of the car, and starts walking toward the young woman. Obviously she's thinking the same thing I am: this is how it happens.

~

Indigenous women disappear with staggering frequency. In 2019 Canada released a report titled *Reclaiming Power and Place*. The report was the result of the National Inquiry into Missing and Murdered Indigenous Women and Girls, which was begun in 2016 by Canadian prime minister Justin Trudeau. The crisis of missing women and girls was so overwhelming it was determined to be "genocide."

South of the Medicine Line the statistics are sobering. Eighty-four percent of Indigenous women have experienced physical, sexual, or psychological violence in their lifetime. In Montana, Indigenous women are four times more likely to go missing than non-Indians. In the fall of 2021, when a young white woman named Gabby Petito went missing in Wyoming under dubious circumstances while traveling cross-country, her disappearance dominated the news and social media cycle for days until her body was discovered. Later, news agencies including the *Salt Lake Tribune* reported that "at least 710 Indigenous people disappeared in Wyoming from 2011 to 2020, according to a report issued in January by the state's Missing and Murdered Indigenous People Task Force." Those disappearances earned little coverage. In fact, this failure to report on missing brown people has carried a name of its own since 2004: "Missing White Woman Syndrome."

As reported in *Red Nation Rising: From Bordertown Violence to Native Liberation*, a scathing discussion of reservation-adjacent communities called border towns, "The movement to get justice for the murders of Native women, girls, transwomen, and Two-Spirits is often represented by the acronym MMIWG2S, but no acronym captures the astonishing scope and scale of the violence." The numbers we know about aren't even accurate, because they rely on data of reported cases or cases recognized as such disappearances. Many attacks and disappearances go unreported or unnoticed outside of the families and communities where they originate. In the case of trans women, who often "do not count as 'female'" in the eyes of the colonial bureaucracy, the numbers aren't even considered.

I bring these statistics up—and there are many more, equally grim—because like so many other elements in the story of European colonization of North America, they're horrors that keep repeating themselves.

Trafficking and abuse of Indigenous women has been part of the interaction between colonial powers and the people they colonize the world over, and it's no different in North America. It's still happening today as the MMIWG2S numbers show us. Hardly a day passes when there isn't an alert going around my various social media feeds about another Indigenous person, usually young, missing in or on the fringes of Indian country.

In his book *Our History Is the Future: Standing Rock versus the Dakota Access Pipeline, and the Long Tradition of Indigenous Resistance*, historian Nick Estes describes the first river forts that defined the fur trade as the original "man camps." These forts and trading posts were, and are, "large, usually temporary, encampments of men working in extractive industries, from the fur trade to oil and gas development, where rates of sexual and domestic violence, and murders and disappearances of Native women and girls are intensified."

The idea of man camps isn't an archaic one. They still exist all over the world anywhere resource extraction is happening. They exist in modern Canada, and they exist in the United States. And wherever they exist, women go missing.

Most of what we know about the role of women in the fur trade comes from journal accounts of the trappers and traders themselves, which means we witness the lives of these women through the lens of a worldview utterly foreign to the Indigenous perspective. Not to mention the patriarchal European ideal of how women are supposed to "be," and generally only from the perspective of literate, educated men.

"Practically to a man," historian Sylvia Van Kirk writes in her essential work on the subject, *Many Tender Ties: Women in Fur-Trade Society*, "fur-trade writers articulate a view of women as being the fragile, weaker sex dependent upon the chivalrous protection of men."

Indian women worked. Hard. They were strong. They carried heavy loads from camp to camp. The work of transporting heavy animal carcasses, skinning and butchering them, tanning hides and making them useful . . . it was all hard work. Not to mention the eternal challenges of raising children. The first European traders to witness all this toil were appalled, and they expressed so in their journals and letters. They felt "the drudgery and hardship" was too much for women to endure, never mind that such lives were also more rule than exception among the women from their own countries.

Yet the horrors that followed the arrival of European men into the region weren't necessarily immediate, at least in this particular region; they were a few decades in reaching their ultimate expression of depravity. The women responsible for the establishment of the fur trade, the early mothers of the Métis culture, were no victims. They were determined and important members of their society who understood what was happening and what needed to be done.

As now, Indigenous women were confident, eager, and initiative-taking participants in their own lives. They had power in their relationships and agency in the subsequent marriages that combined vastly different cultures from distant continents, as well as much to gain from it for themselves. Women were as interested in establishing lines of trade with the Europeans as anyone else involved.

While Indians provided the traders and first-arriving settlers the necessities that came from the region—furs, meat, forage—in turn they received goods they quickly came to rely on: guns and ammo, metal knives and cooking utensils, and new fabrics for making clothing. These domestic goods went a long way toward improving the lives of Indigenous women, and they were keen to take advantage of them. But to trade, relationships had to be established. In the Indigenous cultures of the day, trade only happened among relatives, among family.

That's why these marriages had to happen. Marriages—alliances, really—through established and sometimes elaborate kinship ceremonies were essential to making early trade work. The resulting relationships became both economic and familial and laid the groundwork for an entirely new society in the region. It wasn't European, nor was it Indian. It expanded as the years passed, more marriages happened, and children were born.

If the idea of Indian women marrying into trader households sounds less than charming, it's largely because it wasn't, nor was it intended to be. Europeans and Indians had totally different ideas around sex and marriage (and divorce) and what all it was supposed to mean between the couple. Indians weren't just marrying into European circles for trade, they were also marrying into other tribes for the same reasons. Marriages within their own tribes were largely arranged for one kin relationship advantage or another. It was just part of the way things were done.

But now and then, sweetly, it was for love too.

Sometimes traders sought wives because they were lonely. After a long day—or weeks of them—doing hard, dangerous work in a desperate environment, connubial companionship can be a balm for the soul. For these men, Indian women were the only women around. European women were essentially banned from Rupert's Land for several decades, and not every trader was interested in finding love with the hairy guy snoring and farting in the next bunk. It was lonely out there; men still wanted romantic connection and families.

Sylvia Van Kirk's *Many Tender Ties* references the copious private correspondence from Hudson's Bay Company officers and the regular expressions of concern and affection they had for their nineteenth-century wives and families, as found in these journals and letters. Some of these marriages became true, devoted unions. We see this reflected in the journals of men who lamented the illnesses and mourned the deaths of their Indian wives.

I do love the idea of "many tender ties." I like to think there was abundant love in the lives of my early ancestors despite the hardships, just like love abounds today. Moments of kindness, and sweetness, and shared appreciation for the world around them. This had to be there, didn't it?

There were hurdles, of course. The clash of culture between a European man, puffed up with his own ideas of how things should proceed, and the expectations of the Indigenous family of a potential bride, for example. Rules pertaining to how officers and employees of the major trade powers—the HBC and the North

West Company, primarily—could engage with Indian women were significantly different too. But, as we poets are inclined to say in a multitude of fashions, love finds a way.

Indian women brought into the forts and trading posts were key to helping newcomers assimilate with the wilderness culture surrounding them. The importance of this can't be overstated. All the skills a woman brought to her Indigenous family before Europeans came—foraging of berries and wild rice, skinning and tanning hides, or netting and drying fish; providing familial connections to potentially important trading partners—now benefitted the fur traders, especially during lean times. Frequently, as men fulfilled their terms of service to their employers, many remained in the area as "free trappers" or "free traders" so they could remain with their wives and families. Populations grew and family connections solidified, especially as the custom of marrying "pure-blood" Indian women gave way to marriage with the subsequent generations of "mixed-race" women.

It wasn't long before most marriages taking place were between settler men and the first generations of mixed-blood women. This resulted in "a widespread and complex pattern of intermarriage" in fur-trade communities. These close ties of kinship knit people tightly together from community to community and established families that, while bearing the names of the fathers, are traced largely through the lineage of the mother and her relatives.

This is a subject I've spent considerable time reflecting on: women, and the largely unsung role they played in maintaining who we are as a culture over these centuries. It's why I wanted to devote an entire chapter to the early days that created the Métis people and show how participatory women were in its unfolding . . . and, particularly, its preservation.

I think about my grandma Ruby and her life. If she'd closed her mouth to any mention of her Chippewa family, if she'd turned her back on them like my grandpa Leo did, would I be here telling this story? Probably not. I wonder what difficulties she faced in maintaining these kinship ties in the face of my grandfather's apparent disdain for them. His disdain for Indians, for being Indian. How did it feel for her to see her children, and then her grandchildren, pushed further and further away from their roots? It had to be difficult. This struggle, and the women who maintain the relationships that preserve us—the mothers, the grandmothers, the aunties—are critical to the continued existence of our people, even if it's the men who initially did all the traveling and speaking on our behalf.

I can only speak to how it plays out in Little Shell celebrations, but I've been on the periphery of enough such things in other tribes to think it isn't uncommon. There's a lot of talk about honoring our elders, and our veterans . . . but rarely, if ever, do we specifically speak about honoring our women. During a grand entry at a powwow, for example, or any other event that includes such pageantry, it's overwhelmingly veterans (as represented by men; I've only ever seen a woman once or twice) who carry the flags at the front of the procession. In the United States, Native people volunteer for the military more than anyone else per capita. We take great pride in that.

But I also have to wonder: If there's a black MIA flag for unforgotten Vietnam vets right there next to the US flag and the state flag and the tribal flag, why isn't there a red one for MMIW?

In the introduction to their paper *Demilitarization Is Decolonization*, the South Dakota–based Native organization NDN Collective states:

> having a Relative, an uncle, an auntie, a cousin, a grandpa who served in the military is not uncommon in Indian Country. In fact, seeing veteran service hats that read "Vietnam Veteran" or "Native Vet" combined with embroidered feathers or an eagle is a guaranteed sight at any powwow or flea market. We have love for our Relatives that have seen war and came back; we have love for all our Relatives. We know that there are many unique motivations behind the enlistment of Indigenous people in the military, sometimes influenced by a sense of duty to protect our homelands and a long history of warrior culture. Relatives also enlist due to a lack of financial opportunities, lack of secondary education resources, or from familial influence—all examples of poverty draft. Yet NDN Collective's understanding is that the United States military and the Military and Police Industrial Complex (MPIC) have exploited our circumstances and our connection to warrior culture, and are ultimately pathways for exploitation and destruction of our communities within Turtle Island and internationally. We, as a collective of Indigenous people, stand with all Indigenous people everywhere who face the ongoing effects of colonialism, imperialism, climate change, capitalism, and genocide, in our position for demilitarization and Indigenous liberation as antimilitarist.

I love this statement. I join the Collective in believing we should honor our vets and celebrate their safe return from service at every opportunity. We need to make every effort to support them and see that all their needs, often severe, are seen to for as long as necessary to make them whole and happy members of our civilian community again. I also believe we need to work to create communities where our men (and women!) don't need to enlist as cannon fodder for a colonial empire that has only ever practiced genocide against us. I've heard the sentiment from Indian vets that says something to the effect of "We lost this land once, we aren't going to lose it again." I look around and have to wonder: What have we gotten back since we lost it the first time, and whose concept of "land" are we really defending?

I recall the first time I walked into the Little Shell community center at the base of Hill 57 and saw the enormous United States flag hanging over the entrance hall. I was irritated. Its presence disturbed me because I think there has been no greater impediment to the existence of my people—of all Indigenous people—than everything that flag represents.

If we're going to begin our ceremonies with the presentation of flags and people carrying them, I'd like to see additional honoring of the people who are at least equally responsible for the preservation of our communities, of our kinship networks: our women. Move them from the back of the procession to the front. Let our grandmothers and mothers and aunties carry the flags. And if any are too frail or need help, let them be assisted by our teenage children, boys and girls alike, in hopes of a better future than any of these flags represent.

It's debatable if the lives of Indian women were any better as wives of fur traders than they would've been outside of the forts. Of course they were in some ways; their husbands certainly thought they were doing them a huge favor. But these women yielded a significant amount of freedom to come and go and cultural authority once the gates closed behind them. Many European men, particularly the officers of the trading companies, set about trying to enforce their patriarchal views on the family. This included what freedoms a wife should enjoy (there were few) and how the children should be raised. Boys were often sent away for education, and as time passed the daughters, while largely influenced by and taught the skills of their mothers in the early days, became projects of fathers hoping to "civilize" them. These men thought they were acting in the best interests of the daughters but were instead sentencing them to a kind of liminal space between two worlds; no longer as culturally connected to their Indigenous families but also not European either.

A deep racism and sexism these young mixed-race women were particularly vulnerable to arrived with the coming of missionaries and white women.

The vast majority of European men who came to the region as fur traders were Catholic. When they married Indian women, part of the patriarchal overhaul of their lives was the enforcement of Catholicism in their households. This is how Métis culture became Catholic in the first place, though initially as a curious mix of its folklore with that of existing traditional Indigenous cosmology, as we'll explore more in the next chapter.

By the early 1800s there was a large mixed-race community in the region, more than records from the day accurately indicate. Marriages between the Europeans and both Indian and mixed-race women were now common. These marriages were sanctioned by regional standards, a practice important also to the Indians and based mostly on their customs. But they weren't church sanctioned because these initial marriages came before the arrival of missionaries and "official" church reckoning. The unions were instead marriages as to "the custom of the country" or "of the country," or *à la façon du pays*.

This is how the arrangement typically unfolded: First, the European man had to get permission from his potential bride's family. Approval meant a bride price paid to the Indian family, which could be as simple as a horse in exchange for a wife or a more significant amount in blankets, trade goods, trinkets, and even guns. There were no vows exchanged, at least not in the ways we typically experience today. But it worked for at least a couple generations.

It all started to change, and rapidly, with the arrival of both Catholic and Protestant missionaries. As the trading communities expanded and actual settlement loomed, the church moved in to see to the spiritual needs of the people living there and, more important, lay the groundwork for those to come. The first Red River Catholic mission was established in 1818; a Protestant mission followed two years later.

The patriarchal attitudes of the arriving missionaries changed everything. They viewed themselves as the "upholders of civilization" and acted accordingly. They believed "of the country" marriages were "sinful and debased." These missionaries—who in the case of the Protestants were among the first to bring their white wives to the area—set to attacking existing customs relentlessly under the belief that there was no hope of bringing so-called civilization to the region until marriages were church sanctioned. Even then the missionaries couldn't entirely agree on how to make that happen, a problem exacerbated by the movement and reassignment of the missionaries themselves. Some would baptize the Indian woman immediately preceding the ceremony while others believed doing so with someone who knew nothing of the scriptures was pointless. Meanwhile the European men, some of whom had been in a union with an Indian woman for a decade or more, showed varying degrees of commitment to submitting to church authority.

Does this process sound familiar? It probably does to many of us; I've personally heard of many unions that could only happen if one partner "converted" to the faith of their beloved so their marriage could meet the rules of engagement. This has always seemed absolutely ludicrous to me.

The losers in this new relationship were almost entirely, and not surprisingly, the women. The new wave of arriving traders felt no obligation to follow local customs that had made trade work in the first place, so local women—i.e., Native and mixed-race women—became objects for sexual gratification only and weren't viewed as potential wives necessary to solidify trade arrangements. The clergy identified all Indigenous women as inherently promiscuous and blamed them for the immorality that was taking place, not the traders who sought them out as wives and lovers. Racism and misogyny exploded and remains in many modern communities all across the west in how Native women are viewed.

The missionaries were relentless. In a hard press to bring men in line, they began accusing men of keeping mistresses and concubines, and of living in sin. Many of these men still hoped to maintain their upper-class stations in this new world as they had in the old. So it wasn't long before the only way an Indian woman, even of mixed race, could have any security in marriage was if it were church sanctioned. While more and more traders sought this "new" arrangement themselves, others did not. It was easy for a man moving on to ignore his "of the country" marriage and abandon his wife and family. At least the auspices of the church gave women some, if meager, protection.

Young mixed-blood women suffered most. Their fathers were raising them to be more "European." This largely cut them off from their mothers' traditions while also making them more dependent on, and vulnerable to, the region's changing society. For example, the sexual freedom women enjoyed in Indian society was eliminated as part of the "education" of young mixed-race women.

It wasn't unusual for mixed-race women to have multiple husbands during the course of their lifetimes. Their fathers offered them as wives while they were still young; fourteen- and fifteen-year-old brides were common, with some as young as twelve. (Lest you gasp at this, this was happening to women in Europe and colonial America too.) If a husband left or died, the widow was left in a precarious position, so she typically found another husband as soon as she could. Loving marriages by this point were the exception, not the rule.

While Indian women were the ones accused of perpetuating this "sinful" lifestyle, the double standards were telling. It was largely acceptable for married men to relieve their passions outside of marriage, but woe to the woman who took a lover during the often-long months of separation from her husband. She would be cast out to get along as best she could.

By the time European settlement of the region gathered momentum and assimilation into the landscape was less of a challenge, societal and class distinctions magnified. More and more white women were brought to the area from points east and overseas, and Indian and mixed-race women, with few exceptions, now became something else to European men.

Still, something was taking shape up and down these river valleys: the Métis culture. The agency of Indigenous women during the mingling of cultures in the early years of the fur trade led to the Métis nation. This creation of new settlements of people who found a way to thrive in this new cultural landscape meant that, for a time, things were good for everyone involved. There was much money and influence to be made, and Indigenous populations—particularly among the Métis—swelled.

In the excellent collection of essays she coedited called *The New Peoples: Being and Becoming Métis in North America*, author and historian Jacqueline Peterson writes, "The 'new people' of Red River—not merely biracial, multilingual and bicultural, but the proud owners of a new language; of a syncretic cosmology and religious repertoire; of distinctive modes of dress, cuisine, architecture, vehicles of transport, music and dance; and after 1815 of a quasi-military political organization, a flag, a bardic tradition, a rich folklore and a national history—sprang only metaphorically from the soil."

It didn't last, and one need only look at a map today to see who the winners and losers were. Even so, the unfolding hasn't reached its completion yet either.

~

The young woman Julia and I pick up in Canada is named Crystal, and she's happy to get a ride. I can't help but imagine all the possible ways her story could've played out differently. If a smiling predator had happened along the highway before we did, for example, or any number of other sinister narratives. It's unsettling to think about but part of Indigenous people's, particularly women's, daily lives.

As we drive north Crystal talks on her phone, coordinating with friends and a family member to arrange a meetup so she can begin to make her way home to Prince George some hours farther north. The initial plan is to take her to Elko, BC, just up the highway, but then we decide it's easier to go a little farther instead to where she has family in Cranbrook. At this point I'm ready to drive her all the way to Prince George if that's what it takes, and I tell her so. She laughs and thanks me, assuring me her family will be at the Tim Hortons in Cranbrook when we get there.

The drive allows us the opportunity to hear Crystal's story. She moved south near the blip on the map called Roosville, just this side of the border, to live with her boyfriend. As so often happens in these stories, it quickly turned sour.

"He didn't have a job," Crystal says. "And then he started making me give him money. Today I just left. I don't have any money left even for the bus and I just want to get home. That's why I'm going to my auntie's."

We make it to Cranbrook and stop at the Tim Hortons. It's a perfect time for a coffee and doughnut break anyway. While we indulge, Crystal's family arrives. We hug our goodbyes. Conveniently there's a Jiffy Lube next door, and we pull in and get the oil in the Prius changed. The light on the dash is still on, but I feel more confident. We backtrack a few miles and head to Fernie, then to Calgary, and from there to Banff. It's cost us a couple hours, but we aren't in any hurry. And Crystal, at least this time, doesn't become a statistic.

CHAPTER 15

2019

FRENCHTOWN, MONTANA

On my birthday in April 2019, my mom gave me a little teapot and some tea. I use it all the time now; it's blue, made of earthenware, and has a little basket for the tea leaves to steep in under a closed metal lid after hot water is added. It's sized for about two cups' worth, which is perfect for a little midafternoon pick-me-up, particularly during the cooler months that comprise my favorite time of year. When Mom gave it to me, the box was wrapped with a ribbon and there was an old wooden rosary attached to it. This rosary was my father's. One of his "prized possessions," she told me. I was amazed, as I'd never even seen it before.

The rosary was a gift from his grandmother Margaret Berger La Tray, who lived in Lewistown, Montana. She made the rosary for him. In our box of family photos there's a letter my dad sent her when he was ten or eleven, with a drawing of a farm. I remember being fascinated with this growing up; I still am. My dad never talked about his childhood, so these keepsakes are part of the life of a person I never knew anything about.

Mom tells me my dad was a favorite of his grandma Margaret's. The importance of their relationship to him is reflected in the password she tells me Dad frequently used on the internet: "Yendis."

"That was the name your great-grandmother called your dad," Mom says, "which is just his name spelled backward. He used it all the time."

I never met my great-grandmother Margaret, but my mom did. Over breakfast at the Reno she tells me how my dad took her to Lewistown for a visit a couple years before I was born. Born in 1888, not even a decade after her hometown was settled, she would've been in her late seventies. My folks visited during Halloween. My great-grandmother was terrified of trick-or-treaters, so she asked my folks to take her to her sister's house. As they drove, Mom tells me my dad leaned over and told her, "Now keep an eye on your wallet, we're about to enter the tribe."

"It was something like that; I'm paraphrasing," Mom says. "And it was the tribe! They were all Indians, his whole family, which was a surprise because I'd never been around his relatives at all."

At the end of the visit, as my folks were leaving, my great-grandmother stood on the porch, waving and crying. Mom says Dad told her it was sad because he thought he might never see her again. And he didn't: A couple months later Margaret went into the hospital for a routine surgery. During the operation, the doctor accidentally nicked another of her organs, which became infected and killed her. She died in 1965.

"She was just the sweetest, sweetest lady," Mom says. "She was this little Indian woman, so sweet, and very close to her sister, chatting away in whatever language they spoke."

My dad didn't speak that language, which was likely Ojibwe or Michif. If he did he never uttered it in my presence. That little quip about the wallet provides a glimpse into what he thought of his family. I suspect it reflected what, to his mind, everyone else thought of his family too: that Indians were untrustworthy thieves.

∽

If you recall, my grandma Doris, my mom's mom, wasn't keen on my dad marrying her daughter.

As my mom told me, it was either because he was Indian or because he was Catholic.

It's strange for me to think about my dad identifying in any way as Catholic because, as with his Indian heritage, I never heard him talk about it. It makes sense to me now through the lens of even just our immediate family history. His parents were Catholic; they both had Catholic funerals when they died. I was baptized Catholic when I was a baby. I always presumed it was at the request of my grandparents, but maybe my dad led the charge; I don't know and haven't asked. We weren't a churchgoing family at all, though I remember going with my mom on occasion to the Lutheran church. Apparently faith meant more to Dad than I realized, though.

"He would talk about when he would go to mass even when he was in the navy," Mom says. "At one time I think [being Catholic] meant a lot to him. And even though he tried to say it didn't, I think all through his life, even when he died, it really did mean a lot."

I ponder Dad's rosary, which hangs on the wall in front of me now, and reflect on his Catholic upbringing. I suppose I'm Catholic, too, given that's how I was baptized, though I've never for a moment considered myself such, nor will I ever. I'm too much the tree-hugging dirt worshipper for that. I've even wondered if there's a way I could be washed clean of this baptism, have it reversed, but I've never investigated that either. Ultimately I suppose it's just not that important to me. After all, didn't missionaries question the point of baptizing people who didn't know the scripture? How could it be any different for infants, especially ones who grow up with no association with the church? That's not so different from my Indigenous heritage. It's there, but it's only activated if I pursue it.

I mention the Catholicism ingrained in my dad's family because it has always been a curiosity to me and, at least until recently, I didn't understand where it came from. I knew about missionaries of course, and the role they have played and continue to play all over the world as the bloody spearpoint of colonialism. I've never been able to really understand the hold faith has on people, especially when one applies even the tiniest bit of critical thinking to the peaceful rhetoric of church leaders versus the horrors relentlessly perpetrated, century after century, by the institutions of religion. That's a question for some other day. Most important for this story, I didn't know how big a role the Métis played in helping missionaries, particularly of the Catholic variety, spread their faith.

When Belgian-born Jesuit priest Pierre-Jean De Smet arrived in the Bitterroot Valley of Montana in September 1841, five months after leaving St. Louis, the story is that he, with two younger priests and three lay brothers, brought Christianity to the "savages." This is a common story where I live, one I seem to have known my entire life, so I wonder if it wasn't somehow part of my early education. In junior high I recall De Smet School—a school I still drive by today at least once or twice a week—being one of our opponents. And Stevensville, the site of the original mission, is less than an hour away from where I live and the location of one of my favorite places to go walking and bird-watching: the Lee Metcalf National Wildlife Refuge.

My knowledge and interest in De Smet's mission has blossomed during my time researching this book. I've since learned—by reading and talking to Nicholas Vrooman, not to mention friends in the CSKT community—more details. Importantly, while that first mission was indeed the first of its kind to be erected in Montana, by then the Catholic faith was already well established in the region.

De Smet and his entourage travelled west from St. Louis on the Oregon Trail to Fort Hall, the same Hudson's Bay Company post, you may recall, where Johnny Grant traded for cattle to build his big Deer Lodge operation. These Jesuits were among the hundreds, if not thousands of parties who launched north, northwest, and even south from Fort Hall during those years. And the Red River Métis, who had built the post as part of their service to the HBC, were there all along. It was a Métis guide named Gabrielle Prudhomme who took De Smet to what's now Stevensville. De Smet's people constructed a church out of cottonwood logs held together by wooden pegs, raised a cross, and established the area's first mission, called St. Mary's. But they weren't the first to introduce Catholicism.

My cousin Kim tells me I've met the Métis scholar Émilie Pigeon at a celebration in Great Falls, but I only have the vaguest recollection of doing so. I'm ashamed of that, because the copy of her April 2017 dissertation, "Au Nom du Bon Dieu et du Buffalo: Metis Lived Catholicism on the Northern Plains," has been essential to my understanding of how the relationship between Catholicism and the Métis evolved. If it was a physical book, it would be much creased, highlighted, and dog-eared from my handling of it.

"Like other Indigenous peoples, the Métis were renowned guides and expert hunters, who knew the land, its rivers, lakes, and mountains, and navigated them with ease," Pigeon writes. "In a similar fashion, they affirmed their adhesion to Catholicism by allowing it to become an important part of their daily experiences and communal practices. Métis believers brought their faith with them throughout the northern plains."

And points southward. Métis people carried Catholicism up and down the Bitterroot Valley and all points in between long before De Smet arrived. The Red River Métis were among the people who helped convince other Indians, like the Salish, to go looking for "black robes" in the first place (or fourth, since De Smet's assignment to the area came after three previous Salish delegations to secure a priest).

Indigenous people used prayer, ceremony, music, and rituals as tools in a constant quest for spiritual assistance to overcome the unpredictabilities and hardships of life lived so intimately tied to the land. That should read "use prayer," because we still do. These rituals and ceremonies and prayers were—are—passed along just like everything else in a world rich with interactions between people for the purpose of trade and, particularly between tribes, marriage. The original version of the Catholic faith that the Métis practiced was an element of this network of cultural interaction.

The St. Mary's Mission, then, could be said to be not so much something new related to the spread of Catholicism, just the latest node in growing points of connection for family networks that shared spiritual practices all over the region.

Catholicism arrived early among the people who would become the Red River Métis. It didn't arrive with missionaries, though. Instead it arrived in the practices of the first European men to travel to the region and begin setting up trading posts and forts. Not just among officers and employees of the fur-trade companies, but also among the legendary voyageurs who joined them.

The voyageurs, French for "travelers," tend to be the heroes of the fur-trade era because of their exploits, which exist today in songs and folklore. Described as "French Canadians," their origin predates that of the Red River Métis, though they were largely of a Métis people, too, from European/Indigenous interaction earlier in the colonization of North America. The voyageurs were renowned for their ability to transfer huge loads of furs and supplies over the lakes and rivers at remarkable speed, not just over water, but portaging loads—like ninety-pound bundles of furs carried two at a time—overland around rapids and between waterways.

In his excellent book *Astoria: Astor and Jefferson's Lost Pacific Empire*, the writer Peter Stark describes the joyfully furious voyageur assault on waterways:

> A voyageur canoe, for several centuries, was by far the fastest mode of transportation into the wild heart of the North American continent. Propelled by the powerful arms of the voyageurs, commanded by the steersman, and paddling in exact unison at forty to sixty strokes per minute, these canoes surged through the water at four to six miles per hour, a remarkable speed. Paddling twelve to fifteen hours per day, with short breaks while afloat for a pipe of tobacco (they measured distances in terms of "pipes") or a stop ashore for a mug of tea, they could cover fifty to ninety miles per day, unless they faced strong headwinds or waves that forced them to the shelter of shore.

One of my favorite pictures of myself was taken by Julia in Banff, Alberta, in front of a sign that reads "Voyageur." I stand, bearded and unshaven, in a shapeless hat, smirking with pride over my relationship to the word.

The mighty voyageurs didn't just deliver cargoes up, down, and across the continent. They helped spread religion. Through those early "of the country" marriages they introduced a layperson's version of Catholic rites and practices to their growing families and communities. In the absence of missionaries, Catholicism became to the burgeoning Métis people and culture what Pigeon calls a "lived religion." It existed and flourished outside of a church.

From the 1730s and 1740s the seeds of this lived religion were planted and passed along through familial lines. By 1750, a fully developed mixed-heritage society was well on its way to being established. Yet the Indigenous people who participated in this flourishing weren't interested in replacing their religions; they certainly weren't "converts." Instead, they were looking to add spiritual power to what they already had. It was a hard world, and Indigenous people were happy to take spiritual influence, spiritual assistance, wherever they could find it. They found it in this unique form of hybrid Catholicism that was well established before the first missions in the Red River region in 1818. Digging a little deeper into the relationship between De Smet and the Salish people in 1841, their relationship wasn't so different either. The entire "conversion" model regarding the indoctrination of Indigenous people is largely a false narrative. There are many, many Christian Indians, but it took time, and lots of inflicted trauma, for Christianity to fully establish itself.

When the missionaries finally arrived in the Red River area and began flexing their muscles over "of the country" marriages and all the other ways their faith had taken hold outside of their supervision, they found a community that couldn't be pushed around. At least not yet.

The first priests, thirty-two-year-old Joseph-Norbert Provencher and twenty-five-year-old Sévère Dumoulin, arrived at the Red River in 1818 with specific instructions. They were to erase "Indigenous spiritual practices and livelihoods," which were considered "barbarism." Clearly these were men of a faith that didn't respect Indigenous spirituality and religious practice. Indeed, in this time period Catholic leadership dismissed any nonbelievers as "uncivilized."

There weren't enough early missionaries to impose any of their hardline changes by force, though. So, despite plenty of baptisms and sanctioned marriages, it took time for the more traditional practice of Catholicism to unfold. It evolved more as a partnership that was beneficial to both parties by around the 1830s.

This mutually beneficial partnership, once the two sides relaxed a little in the side-eye they directed toward each other, blossomed as Métis buffalo hunters moved onto the plains in their enormous family groups and invited priests to join them. This passage from Émilie Pigeon summarizes it perfectly:

> The immediate gains obtained by a priest's presence on the buffalo hunt were threefold. First, Church officials provided spiritual comfort, which was especially important when facing the danger of death since the faithful wanted to ensure their entry into heaven and believed in the role of last rites. Second, the medical knowledge of missionary priests healed ailments, treated ills, and mended bones. This contribution was complementary to the Metis men and women, versed in local pharmacopeia, who traditionally occupied these healing roles. An additional curative power was advantageous on dangerous hunting rounds. In addition to the benefits of connecting with someone possessing this skill set, Metis families that welcomed clergy on their expeditions gained a cultural intermediary to both confront settler incursions and help repel attacks by other Indigenous nations.

Everybody benefitted. The clergy could bring the Métis closer to traditional worship while still allowing them their movement. Meanwhile, this movement spread Catholicism all across the region without so many of the dangers small parties of missionaries typically faced. It's hard to pick on the black robe too much when he's surrounded by a few dozen beardy, horse-mounted dudes armed with buffalo rifles, after all. Red River Métis identity and community spread far and wide from its birthplace half a continent away, and family connections extended with it.

But like everything else it didn't last. The clergy could only help against settler incursions for so long. As would-be homesteaders swarmed the landscape and the buffalo disappeared, Métis families split up and lived wherever they could and did whatever they had to to survive. By then, thanks to the influence of actual priests, much of their unique practice of Catholicism had evolved back to a more traditional version of the faith. The result was people like my grandparents and their generation essentially becoming Catholics in the way all the other Catholics of the region are, despite their cultural differences.

~

Dad usually gave two reasons for why he didn't practice his Catholicism, Mom tells me. First, he didn't like going to mass and seeing all the hypocrites there, people who were "holier than thou" at church but shitty the rest of the time. Second, he didn't want to support a church so full of wicked priests.

That last reason is a sentiment I can relate to. I haven't uncovered any evidence in my immediate family of anyone spending time in the infamous boarding schools for Indian children so common in North America. But the families of my Little Shell relatives certainly did, especially as Métis people lost the ability to wander freely and settled into communities near growing white settlements. Dr. Denise Lajimodiere is Turtle Mountain Chippewa, which makes her family, and she documents the abuses in her harrowing and essential book *Stringing Rosaries: The History, the Unforgivable, and the Healing of Northern Plains American Indian Boarding School Survivors*. In the book, Lajimodiere presents sixteen interviews with boarding school survivors, selected from many more, to "investigate the experiences of those attending boarding schools during the years 1921 to 1986 in the Northern Plains region of the United States."

Lajimodiere writes about how children were stolen from their families. She also writes about her research, and how in many cases parental signatures match the handwriting of Indian agents who kept the records, a strong indication of the forging of parental consent. It's harrowing and heartbreaking to consider all these ruptured families.

These children were as young as two years old. They would be away from families for anywhere from four to twelve years. This is genocide that still reverberates today. There remain many, many survivors of the ordeal who carry their trauma into families, trying to learn what it means to be parents, to be elders, to be part of a society that has shown itself to be overwhelmingly callous to them.

The history of boarding schools is one of those dark truths against the "exceptional" narrative so many settlers would rather forget. It's a history our education system ignores. But, as of this writing, the uncovering of thousands of unmarked graves of Indian children across Canada and the United States has brought the horrors into the spotlight.

In a June 2021 opinion piece for the *Washington Post*, US Secretary of the Interior Deb Haaland—the first Indigenous person to hold a cabinet position in the United States government—reveals the history of her own family members being taken away to boarding schools. "I am a product of these horrific assimilation policies," she writes. "My maternal grandparents were stolen from their families when they were only 8 years old and were forced to live away from their parents, culture and communities until they were 13. Many children like them never made it back home." She writes of discussing that history for the first time with her grandmother, how hard it was, how "a priest gathered the children from the village and put them on a train, and how she missed her family."

Haaland pledges to do her part to address this tragic history. "Many of the boarding schools were maintained by the Interior Department, which I now lead," she writes. "I believe that I—and the Biden-Harris administration—have an important responsibility to bring this trauma to light."

Hopefully they, and subsequent administrations, will. But I don't think anyone is going to hold their breath hoping. This is the United States government we're talking about, after all.

~

In October 2021 I sit with Denise Lajimodiere on the back porch of her little cabin overlooking Belcourt Lake where she lives on the Turtle Mountain reservation. Belcourt Lake is named for the town of Belcourt, where the Turtle Mountain Chippewa are headquartered. Belcourt the town is named for Father Georges-Antoine Belcourt, a French Canadian Roman Catholic diocesan priest and missionary who served the Chippewa and Métis of the Turtle Mountains. Denise relays this history, then mutters under her breath, "That shitass."

Denise, also a celebrated artist and poet, has dark, dark eyes and skin, and long, gorgeous silver hair. We sit together in the late morning, sipping coffee and sharing a few tears over the boarding school horrors she has written about. I'm drinking coffee from a white mug patterned in the bright green, red, yellow, and indigo stripes of the classic HBC point blanket. Denise tells me sometimes she gets hassled for having it because of the sinister aspect of what the HBC represents to our people, but she doesn't care because she thinks it's pretty. I laugh because I think it's pretty too. I have a couple mugs of my own with the same pattern. My phone case is also patterned the same, and I show her. Denise laughs.

She has just received the paperback edition of *Stringing Rosaries*, which she signs and gives to me because I've forgotten to bring my hardcover edition with me. In Appendix A, updated in July 2021, the text notes that there are, or were, 406 schools in the United States spread over thirty-one states (sixteen in Montana).

"And I've already learned of four more!" Denise tells me. Because it isn't just the history of what happened in these schools that has been erased, it's that the schools, in many places, even existed at all. It should be noted that they weren't all Catholic schools. But so, so many of them were.

It drags at all of us, knowing what was done to so many of our friends and relatives. It drags at anyone hearing the story for the first time, drags at people of faith who must reconcile the institutions they're part of with the actions in their history. I'm surprised to learn from my mom that my great-grandmother Margaret worked for a time at the St. Ignatius Mission in the town that bears its name, on what is now the Flathead reservation. For how long and what she did there are questions no one is left to answer. That place has its own cruel history in its treatment of Indian children, and I fear for what she was witness to.

"She wasn't really forthcoming," Mom says. "Your dad's family was always very quiet."

Tragically, like so many other families.

~

I've considered several times while working on this book that maybe I should attend a mass or two, just to get a feel for it. The only Catholic services I've attended are a wedding a couple decades ago—which I hated—and the funerals of my grandparents, which were awful. The priest at both funerals seemed weary and disconnected. Then there was so much jibber jabber about everything other than the lives of the deceased that the entire experience felt more in service to a self-absorbed deity than a respectful celebration of a mortal life fully lived. But I still contemplate going every now and then. Inevitably, though, something lands in the news cycle about another priest being busted for something loathsome and I say to hell with it. The church needs to do a lot of internal soul searching—and house cleaning—before I'll ever choose to darken a doorway for any kind of service.

I do love churches, though. I enjoy the peacefulness of so-called holy places. I feel sad that not everyone can feel safe within them. I enjoy the observation of holy days, ritual, and all the associated trappings. I'm just not big on participating in them because they so often feel too much like a performance. I get that uncomfortable feeling even at Little Shell meetings, during the prayers that open and close each session, which aren't necessarily Christian prayers but still feel like it to me. These moments often sound like little more than an approximation of what someone thinks an Indian ritual or prayer *should* sound like. It doesn't move me. The songs, though, are magic. The beauty of traditional language. I'm reminded of sharing a reading stage with the poet Sherwin Bitsui. Sherwin is Diné of the Todích'ii'nii (Bitter Water Clan), born for the Tlizílaaní (Many Goats Clan), and one of this country's most celebrated poets. I enjoy his poetry most when he performs it, because often he writes in his own language, and this experience of the music of his words in his language is deeply moving. It's prayer.

Spirit and contemplation are important to me, and I'm often troubled by this history in ways I find difficult to overcome. I struggle reading Christian philosophers like, for example, Thomas Merton, the Trappist monk who was such a prodigious writer and thinker. I love much of what he has to say, but I often find his sidetracks into strictly religious reflection borderline fanatical, which says more about me I think than it does him. But then, at other times, not so much.

In the book *St. Francis of Assisi: His Life, Teachings, and Practice* by Jon M. Sweeney, the author writes of Francis's teaching being "about acquiring new ways of looking at life that lead to changes in how one lives." Sweeney continues, "Is the purpose of life simply survival? It isn't, says Francis, and of course on this and every point Francis is repeating or reframing the Gospel. Life is not for survival; it's for joy. There is a way of living that is freer, fresher, and more satisfying than focusing on simply how to get through the day."

Living as an effort to just get through the day. How many people's lives does that statement sum up? It's probably familiar to most of us, especially all the people so often lauded for their "resilience" in the way Indians too often are. It was certainly familiar to my dad, though he never would've admitted it. I think by the end of his life moments of joy came fewer and farther between.

So I've taken to compiling a list of things that bring me joy, and I try to make time to attend to them: Walks outside. Occasional vigorous exercise. Sitting somewhere alone and simply thinking about stuff. Making an effort to be kind to people for no other reason than kindness. Looking at the stars and planets and the moon, and considering how that monumental expanse was once as familiar to us as the home screens on our stupid smartphones. Expressing love and gratitude to the people who deserve it. Reading for the love of reading. Observing. Petting and roughing up my dogs. Afternoon tea out of the pot Mom gifted me for my birthday, sipped from the coffee mug my dad brought home from the navy.

My greatest defense against the despair of having Catholicism largely replace the Indigenous spirituality of my people is that the wild world still exists. I make a point to be out in that world whenever I can—in forests, on riverbanks, even immersed in the cold water—in hopes that whatever whispered to my people from those places is still there whispering to me. I'm doing my best to listen.

CHAPTER 16

2019

LEWISTOWN, MONTANA

THE JUDITH BASIN REGION of Central Montana is a gorgeous representation of Montana pretty. The basin—a bowl-shaped dip in the landscape, with sides higher than the bottom—is surrounded by the Judith, Little Belt, and Big Snowy Mountains. The Judith River, named by William Clark in May 1805 after his cousin (and future wife) Julia "Judith" Hancock, originates in the Little Belts roughly 60 miles southwest of the city of Lewistown and flows 130 miles north to the Missouri, draining the entire basin along the way. Its natural abundance has attracted people for centuries, both as shared and conflicted territory. Here, at the mouth of the Judith River at the Missouri, is where Isaac Stevens negotiated the Lame Bull / Judith River Treaty with the Blackfeet (and the Nez Perce, Salish, and Pend d'Oreille / Flathead tribes) on October 17, 1855, to make way for the railroad. This land was identified as "shared" hunting ground to be guaranteed accessible to all the tribes for a period of ninety-nine years. But of course an influx of settlers and homesteaders put the kibosh on efforts to uphold the treaty for even a fraction of that time, if that was ever the intention.

My ancestors looked for a home here too. In the spring of 1879 a group of Métis families, twenty-five of them, made their way into the Judith Basin country in pursuit of a new way of life. They had already been in the area more than a decade—longer, in many cases—if we use "area" loosely and include the Milk River country to the north. That river, which originates in the Rockies, waters land in both Montana and Canada until it dumps into the Missouri River near what is now Fort Peck, Montana.

These families all had deep ties to the Red River Valley Métis communities to the east on both sides of the still-new international border. They moved in small bands and family groups related in tangled ways that connected more through mothers and sisters than fathers and brothers. They were buffalo hunters too. As the herds dwindled in the Dakotas, the entire Métis economy, born in the fur trade and refocused on buffalo since the 1840s, moved westward. There were still buffalo for a while around the Milk River, but the herds dwindled there too. The Métis would hunt during the summer for meat that could be dried and turned into pemmican and jerky for trade, and again in fall when buffalo hides were more robust in preparation for another formidable winter. During that season, the hunt served to replenish meat stores and provide hides that could be turned into luxurious robes that fetched a high price. Notably, the Medicine Line meant nothing to them. It was all just home.

These families settled on Big Spring Creek at what is now the city of Lewistown. The migration to and establishment of this community was led by Pierre and Judith Wilkie Berger, both middle-aged at the time. They were accompanied by a number of their adult children and extended family and friends. Of those adult children, Jean Baptiste Berger and his wife, Betsy Keplin, had a daughter named Mary Margaret Berger, who became Mary Margaret La Tray. My dad's grandmother. My great-grandmother, the same woman who was fearful of trick-or-treaters.

On a hot, sunny day in late August 2019, I'm coasting down the long hill into Lewistown as the highway turns into West Main Street. I pass vibrant green trees and then, on the right, the Lewistown Lodge motel, the McDonald's, and the beautiful Carnegie Library, then on past the old brick buildings at the heart of town. I'm astonished that this is the first time I've ever been here, because so much of my family history springs from the area.

It was inevitable that I would come here; it's a kind of homecoming. My dad and his dad, my grandpa Leo, were born here. My grandma Ruby was born in Roy, a blip on the map not far north and east. Her family, the Doneys, among the original twenty-five families who established Lewistown, are all over the state—including among the people of the Flathead reservation north of Missoula—and I'm certain most trace their origins to kinship ties here too. Same with the La Trays. Mose and Susie La Tray were part of this community, arriving with four of what would ultimately be over a dozen children in tow.

Given the small number of families who first established themselves here and their good Catholic habit of having piles of children, it's no wonder so many of us Little Shell are related in varying ways. In talking to people related to the wider Little Shell community, it's like Six Degrees of Kevin Bacon. You know that game—it's where you start naming people and within six names you find a connection to the actor. For us, it's family names, and for those of us with even the slightest knowledge of our family trees it's usually only a generation or two before we find a common ancestor.

I didn't know anything about Lewistown growing up. The only reference I have to it is an old letter we keep in the family photo box. The letter is from my dad, the envelope postmarked August 30, 1951, from the State Fish Hatchery in Hamilton, to Mrs. Margaret La Tray in Lewistown, Mont. Dad would've been two months shy of eleven at the time. He drew her a picture of a farm. For years, the letter lived in a shoeshine box my dad had from his navy days that contained a small collection of personal keepsakes. I can remember gazing at the farm as a child, in a state of wonder that my father could've ever been so young, let alone capable of drawing a picture just like any other kid.

I also have vague recollections of our family occasionally being visited by cousins from my dad's side, all Doneys. Still in my single digits, I was too young to pay much attention. Dad never talked of Lewistown. My grandma Ruby kept in touch with her family and often referenced sisters and brothers in conversation, but that they lived in Lewistown escaped me. They were just names dropped in conversations I wasn't part of.

My dad hinted sometimes of training horses. This was a Lewistown activity, my mom tells me, as were hunting trips with his brother. Both ideas were ludicrous to me as a child. Dad had a couple rifles, but I never knew him as a hunter at all. And riding horses, let alone training them? When my sisters and I get together, we like to laugh about the time one of our 4-H pigs got loose and lit out for greener pastures. Dad jumped bareback onto our black little half pony, Amigo, and took off after it. The image of Dad bent over that hustling animal, his feet all but dragging along the ground, is hilarious. That piece just doesn't fit the image we had of him. Like so much of his life, this town, this pivotal place in our family history, and my dad's place in it, baffles me.

Lewistown isn't a large city by anyone's measure, but at roughly six thousand inhabitants, it's still bigger than I imagined it to be. The city serves as the seat for Fergus County, with a total population not even double that of Lewistown spread over 4,350 square miles of wide-open grasslands with horizons interrupted by mountains and badlands, frigid in the winter and scorching hot in the summer, and more cattle than people. That's a lot of open space with not many folks inhabiting it, and the population, like so many rural communities in a state increasing overall in population, is shrinking.

I check into the Trails End Motel, then drive around looking for landmarks like the Catholic church St. Leo's, where my father was certainly baptized. I see murals in two different locations—one on the side of the Albertsons grocery story, another on a wall facing a coffee shop—that depict early settlers arriving in Red River carts. It seems surreal, that this has been here all along, waiting for me to discover it.

~

I need to talk more about the history of the place. It's uncommon-enough knowledge to most people how Lewistown was settled, but even among those who know some, the deeper details have been obfuscated by history. Though still almost two decades away from the final scorched-earth policy of "Canadian Indian" removal on the northern plains, the attitude toward Métis Indians was far from friendly as these families moved into Spring Creek. This was no bucolic cart train to greener pastures. This was an uncertain scramble into a questionable future.

While the Spring Creek families were the first to establish a true settlement in the Judith Basin, there were plenty others already active there. Métis hunters and traders had been in and around the area for at least a decade or two; certainly that's how the Bergers knew about it in the first place. The Reed and Bowles Trading Post already existed. These sketchy proprietors resupplied travelers on the Carroll Trail—built in 1874 to connect Missouri River ports to the mining camps around Helena—with various and sundry items, plied Indians with alcohol and probably guns and ammo, too, and did their best to exist below the gaze of the various military posts that popped up here and there and then disappeared.

Most important, the last remaining buffalo herds on much of the continent were concentrated in Central Montana, which also concentrated the remaining Indigenous people whose lives hinged on their access to these animals: the Lakota, the Blackfeet, and their various allies and rivals. There were those among the Métis people who wanted to maintain their share of that action as long as they could too. Nor was anyone prepared to show anyone else much quarter in accessing them either.

Settlers were eager to get at all this fertile land, but the Indians were still there, and no one could abide that. The Indians had handed Custer his ass just three years earlier in 1876, at the Greasy Grass, and following that great victory Sitting Bull and his people lurked just north of the Medicine Line in Canada. It can't be underestimated just how terrified settlers were of the looming threat the Hunkpapa leader presented, and rumors of his return abounded. US military presence went from around seven hundred troops pre-Custer to over three thousand in the aftermath of his comeuppance.

Chief Joseph and the Nez Perce nearly made it to Canada themselves just two years earlier, coming up a mere forty miles short. They were forced to surrender to Colonel Nelson Miles (soon to be general) after he surprise-attacked their camp in the Bears Paw Mountains near present-day Chinook, Montana. The Nez Perce held strong for three days until Miles was reinforced by troops under the command of General Oliver Otis Howard, who had chased the Indians all the way from Idaho. Chief Joseph formally surrendered on October 5, 1877, after one of the most desperately heroic multimonth efforts in the history of the world.

For the next two years, Miles—who would go on to become one of the more infamous names associated with this whole "Indian Wars" period, both here and in campaigns in the Southwest—and his army prowled the border, playing a chess match against the rumors around Sitting Bull's intentions. Miles essentially laid siege to Sitting Bull and his people, doing everything he could to sever access to supplies and resources the Indians needed that came from the American side of the border.

Miles wondered where the Indians had gotten their weapons and laid a suspicious eye on the Métis; everyone did. There was a common assumption that Métis traders, who continued to move freely back and forth across the border as they had always done, carted supplies for "renegade" Indians on both sides of the border. Nor could Canadian and American officials agree on who the Métis even "belonged" to. Americans—Montanans, really—wanted these "Canadian Indians" expelled because they wanted a monopoly on the growing trade industry. The rhetoric was ugly.

Historian Martha Harroun Foster, author of *We Know Who We Are: Métis Identity in a Montana Community*, writes, "Tirades appeared in Montana newspapers, including the *Benton Record*, whose editor accused the Métis of carrying on 'an illicit trade with hostile savages.' 'These Canadian half-breeds pay no taxes,' he claimed. 'They produce nothing but discord, violence, and bloodshed where ever [sic] they are permitted to locate, they are a worthless, brutal race of the lowest species of humanity, without one redeeming trait to commend them to the sympathy or protection of any Government.'"

Foster's book, along with references in Vrooman's *One Robe*, are essential reading for learning this history. More details pop up as "Easter eggs" here and there, too, and it all jumbles around in my head. There's even a lovely little book funded by the Montana Committee for the Humanities called *1879 Metis Trek to the Judith Basin* by Mary Jean Golden that includes some first-person narratives from people who were part of the journey, as well as complete lists of names of who arrived and when. I look at all this stuff over and over again.

We know Colonel Miles was happy to see the Métis column roll out of the Milk River area that spring of 1879 and certainly encouraged them to do so. For those in the first wave the decision to leave hadn't come a moment too soon. In the fall, Miles moved once and for all to break up all the remaining Métis settlements up and down the Milk River. He forced them either to Canada or "encouraged" them to join their relatives in the Judith Basin, going so far as to provide "escorts" to see them safely there.

The Métis settled in quickly, clustering in loose, family-based enclaves spread out around the basin. Those who still leaned more toward hunting found game plentiful and settled close to those areas that allowed them easiest access to the animals. Meanwhile families like the Bergers and their closest relatives set to building houses and homesteads in the vein of a more traditional settlement community. A man named Francois Janeaux and his wife, Virginie Laverdure Janeaux, arrived shortly after the first wave and established a trading post. It was a bustling time. Everything was made with wood, and tools were hardly more advanced than a simple axe. But they got the job done.

Miner and cattleman Granville Stuart, who established a cattle ranch nearby in late 1880 (and then lost essentially his entire herd in the apocalyptic winter of 1886/87), first passed through in May of that year, barely a year after the existing community had migrated from the Milk River. Martha Harroun Foster reports that Stuart was "favorably impressed with the village, noting that it was 'quite a settlement.' He approved of the plowed fields and the neatness of the post and homes . . . the community was more to Stuart's liking than the rough Missouri River trade towns, and he commented dryly that 'the houses of the Red River half breeds are in marked contrast to the posts of the white men through here.'"

My driving around Lewistown leads me to the Central Montana Museum. This enterprise is administered by the nonprofit Central Montana Historical Association. I'm also fortunate, because the weekend I arrive is the last one they will be open until Memorial Day in the spring. Doubly fortunate, in fact, because at the time none of us know that in almost exactly six months, the COVID pandemic will shut the entire world down.

I'm eager to check the museum out because more than once I've had friends who visited text me photos of various displays that depict the La Tray family; specifically, an old-timer named Mose La Tray, my great-great-grandfather. He, with his Assiniboine wife, Susie, participated in the initial settlement of the town as well. It's their son, Frank, who marries Mary Margaret Berger to begin my immediate, specific branch of the family tree.

I love small-town museums, and this is a particularly good one. There are collections focused on every era this part of the state has weathered, including the skull of a triceratops. The best part though, and the section I spend the most time in, is devoted to Lewistown's earliest settlers. Display cases show off arrowheads collected in the region, beaded moccasins and other accoutrements, weird student-made dioramas, and all the usual stuff one might expect in such a place. But the attention devoted to the original Métis settlers is better than I had hoped for.

There's a life-size replica of a Red River cart with a mannequin for a driver, complete with a broad-brimmed hat and a snappy Métis sash, and a detailed description of how the carts were made. A couple beautiful paintings depict life in the early days of the settlement, and plenty of old photographs and historical details printed out and pinned to the walls provide a decent idea of what went down here. There are photographs of Pierre and Judith Berger—stern of visage and dress, rendered in what looks like tintype—with short biographies identifying them as the founders of Lewistown before it became Lewistown.

Finally, in a photograph next to a display that depicts what the trading post (and first post office) called Reed's Fort looked like, is a photograph of Great-Great-Grandpa Mose, who was hired to build the structure. Here he is old, beardy, and smiling. Then there's a photograph of Mose with his wife, Great-Great-Grandma Susie, both looking grim and stiff like the subjects of any photograph from the era, as well as a photo album full of other images from the period, including more references to the sizable La Tray family.

Visiting the museum is wonderful, and I come away with a warm feeling for having been there. Yet the picture it paints is still incomplete. There are references to the hardships faced in establishing such a community, sure, but they don't really extend beyond what we've been conditioned to think of frontier life. These people faced hardships not mentioned. It wasn't an easy time to be Métis, chased here and there by the US Army and surrounded on all sides by people who want you gone so they can take what you have.

I have other family to look for. After the museum I drive out to Roy, maybe thirty minutes distant by highway. Its heyday was in the early 1910s, after the railroad came to town, but that was short lived. I'm interested to visit because around the late 1890s, it became a Métis settlement enclave particular to the Doneys—my grandmother's people—and their relatives. Specifically, they were ranchers and sheep farmers.

It's beautiful, this valley, even in late summer, with stormy, iron-gray clouds that gather behind the Little Belt Mountains to the west. Central Montana is a revelation to me, and I long for the chance to spend weeks just poking around, seeing what I can pull free that's relevant to me from the fog of history. After all,

150 years doesn't look quite as distant out here as it does in a city that tends to puff up and expand every decade or so like Missoula.

Roy itself seems hardly a town at all. I park in front of Roy Grocery, get out of the car, stretch, and start walking. I have a vague idea I might stumble on the cemetery but have no clue where to look. There are a few houses scattered over a small grid of city-sized blocks and plenty of trees and shrubs. Some beautiful, boarded-up old buildings. A bar. A weary park. A field stacked with old tires and some Angus cattle peppering the distant hills, one of which displays on its sloping face a collection of white-painted rocks formed into an "R" for Roy. It's quiet; maybe one or two other vehicles crunch by on the gravel, and vehicles roar by intermittently on the 191. After thirty minutes or so I walk back to the grocery store and inquire after the cemetery. The woman working the checkout counter directs me just across the highway onto the dirt road that leads over the railroad tracks and up the hill behind. I get back in my car and follow her instructions. At the final turn it seems hardly more than an overgrown dirt two-track, and for a moment I feel like I'm trespassing in some potentially trigger-happy farmer's field. There isn't anyone else around.

The cemetery occupies the top of a hill that overlooks the entire valley. The view is gorgeous. This entire knob is basically dirt covered with a thin layer of dry, close-cropped weeds and little lumps of prickly pear cactus. In the distance large loafs of hay are stacked all over in looming piles. As I get out of the car and walk toward the wrought iron cemetery gates, grasshoppers explode with clicking wings in every direction from my steps.

I'm casting about the space, reading headstones. There are many tiny markers all over, some relatively grand headstones and crypts, and several exhausted trees and bushes. I'm not even certain what I'm looking for as I zigzag about, taking photos here and there. There's a hot breeze blowing and the weeds crunch under my feet. None of it's totally overgrown, but it isn't that well maintained either. My spatial reckoning is terrible, but I'm guessing the entire cemetery encompasses maybe an acre or two.

I start making my way back toward the front gate. Then I see one, just behind a brittle, dull green shrub I've already passed once: a marker with the name Doney. I kick away dirt and debris to be sure. Beside it, another. Soon I realize I'm standing in a section of what must be a dozen or so Doneys. Here is Eli Doney, killed in action in November 1944 during WWII. Donald J. Doney, another WWII veteran, born in 1910, died in 1993. Children, too, like Anna May Doney, born in 1924, died in 1925. And Terry Doney, born in 1934, died in 1936.

My breath quickens; here is Joe Y. Doney, my great-grandfather. His grandparents were Joseph Doney and Philomene Doney, members of the original 1879 Spring Creek settlers. Great-Grandpa Joe was born in 1891 and died in 1965, two years before I was born.

These are *my people*. Despite not knowing them, I'm moved to be in their presence. Yes, many of them were gone before I arrived on this earth, but what of their descendants? The keepers of their stories, their histories? Where are they now? Still here in Roy? In Lewistown? What about the Doneys in Arlee, on the Flathead reservation, that a friend asks me about?

Through some tall brown weeds I see it: a small, unassuming marker, almost hidden. But I can read the letters even from several paces away. I walk over and kneel beside it, pull aside the desiccated stalks and leaves and dirt, and brush it clean, getting a palm full of nettles for my trouble. Tilley Rose Doney, Jan. 2, 1896, to Sept. 26, 1989. My great-grandmother.

I met Grandma Tilley once, at least one time I can recall. I was young, and she was staying at my grandparents' place on Flathead Lake. I can see her so clearly, shoulders hunched, a tiny woman, smiling, standing in the shade of the big log house. She kept to herself while the adults visited and us kids ran roughshod. She hardly spoke and I couldn't understand her when she did, which makes me wonder if she was speaking Michif, which makes me wonder if my grandmother did, too, unbeknown to me. I was mildly afraid of her because she was old. Because I didn't know her. And because she was so clearly, gloriously Indian.

Mom tells me Dad went up for Grandma Tilley's funeral in Roy in 1989. The church was right across from the bar, and there was a huge crowd. So many people moved back and forth between the bar and the church that they decided to just move the entire service to the cemetery. So Tilley's homemade pine box—built by one of her children—was loaded into the back of a buckboard and pulled by a horse up the hill to the gravesite, with "the whole tribe following."

My mom pauses in the telling. "That's what he kept saying," she says. "He said, 'The whole tribe was there.'"

Who is this "whole tribe" then? The area nearly became a reservation specifically for Métis Indians in 1880. No less important a person than Louis Riel, in Montana between leading Canadian Métis uprisings, drew up a petition asking that land be set aside for the "half-breeds." He gathered many signatures for his petition from the wider Spring Creek community, including men of my ancestry. Colonel Miles supported it, but the effort ultimately failed. Granville Stuart, speaking for the area cattlemen, opposed it. That crowd wanted less land for Indians than there already was; they certainly didn't want to set aside more. More important, Crow reservation Indian agent A. R. Keller opposed it, falsely claiming that the Métis were British and Canadian with no right to land in the United States. Furthermore, he accused the Métis of being poor citizenship material, citing their reputed connections to the whiskey trade.

Imagine that: a white guy accusing Indigenous people of plying the locals with alcohol.

This is an example of the still-growing racism directed at the Métis people. Yes, the Métis referred to themselves as half-breeds—more of a translation from their native French or Michif language—but "breed" became a derogatory term used to identify them by just about everyone else.

Other events as early as 1880 began to whittle away at the control the families exerted over their own community. Granville Stuart established his DHS ranch nearby. He proved to be no friend of the Métis, whether he respected their settlement or not. Gold was discovered in the Judith Mountains, and the town of Maiden was established, drawing many prospectors. More and more settlers moved in and established sawmills up and down the waterways, claiming homesteads and gobbling up land. And finally, the last of the bison disappeared from the landscape.

The community had a good run. One hundred and fifty families lived there before the influx of settlers overwhelmed them. Then these factors—the disappearance of bison and other game, the press of arriving homesteaders—overwhelmed the settlement and "precluded Métis economic, social, and political dominance in their new community."

The descendants of the original Métis families still live there. That's the tribe my dad was talking about when he told my mom they were all there for Great-Grandma Tilley's funeral. Many today are Little Shell members, or could be if they chose to be. But there was so much hardship and negative public opinion directed at Métis people just because they were *Métis* that the trauma of those associations was too much to overcome for entire generations of people. It's only now, with those of us removed from those times yearning to be part of a wider community again, that these truths are being revealed, and we are ready to reclaim what was lost and be proud of what our people accomplished.

CHAPTER 17

2020

CHOTEAU, MONTANA

It's a midmorning in February with a storm barreling toward me from off the Front Range of the Rockies when I pull up in front of an unassuming ranch house on a quiet street in Choteau, Montana. Despite being so deep into winter there isn't any snow on the ground, and it really isn't that cold . . . yet. By the end of the day that will all change, and, being a three-hour drive from home, I'm trying to stay ahead of it.

I park my car and get out. I start up the walkway to the entrance of the house. From inside the inner door opens, and a figure appears behind the storm door. That door swings wide with a springy rasp and a tall, lean man in denim and a blue western shirt with colorful patterning across the chest and sleeves steps outside and holds the door open. He has clean-shaven, angular features over a rectangular face and wears wire-rimmed glasses. His white hair is close-cropped. He looks at his watch, then at me, and flashes a crooked smile. "You're right on time, on the dot!" he says. He offers his hand. We're off to a good start.

The man's name is Al Wiseman. I've known *of* him for far longer than I've known him. Few have done more to keep the story of Montana's Métis people alive than Al. He was one of the first people Nicholas Vrooman told me I needed to meet, and the two men have done many presentations together. I met Al briefly once before, and we spoke on the phone to coordinate this sit-down, but this will be the first time I get to spend significant time with him. The opportunity, I soon realize, is a gift. This meeting marks the beginning of one of the most important relationships of my life.

"Our people settled west of here years ago, but it wasn't until later years that they came into town," Al tells me from a chair at his kitchen table just a couple blocks shy of downtown Choteau. Coffee has been offered and accepted, and the small talk is behind us. "They came to the canyon later in the 1800s. They weren't all involved with the Riel thing in Canada, they were always here. I myself knew some people who were involved when they were little kids."

Al is referring to a Métis settlement in a place called Teton Canyon, tucked away against the eastern face of the northern reaches of the Rocky Mountain Front. At its height, over a hundred people lived in this community along the South Fork of the Teton River, approximately thirty miles west of Choteau, less than an hour's drive over mostly dirt roads from Al's home. It's beautiful country, and no one alive knows it or its history better than Al does. It's his family history.

"My mother always made sure that she told us, even when we were little bitty kids, who we were, where we come from," Al says. "We know a lot about what went on up here because we had so many good teachers. But now all the good teachers are gone. Now I'm the teacher."

A lot went on "up there," and Al Wiseman is an excellent teacher. I learn this firsthand when, months later, we make a summer visit to the old Métis community. By now, over subsequent encounters and several phone calls, we've become friends, and Al, along with my cousin Kim, is probably the person in my wider Native community I talk to most.

On this particular hot, smoky day, we're walking through a narrow, weedy stretch of grass that just looks like unused pasture to me. Al sees something different. He points out serviceberry bushes whose ancestors provided much-needed sustenance during lean years to his. Gesturing at a depression in the ground, Al asks me what I think it is, and when my imagination falters he describes it as the remnants of an old root cellar—suddenly I realize there are several in the immediate vicinity—then tells the story of how he once stopped a young man from the nearby Pine Butte Preserve, a conservation area owned by the Nature Conservancy, from "filling in the holes" with a tractor. He laughs and shakes his head.

The Conservancy actually owns all this land, which was never "technically" owned by any of the Métis families but one: the Bruno family (Little Shell enrollment officer Linda Watson's family, to be specific), who relinquished their final claims in 1930. The rest of the land was simply taken out from under the Métis settlers by homesteaders filing claims to this already-occupied land, as if the people there were mere squatters. Then the land changed hands over the years, as all the stolen land in America has, until we reach the current owners: groups like the Nature Conservancy, whose website describes the area in this way:

> Pine Butte is part of a landscape that the Blackfeet people have called home for countless generations. The Old North Trail, used by Native Americans for thousands of years, cuts through the preserve. Tipi rings and a buffalo jump and associated drive lanes testify to the presence of prehistoric plains dwellers. Scant remains of homestead structures dot the preserve, while ranching activities continue as they have for the past century. The location of a Metis settlement from the late 1800s and early 1900s along the South Fork of the Teton River now serves as our management headquarters.

We're standing in the middle of that settlement. From here, we can see the log cabin where the writer Joseph Kinsey Howard lived, near the Nature Conservancy buildings. On the way up from Choteau we also passed the larger cabin where A. B. Guthrie—author of the classic fur-trade novel *The Big Sky* as well as 1950 Pulitzer Prize–winner *The Way West*—once lived.

It's generally accepted that the community began in the early 1870s, but Al, whose family arrived via social connections made just a short jaunt south at St. Peter's Mission in the 1880s, says he's seen documentation that establishes settlement as early as 1862, and probably earlier. Either way, when the Métis founders first arrived they lived in tents and tipis, but over time those dwellings were replaced by cabins. It was hardscrabble, subsistence living. Water came from the river, and there was no electricity. The people grew what food they could, supplemented by foraging, and they hunted and fished.

Even through the haze of wildfire smoke the view is breathtaking. Craggy mountain peaks rise all around us, and the South Fork of the Teton River is both visible and audible from where we stand, rushing over and around rocks and deadfall pine and cottonwoods, even at this point in the summer when flows are low. It's as beautiful a spot as I can imagine living in, and I tell Al so much. He nods, and tears well up in his eyes.

"These mountains kept our people alive with food and with their timber," Al says. "We always had horsepower. When homesteaders came in and started making claims they had to make improvements on their places to keep them. And they wouldn't have survived their first winter without us! So that's where our people fell in with [selling] fencing material, house logs, corral poles, just generally anything to get [a homesteader] set up. And then they sold firewood. They called themselves woodhawkers. A lot of the women went out right with the men. A double-bit ax and a crosscut saw, that's all they had."

These woodhawkers (like my Grandpa Mose not so far away in Lewistown) would load their wagons and head for the growing town of Choteau, making the twenty-five-to-thirty-mile trip in one or two days. ("I can show you where they camped!" Al tells me. "My grandfather showed me!") They might make ten dollars a load, or perhaps barter the wood for other needed supplies like groceries, harnesses, or oats.

They were known then as the "Canyon People." Over time, and as attitudes toward them changed, their community became known as "Breed Town."

"You don't hear too much anymore about that half-breed stuff, you know," Al says, not without some bitterness. "When you were calling us half-breeds, if you're more than one blood [of anything] you were talking about yourself! But back then, you know, we were just 'dirty old half-breeds,' and 'drunken half-breeds.'"

It's astounding to look closely at a map that shows all the places the Métis people spread out across the landscape to either establish settlements or live on the fringes of existing ones, even if one merely focuses on Montana. Métis were well established in the state before it became a territory in May 1864, let alone by the time it became the forty-first state in November 1889.

From the extreme upper-northeast corner of the state—like the towns of Plentywood, Scobey, and Opheim—all the way to the western border with Idaho and beyond in towns like St. Regis and Stevensville, Métis lived here. Settlements across the Hi-Line that are connected one to the next by Highway 2; places like Glasgow, Malta, Harlem, Chinook, and Havre. Towns on the other tribal reservations—Poplar, Wolf Point, Hardin, Browning,

Heart Butte, Pablo, and St. Ignatius—to such an extent that we are as deeply entwined as marriage-related people; we are family.

There were settlements near what passes for cities in the state today: Butte, Missoula, Billings, Helena, and Great Falls. Various forts, missions, and trading posts whose histories tend to leave out mention of the Métis at all and, when they don't, still call us half-breeds or even just "breeds." There are the towns of Lewistown and Roy, where my closest generational relatives established themselves, and places like Plains, where my grandparents are buried, a community resettled from White Horse Plains way up in Canada near the original Red River settlement, now known as Winnipeg, by people who carried the name of their home with them.

The Métis Archipelago. Or, per another word that comes to mind, the Métis "diaspora." We usually think of that term as it relates to the scattering of people in other parts of the world, not here in the United States. But according to Dictionary.com, it can also mean "any group migration or flight from a country or region" or "any group that has been dispersed outside its traditional homeland, especially involuntarily, as Africans during the trans-Atlantic slave trade."

The Métis and our Plains Chippewa relatives exemplify the criteria for that latter definition, and the dispersal, the forcing out, began long before the events of the late 1870s into the early 1900s. Our search for a place we could call home, a new place because the original was being overrun by strangers who had no interest in sharing the land, began with the first screeching wheel of a Red River cart rolling onto the plains. As each season passed and new expeditions embarked, more families stayed "out there," or moved on even farther. Change came fast, and Métis people are nothing if not survivors. We found places we could live and dug in as long as we could.

From the settlement clearing Al leads the way along a short path that winds through brittle shrubs and aspens up a short hill to the old Métis cemetery. Halfway up he stops and points to a spot high on the hillside. "You see that outcropping there?" he asks. "They [the Métis community] would always have a lookout up there, after the government started rounding the people up and shipping them to Canada. If anyone started coming up the canyon, they'd race down and let the people know and everyone would scatter." He flashes his hands out for dramatic effect.

The cemetery is a small, sloping, rectangular place with several grave markers. The grass, what there is of it, is cropped short. Al, the caretaker here, has constructed not only a split rail fence surrounding the area but also a rough-hewn replica of a Red River cart. A signboard identifies who's buried where. It's beautiful and peaceful. Aspens with mottled, glowing white bark surround it on three sides. It is sublime in its beauty, quiet except for the rattling of the bright green aspen leaves.

Al tells me the story of an old woman he knew when he was growing up. She had come down from Canada after the North-West Rebellion of 1885 after it became too dangerous to stay. A Métis settlement on the American side of the Medicine Line west of the town of Dupuyer she called "Little Chicago" was already there, and her family decided to head for it.

"This woman and her family came down and had ten head of stock with them," Al says. "They only traveled at night, and they traveled in Red River carts. That's one of the few people I ever talked to who ever traveled in one. I think she told me she was six years old. She never did say what they ate along the way because what do you carry? So I asked her one time, what did you do for food? She dropped her head and said, 'Al, I don't like to talk about this, but we ate a lot of gophers.'"

Al tears up as he relates the story. It took them three months to complete their journey to Little Chicago, he says. The family ended up in Teton Canyon.

"I often think of this stuff, you know," Al says. "If it hadn't been for their will, none of us would be here."

Al Wiseman was born in Choteau, one of five children. His father was a German from Indiana, and his mother was Métis. The family moved from Choteau just down the road south to Gilman, near Augusta, when he was two or three. Growing up there were plenty of Indian kids around, and plenty of mixed-race kids too. Some were sent to boarding schools and came back changed.

"Boarding school kids were disconnected; they didn't know who they were," Al says. "So they turned to alcohol, and drugs."

His mother made sure her children knew where they came from, but there were limits. For example, Al doesn't speak Michif or any of the other languages—Cree maybe, or Ojibwe—that the Teton Canyon people spoke.

"The older people wouldn't teach the language to the kids," Al says. "Old folks would be in the cabin, visiting, playing cards, and the kids would come to the window and listen to try and learn. But they didn't want the kids to know."

He understands why and doesn't blame the older folks. Think of the boarding schools. Of the punishment Indian children endured for merely speaking the languages of their ancestors.

"When you get burnt, or hurt, or however you want to say, when you're young, you don't want to pass that on because you don't want your kids to go through what you went through," he says. "If [children] don't know it, they can't be punished for knowing it."

Al had his share of encounters with anti-Indian racism too. He tells me a story from when he entered high school in

Augusta and signed up for a class taught by an instructor from Fort Benton. It wasn't unusual for what all Native children experienced growing up.

"There was quite a few mixed-blood kids [in the school], but in this particular class I was the only one," he says. "I took Spanish. Don't ask me why because I don't know, but at this time anything about Indian culture I could have benefitted from was taboo, you know? No one even liked to say the word 'Indian.' Anyway, I take Spanish and I didn't last too many days in there. This teacher would come by and just bypass me. He wouldn't even look at me. I think it was the third day maybe, and he came by and he stopped at my desk and he says, 'Al, I don't know what you're doing in this class.' And I thought to myself, I don't know what I'm doing here either. 'I don't think you Indian kids would understand anything about Spanish. You know the best thing you could do is go back to the reservation where you come from.' I said I don't know anything about any reservation, I've never been on one in my life, I've only heard about them. I'm not from a reservation, I live right down the street here. The next day I didn't go back to his class."

Al had seen the older generations go out and make a living doing manual labor and figured he could too. So at sixteen he quit school and got a job doing carpentry for a local builder.

"I went to a guy here in town who was a pretty good-sized builder and I said, 'Bob, I never finished high school and I don't have much education, but I'm willing to work.' And he said, 'By God, that's what I'm looking for and I'm willing to teach. You've got a job.' I worked for him for years."

In the 1950s when Al was drafted into the army, Bob said he could get him deferred. But many of Al's friends had joined the army, and he knew veterans who had gone to WWI and WWII, so he couldn't stay behind. Al put in two years in Korea, then came back and went to work with Bob again right away.

"The last twenty-two years of my working life, I run my own business," Al says. And he beams with pride.

Al's wife, Elaine—a beautiful, kind, and soft-spoken woman who constructs a mean Spam sandwich—has been part of that business, too, handling the books and keeping things on track. Her family has deep ties to Teton Canyon and to the Little Shell, with her family roots in the Turtle Mountains.

"I honestly never heard the word 'Métis' until recent years," Elaine says. "As I was growing up I knew I was Indian, but I never ever . . . I can't remember my dad, my grandma, anyone saying Métis. Chippewa and Cree is what I was raised up hearing. I guess I am Métis, but I never heard of it."

Elaine says both of her parents were very quiet. Her mother also lost her own mother at a very young age, so she didn't learn anything to pass along.

"From the time I was little we used to go to [landless Indian] meetings in Great Falls," she says. "Other than that, nothing."

Al Wiseman learned what he knows from growing up around it. There was never any concentrated study, it was just "a matter of living," as he says. The Métis were forced out of the canyon by homesteaders assisted by the US Army and assimilated to varying degrees into the surrounding communities. Many who could pass for white did, if only to make their lives and the lives of their children easier. Others had to get along as best they could. All these people are the ones Al Wiseman grew up beside, and there aren't many left who can, or are willing to, tell the story the way Al can.

"I've known this stuff all along, but I never stepped out with it or anything," he says. "I didn't learn this stuff overnight; I lived it. I heard these old people talk and was always interested in it.

I figured I better try and do something here because our older people were so reserved, you wouldn't get much out of them. Especially if you were non-Indian they wouldn't tell you much because they didn't trust you."

Why should they have?

~

Two years into this book and reflecting on my dad's life as part of a family that absolutely experienced the scattering, the diaspora, of our extended relatives from the lands that defined them, a thought occurs to me for the first time. It manifests as I write and reflect on the stories Al Wiseman told me of his life.

Because my dad is no longer someone I can see and connect with physically, there's an image of him that lives in my head. It's not the older version of him, the one who finally declined after decades of poor health and alcohol abuse. It's the robust man I always counted on when I was younger, the version of him that's about the age I am now. Thirty years younger, healthy, and something of a force of nature.

The reality is, he isn't my contemporary. If he appeared again before me, he would be of Al Wiseman's generation. Al is less than four years my dad's senior. They could've been classmates. When Al was sixteen and leaving high school my dad was thirteen, already drinking beer and smoking cigarettes and tinkering on cars. Both men left high school early, Al to work as a carpenter, then the army, then back to work, and my dad to the navy and then work.

But man, did things go separate directions when it comes to how they were raised, how they were encouraged to stay connected to their ancestors. It seems that Al's Indian mother passed down a measure of pride for where he came from that he was able to connect with. My grandmother is the only person I recall from my family who openly talked about being Chippewa, and I don't know much of what her relationship with my dad was like. Perhaps my despotic grandfather forbid such sharing; I know he physically and emotionally abused my dad. My dad was constantly berated as "worthless" and "stupid," so my mom tells me, both of which he absolutely was not.

What if my father had received some encouragement? What if his family had remained closer in proximity to the La Trays and Doneys so there was some kind of community around him for a larger percentage of his life? People sharing the experience of being Indian in the fifties and sixties and seventies and watching each other's backs—what kind of difference would it have made? This disconnect and shame is what happens when communities are broken up. When connections are lost and rituals and rites of passage aren't practiced.

My dad loved his immediate family, my mom, my sisters, and me . . . and his own parents, I guess, unless his time with them was merely him doing what he thought of as his "duty" since he was the only one close by. In her bleeker moments, my mother tells me she never felt part of the La Tray family, that she was assured by both my father and his parents that this was the case. But I also know how bad my entire family is at being close, not just to others but to one another. I talk to my mom fairly regularly, but I can count my interactions with my sisters on one hand every year. My mom is now estranged from her family, too, near as I can tell; I haven't seen any of them for years. So there's only the four of us to *be* connected, and we just . . . aren't. Not really. It doesn't seem weird to me because I don't know any different, but maybe it is.

This all stems from the generations stacked up against us who chose to disavow where they came from so future generations wouldn't have to endure what they did. We can't be angry about that either because they were as trauma-struck as we are. We have to have compassion for what they endured, no matter how angry it made them, and try to be the generations where the disconnect ends. But it's hard when you don't know any different.

Al Wiseman and his wife, Elaine, are true Métis elders, and their value to our community is immeasurable. But they're members of just one community. Certainly there are others scattered about with the rest of our Métis relations with similar stories to tell. Maybe stories they've never told at all, like the boarding school survivors my Turtle Mountain friend Denise Lajimodiere talks about. One benefit I'd like to see from a Little Shell federal recognition is that it would hopefully give more people the courage to open up about their experiences. That might help people heal, whether they're like my dad, who had his pride for where he came from tormented out of him, or people like me, who never had a chance to celebrate that part of who we are.

"When you talk to elders, you'll hear different things," Al Wiseman tells me. "What I'm saying, I'm not saying this is the only way it was, because it's not. You get outside of this territory, our own people did things a little different."

What they had in common is they banded together and formed enclaves on the outer edges of the newly forming settler communities and had to make a go of it on their own. All those familial, matrilineal ties that created a web of community across distances were stretched near to breaking, but they endured, if quietly and largely underground. Importantly, the people survived, and with them stories like Al's. That's what's important, because sometimes when it comes to the long game, the people who hold out, whatever it takes, often come out ahead.

"I seen a lot of stuff," Al Wiseman says. "I heard a lot of stuff. Both personal and not personal stuff. I carry it here," he says, pointing at his heart. "And I will until I die."

CHAPTER 18

2021

MISSOULA, MONTANA

I'M DRIVING WESTBOUND after dark on Broadway in Missoula in the days following Christmas, just after the winter solstice, when the night finds its darkest. There are clouds and no stars. It's cold and getting colder. Silhouetted against the orange glow of streetlights a bulky shape, also headed west, lumbers along the sidewalk; the outer edge of my headlights can barely make a sketch. I see a person in an oversized coat, a thick bag of some kind—like a stuff sack, or duffle—clutched in the left hand while the right holds an undefinable lump over their back and shoulders. As I pass it looks like a white comforter similar to the one on my bed at home. Not a block farther along is another figure, blanket wrapped and shuffling, heading east. I wonder if the two will greet each other when they pass.

I wonder where they plan to sleep.

Living on the street, on the fringes, I suppose you learn the better places if you survive long enough—the best doorways, the best covered parking areas. If these two plan to join their fellows at the outdoor camp off Reserve Street, at times occupied by well over one hundred people, one has a long way to go, and the other is headed in the wrong direction. It's probably too late to find a space in the homeless shelter or anywhere else the city offers "authorized" space to take cover from the cold. If they're lucky maybe they have a car or RV parked on a side street that they can hunker down in for the night. If they're very lucky, maybe there's a person they can call who will offer a spare couch or stretch of floor to sleep on. There remain many hours until morning.

There are a heartbreaking number of houseless people in Missoula, but it's nothing like other northwest cities. My last visit to Portland, Oregon, for example, I was stunned by the number of camps in the city, on the slopes along the network of highways and interstates that connect north to south and west to east. "It's a problem!" the public cries, but not in the way the loudest voices portray it. They see vagrants, addicts and deranged and irredeemable souls that need to go somewhere their plight is less visible.

Not me. When I see these people, no less beautiful in their humanity than anyone else, I see echoes of mine, the Little Shell Tribe of Chippewa Indians, during those unfortunate years as landless Indians.

I've mentioned several times how the Little Shell were known as the landless Indians, and how we lived on the fringes of communities. None of that happened overnight, and none of our ancestors chose to live that way. Like our houseless relatives today, it was almost entirely the result of forces beyond their control. Beginning as early as the 1850s, settler pressures pushed and divided our traditional communities. But things accelerated over a twenty-year period that flooded the landscape with refugees from these conflicts, and this book wouldn't be complete without an account of it.

From 1872 to 1874—about the time our Chief Little Shell took over for his father as chief of the Pembina Chippewa—the United States turned its eyes northward to focus on establishing a border with Canada that would run along the forty-ninth parallel. The border had existed for years, only now the United States was determined to bring some enforcement to it. Native tribes would come to call this ethereal boundary the "Medicine Line" because of its ability to halt the pursuit of American troops—"bluecoats"—as if by magic. And there was a lot of pursuit, particularly because, to the people living in the area, no border existed. This countryside was their home, and they moved back and forth at will, as they had for centuries.

There were already reservations in the regions, notably for the Blackfeet and those tribes living on the Fort Belknap reservation. There were also Cree and Chippewa people whose territory straddled the border, those people Isaac Stevens had never gotten around to stealing land from before he went off and got himself killed in the same Civil War that was flooding the continent with trigger-happy malcontents. There were the Métis people, who had been settling in for decades along the Milk River, some creating communities, some hunting buffalo, most doing both. They had never signed any treaty that would put them on a reservation. Therefore, in the eyes of Washington, DC, they didn't have rights to any of their land. The government's solution to the "problem" became a period of ethnic cleansing against border people that began in the 1870s and continued through 1896.

Fort Assinniboine was established near the Hi-Line town of Havre in 1879, built specifically to clear Indians from the border once and for all. As I've mentioned, Colonel Nelson Miles was in the area too. Fearing Sitting Bull's return and fresh off capturing Chief Joseph and the Nez Perce in the Bears Paw Mountains in 1877, he started wreaking havoc on the Milk River settlements. Troops would ride into a community, burn villages and towns to the ground, strip them of all their possessions, and drive the residents into dispersal or back over the Canadian border. If the people came back, which they typically did, the process would be repeated. Many settled with my ancestors at Spring Creek in what would become Lewistown. Others joined family on established reservations. Others still kept trying to make a go of it on their own.

These were people accustomed to living in communities, in a "band" environment. It was the only way of life they had ever known. But their communities were smoking ruins, and new towns, settler towns, sprang up in their place. The flood of white homesteaders continued unabated. There were no remaining natural resources sufficient to sustain large groups of Indigenous people, so the close ties of family and community broke down. The buffalo were essentially gone, so subsistence living was rendered impossible. Some, like my family, managed to find agricultural work in the new white communities, working as cowboys on cattle and sheep ranches or simply as laborers. But there wasn't enough of that work for everyone.

So people moved to where the resources, any resources, were. Generally this meant the outskirts of settler communities, near places like town dumps and slaughterhouses where they could scavenge for scraps, or worse. Winter on the northern plains is particularly severe, and families faced disease, exposure, and starvation, eating dead horses and dogs to survive. They took shelter where they could, temporary jobs if they were available, charity when it was offered.

Meanwhile, north of the border in Canada, tensions were building as well, for many of the same reasons. In 1883, Cree Indians, generally thought of as Canadian Indians, were struggling. They couldn't find enough bison to feed their people, and crop failures exacerbated the problem. The previous winter, as many as one quarter of Montana's Piegan Indian population died of starvation. In an effort to avoid that fate, the Cree resorted to raiding, even against other Indians, to secure what they needed to survive: Horses. Weapons. Food.

The Canadian Métis were being squeezed by the same factors. Poverty, lack of food sources (like those bison herds), and treaty betrayals by the Canadian government stirred a boiling pot of anger. The North-West Rebellion erupted in 1885 when, under a visionary leader named Louis Riel, the Métis decided to carve out their own existence separate from Canada. It was a short, bloody affair ending in the crushing defeat of the rebels at the four-day Battle of Batoche in Saskatchewan in May 1885. Survivors scattered, and Riel was captured and put on trial. Convicted of treason, he was hanged.

~

I'm sitting on the curb across from a pale, two-story stucco-covered building at 203 North Rodney Street in Helena, Montana. It's the first of October 2021, and it's gorgeous. It's in the high seventies, and the skies are blue and beautiful. I'm in shorts and a T-shirt. Rodney Street is under renovation, and the road is torn up so only dirt and gravel remain. It's closed to traffic.

It's a pilgrimage of sorts, my being here. I'm staying just a couple blocks down in a bed and breakfast that, while well appointed and historic itself, also freaks me out a little with all the portraits of stern-looking Victorian-era white dudes and the puffy-dressed women they probably treated horribly. I've wandered up to this spot because this is where, in a long-gone establishment called the Iowa House Hotel, Louis Riel lived for a time in 1882.

Louis Riel is a curiosity to me. His name still riles people up in Canada, but he's hardly known of in the United States. He's one of the most important people in Métis history, but his role as it relates to the Little Shell is more disruptor than leader. The waves of his activities certainly impacted our story here, but his direct involvement is minimal. Given how much ink has been devoted to him in other places—I keep mentioning Joseph

Kinsey Howard's *Strange Empire*, for example—I don't want to spend a lot of time on him here. But this story can't be told without mentioning him.

Riel was in Helena as part of his five-year exile from Canada after the Red River Rebellion of 1869. This rebellion was Riel's first attempt to secure a Métis homeland at the Red River Colony separate from Canada, which had just purchased Rupert's Land from the Hudson's Bay Company. His efforts there led to the creation of the province of Manitoba . . . and also got him run out of the country.

His time in Montana was productive. Before ensconcing himself in Helena he spent time in Lewistown, drafting a petition for a Métis reservation there. When that proposal, supported by Nelson Miles, wasn't upheld by the federal government (or by the local movers and shakers, who had no intention of sharing real estate they had only just acquired), Riel moved on. In Helena he became a father twice over with a Métis woman, Marguerite Monet dit Bellehumeur, whom he married in 1881. Riel was active in local politics. He also became an American citizen. He took a job as a schoolteacher at St. Peter's Mission north of Helena, near the town of Cascade, Montana.

In 1884—the year Chief Little Shell saw the reservation he'd fought so hard to preserve reduced 90 percent by the US government—the Canadian Métis came looking for Riel. A delegation led by legendary Métis buffalo hunter and guerrilla fighter Gabriel Dumont visited Louis at St. Peter's and asked him to return to Canada to lead efforts for another try at a Métis homeland, this time in Saskatchewan. Riel obliged. A series of events led to open rebellion, ending in complete defeat and Riel's death. It was an illegal death too: Riel couldn't be guilty of treason against the queen because at that point he was technically American. The US government chose not to intervene.

The decade after the North-West Rebellion brought even more chaos along the northern plains because it exacerbated the diaspora of people looking for somewhere to live. Métis bands and families, fearing retaliation from the Canadian government, fled south. Bands of Cree raiders were lumped in by the Canadian government as part of the rebellion, even though they were engaged in separate conflicts. A Cree chief named Big Bear was captured and sentenced to three years in prison for his part in the rebellion, even though he'd had no part in it and had actively worked to prevent continued bloodshed. Other Cree leaders, including Chiefs Little Bear and Little Poplar, escaped across the border into the United States with hundreds of their followers. They spent weeks on the trail and arrived, worn out and starving, on the southern side of the Medicine Line, where they found themselves utterly unwelcome on their own traditional lands by flush-faced, indignant newcomers we now tend to revere as "brave homesteaders."

To the east, Little Shell and his Pembina Band in the Turtle Mountains weren't doing any better. In calculating the land they determined "necessary" for the people living there, DC bureaucrats didn't count any of the Pembina Chippewa who weren't present on the reservation at the time, nor did they count the Métis, many of whom were certainly mixed up in the Riel conflict, so they reduced the reservation to the tiniest fraction of what had originally been allocated. The resulting postage stamp parcel of land was entirely too small for the number of people who called the area home. The stolen land carved off the reservation—because certainly "stolen" is what it became—was immediately opened up to white settlers.

The United States refused to offer any support to Little Shell's people, who were trying to subsist on a much-reduced range. The residents struggled mightily; in the brutal winter of 1887, 151 Pembina Chippewa died of starvation. These conditions contributed to the spread of even more people heading west—following relatives already abroad who still considered the Turtle Mountains their home—looking for any means of survival: hunting where they could or scavenging on the fringes of growing settler communities in Montana.

Settlers coveted the rest of the rich farmland that comprised traditional Pembina territory, and the government was set on them getting it. In an effort to halt the onslaught, Little Shell and his subchiefs scattered signs all over the Turtle Mountains that read, "It is forbidden to any white man to encroach upon this Indian land by settling upon it before a treaty being made with the American government." This was in July 1892.

In September 1892, a commission of three men arrived at the Turtle Mountain Indian Agency. They were led by a federal commissioner named Porter J. McCumber. The entire situation was essentially a setup against Little Shell and the Pembina people. Over a year prior, United States Indian agent John Waugh had appointed a committee of thirty-two men—sixteen full-blood Chippewa and sixteen Métis, selected while Little Shell was away hunting on the Fort Peck reservation in Montana—to represent the interests of the Turtle Mountain people in dealings with the federal government, even though Little Shell and his subchiefs were the recognized leaders. The efforts of this committee saw over five hundred people struck from the Pembina rolls.

When Little Shell learned that only the members of this committee of thirty-two would be allowed to speak to McCumber and his commission, he left representation in the hands of his lawyer, John Bottineau, and departed in a state of outrage without signing the agreement. Three days later, on September 24, the commission posted the new membership roll on the door of the church. Any Indians not on the roll were instructed to leave the reservation.

A month later on October 22, 1892, the McCumber Commission announced the results of its mission. In addition to drastically reducing the recognized population of the Turtle Mountain Chippewa—splitting families, ignoring protests, and writing off Little Shell, his followers, and the Métis completely—they reported that the tribe had sold just under ten million acres of land to the federal government for the paltry sum of $1 million. This became infamously known as the Ten-Cent Treaty.

Imagine how this might feel. Imagine you're abroad somewhere, vacationing, visiting family, or working . . . and return to find someone else in your house, it having been sold to them out from under you by someone who never owned it in the first place. And what if it turned out your neighbor, or even a family member, was in on the deal? How devastating would that be when you realized there was absolutely nothing you could do about it? This was the reality for a large percentage of people living in the region of the Turtle Mountains. They were forced to leave.

It didn't end there. Years of wrangling ensued. Little Shell was aghast and sent an impassioned letter of protest to Congress, who ignored it. He sent another letter two years later, this one through Bottineau, who was in DC trying to make things right—nothing. Little Shell's people, forced from their home, were scattered and landless.

The agreement wasn't ratified until April 1904, after Little Shell's death. Even then litigation continued, and details over this stolen land and who should get what are still debated today. Still *litigated* today. In the summer of 2023, I received a $50 check as my share of compensation for the latest class action lawsuit related to the Ten-Cent Treaty. Others got upward of $1,500. People were happy about this, but it's not exactly enough to buy a house and a little piece of land with. It's worth noting, I occasionally pay $48 for a slab of bison ribeye at the steakhouse I occasion. My check has become a bookmark. After I mobile deposited it and ate that steak, of course.

The United States saw all this sorrow as a perfect opportunity to deal with the Indian problem in the area once and for all. The American government labeled the wandering Cree and Chippewa and Métis "undesirable refugees" and offered them no assistance. Instead, under the Cree Deportation Act of 1896, $5,000 was appropriated by Congress to rid the area of these refugee Indians. Operating out of Fort Assiniboine, First Lieutenant John J. "Black Jack" Pershing and his Tenth Cavalry Regiment—the African American Buffalo Soldiers—captured and deported Crees and any other landless Indians they found. All the "half-breeds" scattered around Montana were rounded up and driven like cattle to Great Falls, where they were loaded on railroad cars and shipped to Lethbridge, Alberta. When the money ran out, they were force-marched the entire journey on foot. This roundup occurred all over the state, including an incident of around 150 Cree and Métis "prisoners" (including a few French tourists who found themselves definitely in the wrong place at the wrong time) being marched through downtown Missoula to Fort Missoula, then forced to walk all the way north to the border.

A majority of Montanans were in favor of the effort. Martha Harroun Foster sums it up in an essay for the anthology *Montana: A Cultural Medley*: "By ignoring their long history in US territory, Montanans were able to rationalize Métis removal to Canada. Although this scheme ultimately failed, the perception of Métis as illegal immigrants lived on. Euro-Americans who settled in Montana and the Dakotas after the 1870s were celebrated as 'pioneers.' The Métis, who made the area home decades earlier, were labeled illegal Canadian aliens."

This heartless, violent campaign, the last significant military action in the region, resulted in hundreds of Indians, many of them American-born Chippewas, Assiniboine, and members of other related tribes, being sent to Canada. Hundreds, if not thousands or more, were driven from established communities where they had lived, untroubled, for decades. They were rousted from their ramshackle dwellings wherever they had constructed them.

Still, the Indians persisted. A large percentage of them made their way back to Montana, hiding among relatives on the reservations of other tribes, or returned to and rebuilt the camps they'd already established around the perimeter of larger cities.

Lacking funds to continue rounding up people who would make their way back anyway, the American government essentially threw its hands in the air and hoped the problem would go away on its own. Cree Chief Little Bear was still in the area with his people, as was a Chippewa chief named Rocky Boy. As the years passed, they kept steady pressure on the government to make a place for them.

The Cree Deportation Act of 1896 was an absolute failure. For all the hardships the government visited on the Indigenous people, the ultimate result was more refugees, more people living on the fringes of white communities, and more clamor from people living in those communities to "do something" about it.

Decades removed from the bloody fights that raged across the plains in the 1870s, public opinion toward Indians shifted from fear to a kind of pity. Fort Assiniboine was decommissioned and transferred to the Department of the Interior in 1913. Indian agent James McLaughlin, working with Little Bear and Rocky Boy, established Montana's Rocky Boy's reservation (Chippewa Cree) in 1916, which included federal recognition of the tribe. The reservation had enough resources to support the 425 or so members of Rocky Boy's band on the initial tribal roll, but there were at least five times as many Indians still looking for a home.

I've said it before, and I'll say it again: those people left out at Rocky Boy's, two thousand or more at minimum, and their subsequent progeny largely comprise the people we now call the Little Shell Tribe of Chippewa Indians.

~

It's not a stretch for me to liken the tribulations of my ancestors to what we see on the streets of our cities. The houseless people in my Missoula community are a diaspora of sorts too. They gather here not only from other parts of Montana, but also from around the West, from around the entire country, for many of the same reasons: Untreated mental health crises. Trauma-inflicted addictions. And many, many instances of people forced from their homes for reasons that include collapse of traditional industries or even, far more common than most understand, folks who have jobs that can't keep up with the rising costs of any kind of housing.

Is the tide turning in their favor or looking to drown them? Missoula created a new authorized camp in another part of the city and moved all the people living near the Reserve Street Bridge away from there. Besides the forced removal from that camp, law enforcement is now cracking down on unauthorized RV parking and camping all over the city. Such camps are deemed a "public health crisis." In Portland, the mayor is proposing large structures for housing the homeless. In return, the city can make camping illegal. Is this progress or a sweeping away? Are these projects livable spaces or concentration camps? Are we solving anything or just moving a tragedy out of sight, out of mind? It's too early to tell, but without budgets federal, state, and municipal pivoting toward compassion and healing instead of militarization and incarceration, I remain dubious. Without spirited civic engagement there's far more suffering to come.

The Métis diaspora I've been writing about, our 150-plus years of landlessness, has been the overriding problem of our time for generations. Now we see the same struggle playing out in the broader culture, reaching higher and higher up the rungs of social status. It isn't just poor Indians who get caught up in the suffering anymore, it now includes folks who as recently as a decade ago might've considered themselves firmly ensconced in the middle class.

This is becoming the problem of all of our times, I think.

CHAPTER 19

2019

MISSOULA, MONTANA

On the afternoon of June 26, 2019, I'm walking to my car where it's parked along Higgins Avenue in downtown Missoula when my phone rings. The ID tells me it's my friend Aaron Parrett, a writer/musician/renaissance man of sorts who lives in Helena and runs a letterpress business there. I'd just seen him at the Helena library a few days earlier during a reading I did in support of *One-Sentence Journal.* When I answer the phone he says, "Hey, man. I have some terrible news: Nicholas Vrooman died this morning."

I'm stunned. Vrooman was just shy of seventy and seemed healthy every time I saw him. But he suffered a stroke, Aaron says, while driving to his office earlier that day.

I know the office, on the second floor of an old building in downtown Helena, just off the main drag of Last Chance Gulch, a street name that carries all the weight of the city's mining history with it. The cramped space, which has a desk and a couple chairs, is crammed with shelves and books and posters and maps. I spent several hours in there with Nicholas over a couple occasions, discussing the Little Shell and Métis, opining on what we thought the tribe could become ("You need to run for tribal council, my friend!" he regularly urged me), or even just loudly sharing the joys of a couple book nerds with time on their hands talking literature. The last time we met, we went downstairs for lunch just across the street. When I tried to pick up the check, I was embarrassed to discover it was cash only, and all I had was a credit card.

My first thoughts are to his family. While Vrooman and I interacted on several occasions, we weren't so close that I had opportunity to meet them. I know he's married, but I don't even know if he has kids. He does, I learn, three, and ten grandchildren. He's also survived by four sisters and a brother, and many nieces and nephews. Finally there's his wife of thirty years, Linda. What is it like to lose somebody suddenly, and so unexpectedly? I can only imagine what they must be going through.

Just weeks earlier, I received a letter from Little Shell Chairman Gerald Gray inviting me to the tribe's next quarterly meeting, scheduled for later in the month. In the letter he congratulated me on winning the 2018 Montana Book Award for *One-Sentence Journal*. "Your work is an inspiration to Little Shell people," the letter said, "and we would like to honor you with a token of our appreciation at our quarterly meeting." I planned to attend anyway, and I responded it would be my pleasure to attend, and to accept.

When Nicholas died, the meeting was postponed for late July. As the meeting neared, it was announced the agenda would include a memorial and honor ceremony for him. I assumed that would supersede any recognition I was scheduled to receive, but I was wrong.

During the meeting I was surprised to be honored, along with two others, by an eagle feather ceremony for doing work important to the Little Shell people. There was smudging, an honor song, and a solemn presentation. I received a gorgeous braid of sweetgrass and an eagle feather carefully wrapped, as per tradition, in red cloth. Standing in front of these people, my people, drums beating and voices raised in song, was one of the most powerful moments of my life. It was all I could do not to heave with sobs at the enormity of it.

Immediately following, the meeting adjourned and we moved on to the ceremony for Nicholas. There were more songs, and a meal was laid out in the center of the room. Every step taken—from the pipe ceremony to the blessing of the food with sacred smoke to the sharing of the food by servers—was per Chippewa custom. Nicholas's family was there, and many of us, including myself, got up and spoke to them about what he meant to us, what he'd done for us. It was very moving, and there were many tears.

During the event Kim McKeehan, an even closer friend of Nicholas's, told me the ceremony with the eagle feather had all been his idea. It was something he thought the tribe should be doing. He suggested it, procured the feathers, and made it all happen, but he hadn't lived to see it come true. But he was there in spirit, still urging us to embrace our cultural heritage with joy and compassion.

Another thing Nicholas didn't live to see was the federal recognition of the Little Shell Tribe. It's a tragedy, certainly, because it remains doubtful how soon, if ever, it would've happened without his tireless advocacy for our people, not just as a folklorist and historian but as a force of nature. I put the blame for this lost opportunity on one person: Senator Mike Lee of Utah.

I can't say enough bad things about the senator from Utah, so I won't even start. But he had it in his hands to do something historic and chose otherwise. In the dwindling hours of 2018, under a standalone bill called the Little Shell Tribal Recognition Act, the tribe was one vote away from finally being federally recognized. The bill was submitted to the US Senate floor as a "unanimous consent" agreement, a process the Senate uses to move bills forward that may never reach the floor for debate due to time constraints. In this case, it requires a unanimous vote in favor of it; all the lobbying and explaining and cajoling happens outside the chamber, and it appeared the thing was going to pass.

I called Little Shell lawyer Josh Clause in 2020 to get the context. Two years removed from the events, his voice still reveals obvious irritation.

"When the bill passed the House in September, we had all kinds of momentum," Clause tells me. "We ran into an issue with a Senator from Utah, Senator Mike Lee. I spent hours and hours and hours with his staff explaining the legal case for the tribe, the tribe's history. We sent him historical documents, we pulled in the NARF [Native American Rights Fund], we brought in [lawyer and Lumbee Tribe member] Arlinda Locklear, the first Native woman to argue before the Supreme Court; we had a very tense meeting for about forty-five minutes where we made the case and answered all the questions."

Despite every other voting member of the Senate being in favor of the bill, Lee blocked the effort. It was exasperating because the process, which had seemed inevitable, had to start all over in 2019. Numerous people worked hard to get the bill so close to the finish line only to have it snubbed by one man's ego.

I think of the elders we lost the following year, who were so close to the recognition they'd sought their entire lives. I think of Nicholas Vrooman not seeing arguably his life's work come to fruition. I hold Mike Lee solely responsible for this suffering, and I'll never forgive him for his cruel arrogance.

The bill was reintroduced in 2019, this time attached as a rider to the $738 billion National Defense Authorization Act (NDAA), a must-pass bill that funds the entire United States military. Still, even as an attachment the bill needed to survive all the back-and-forth shenanigans of our aggravating political operatives jockeying for power and influence. Thankfully when the dust settled, the attachment was intact.

US senator Jon Tester, a Democrat, often relates the story of Chairman Gray visiting his office with an empty tin can. Gray placed the can on Tester's bookshelf to symbolize his frustration that the tribe's recognition bill had been "kicked down the road for more than a century." So in 2019 Tester, with Republican junior Montana senator Steve Daines as cosponsor, got the Little Shell Tribal Recognition Act added to the defense bill in the first place.

"There was a catch, of course," Tester writes of the events in his 2020 memoir, *Grounded: A Senator's Lessons on Winning Back Rural America*. "Senator McConnell [Senate Majority Leader, and a Republican] agreed to include the Little Shell recognition language if we changed it from a 'Tester–Daines' amendment to a 'Daines–Tester' amendment. Of course I agreed. And President Trump signed the legislation into law on December 20, 2019."

Tester, a farmer from the tiny Montana town of Big Sandy, which directly borders the Rocky Boy's reservation of Chippewa Cree, has been a staunch ally of the Little Shell since he was elected to the Senate in 2006. The first bill he introduced in March 2007 was a bill seeking federal recognition for the tribe, and he followed up every year after. Tester was also the first candidate I ever really got behind; I donated to his 2006 campaign and showed up at rallies for him from the primaries through the general election. I have a photo of the two of us at a Missoula fundraising event. We're laughing at the camera, both of us looking much younger than we do now. I remember telling him, "Let's get a picture, Jon. I'm the only guy in the room who's going to make you look skinny!" Chuckles all around. "Click" goes the camera.

"I still keep Chairman Gray's tin can on my bookshelf as a reminder that diligence and patience pay off in the US Senate," Tester writes in his memoir.

I was happy to have an opportunity to help Senator Tester sign a pile of copies of his memoir and thank him personally for his efforts. It meant a lot for me to be able to do so.

Diligence and patience pay off for a tribal nation vying for federal recognition for over 150 years too.

What is federal recognition anyway, and why should anyone care when clearly we know who we are? It is, like everything else in Indian country, extremely complicated.

The federal Bureau of Indian Affairs (BIA) is under the auspices of the US Department of the Interior. Founded in 1824, the BIA's mission is "to enhance the quality of life, to promote economic opportunity, and to carry out the responsibility to protect and improve the trust assets of American Indians, Indian tribes and Alaska Natives." The role and responsibilities as they relate to the agency's interaction with tribes have evolved over the two hundred years of its existence, but one constant is that the relationship has always been, at best, rocky.

The BIA defines a federally recognized tribe as:

> an American Indian or Alaska Native tribal entity that is recognized as having a government-to-government relationship with the United States, with the responsibilities, powers, limitations, and obligations attached to that designation, and is eligible for funding and services from the Bureau of Indian Affairs.
>
> Furthermore, federally recognized tribes are recognized as possessing certain inherent rights of self-government (i.e., tribal sovereignty) and are entitled to receive certain federal benefits, services, and protections because of their special relationship with the United States.

The vast majority of federally recognized tribes received their recognition before there was an official policy for doing so, through acts of Congress, treaties, federal court decisions, etc. But many were left out, and as more and more tribes began to demand their recognition, and the benefits that come with it, the government recognized that something needed to be done. So in 1978, the Department of the Interior "issued regulations governing the Federal Acknowledgment Process (FAP) to handle requests for federal recognition from Indian groups whose character and history varied widely in a uniform manner. These regulations—25 C.F.R. Part 83—were revised in 1994 and are still in effect."

This is why, as mentioned previously, it was 1978 when the Little Shell became a tribe rather than just the title of a hereditary chief. This consolidation as a tribe under a specific name—rather than just "the Landless Indians of Montana"—was a means to gather this broad diaspora of people into a single entity that could then be recognized for who they actually were.

As part of that 1994 revision to the FAP, Congress enacted Public Law 103-454, the Federally Recognized Indian Tribe List Act. This act formally established three ways in which a tribe could become federally recognized: by an Act of Congress; by an administrative procedure through the BIA under 25 C.F.R. Part 83, or "Part 83"; or by decision of a United States court. Until 2009, while Tester introduced bill after bill for recognition during each Congress, the Little Shell also tried for recognition administratively via Part 83. That effort only led to frustration.

I say "until 2009" because it was in that year that the tribe was dealt a blow. In a surprise ruling, the BIA under President Barack Obama announced that, per its findings, there was "not enough evidence to meet the legal requirements for federal recognition" and that the "Department of the Interior, therefore, has issued a final determination not to acknowledge the petitioner group as a federally recognized Indian tribe." The BIA claimed the Little Shell met only four of the seven requirements necessary for recognition under Part 83. They believed the Little Shell could only prove existence after 1935, when the requirement was existence as of 1900 and therefore did not "comprise a distinct community since historical times"; did not "maintain significant social relationships and interaction as part of a distinct community" since their migration to Montana; and "did not demonstrate that the petitioner [the Little Shell] maintained political influence over a community of its members at any time or over communities that combined into the petitioner."

The tribe immediately challenged the ruling, citing in particular that in 2000 under the Clinton administration, the BIA *had* recommended the tribe for federal recognition, but it never happened. Regardless, the conflict seemed destined to head for the courts, where historically such arguments go to die. But the effort wasn't dead, because regardless of the BIA ruling the tribe could still be recognized legislatively by the US Congress. So the Little Shell swallowed their frustration and a few angry tears and kept at it. But in 2018, it was the 2009 ruling that Utah Senator Lee based his no vote on, even though the tribe had proof the BIA had made a mistake in its determination.

I met the LST's DC-based lawyer, Josh Clause, for the first time at a quarterly meeting in January 2019, just after the disappointment of being denied recognition because of Senator Lee. Clause was in attendance to try to explain to the assembled tribe members what had gone wrong. Before he spoke I saw him at the front of the room with Chairman Gray and the rest of the council, and I wondered who the heck he was. Medium height or so and stocky with reddish-brown hair and wearing a thick, heavy sweater, he looked completely out of place. Appearances can be deceiving; there are few players in this drama more important than Josh Clause. In fact, if the tribe ever put up a "Wall of Fame" of portraits, Clause's would certainly be among the first to be commissioned. He has been utterly committed to our cause for many years, is always quick to answer emails and phone calls, and is generous with time I'm certain he has very little of. I'm grateful to have cultivated a degree of friendship with the man, and I have abundant respect for him.

Josh Clause is a citizen of the Mohawk Nation, enrolled at Six Nations of the Grand River Territory in Ohsweken, Ontario, Canada. After years of honing his expertise in federal Indian law and policy, he started Clause Law PLLC to provide legal and policy solutions to tribal nations, tribal organizations, and tribally owned businesses. Most important, he has been intimately involved in Little Shell legal efforts for more than a decade.

And as Gerald Gray told me, "He's a little fucking bulldog!"

Between 2007 and 2008, Clause worked as a legal intern at a larger law firm that had taken on the Little Shell recognition effort as a pro bono client. When he finished law school in 2010, the firm hired Clause so he could keep working on it. It was during that period when then-chairman John Gilbert, in town testifying on behalf of the tribe, visited the firm in DC and met Clause in person. The two men, generations apart, hit it off.

"I was the most junior member on the [legal] team," Clause tells me over the telephone. "For whatever reason [Gilbert] started calling me for explanations on things, and I developed a good relationship with him. I think because it was pro bono I had a little more time on my hands, and it was fun to work on something where I could kind of make the calls. For the most part I think the partners were fine with it because I was taking stuff off their plate."

I understand perfectly why Gilbert connected with Clause, and why Gerald Gray has too. Hell, I connected with the guy. He's an interesting and intelligent person, and he tells things like they are. I appreciate that, as I'm sure my Little Shell relatives do.

Clause's ambitions grew beyond the work he was allowed to do in the larger firm, and he decided to strike out on his own. By then Gerald Gray was chairman of the Little Shell. When Clause called Gray to tell him he was leaving the larger firm, and presumably the Little Shell as well, Gray said, "The hell you are, you're taking us with you!" Clause wanted Gray to know that while he'd be happy to take the tribe with him, and keep doing it pro bono, the truth was he wouldn't have near the resources the big firms have.

"By that point I'd become really invested in trying to get this [recognition] done," Clause says. "And Gerald said, 'No, I trust you.'"

So Clause kept hustling.

When it comes to seeking federal recognition through legislation, there really isn't a rule book because it hardly ever happens... and it's a tough sell. There are a few reasons for this. First, in some instances there are local communities that may not want a new jurisdiction popping up next to them with competing sovereignty (for example, a state government conflicting with a tribal government). And sometimes other tribes are against it, not just because of the perceived dilution of federal funds—for housing, health services, and other programs only available to federally recognized tribes—but also because in areas where casinos are an option, they don't want the competition. Finally, there have been claims made in the past for scurrilous reasons by people claiming to represent tribes they actually don't.

"The most frustrating thing about this entire thing is no one was against you," Clause says. "No one was against the Little Shell. They were against the *idea* of any more tribes. They were against the idea of the sort of slippery slope of recognizing other tribes."

What we Little Shell had going for us was that every other federally recognized tribe in Montana supported us. A series of state governors and attorneys general supported us. We had many allies. Clause used these facts to bolster his effort to get us recognized.

"I'd tell people I don't want to talk about other recognition issues," he says, "or what's happening in North Carolina or Southern California with their tribes. None of that matters. What matters is Montana, and this is a Montana-specific issue."

Clause's goal was to meet with everyone in DC and make this pitch to them about the Little Shell every time. He wanted our story on everyone's radar because once they learned what was going on, he felt they would be compelled to act. And ultimately, they were.

"When I started working on this I was twenty-five. I'm thirty-five now, with a kid and married," Clause says. "I have stories and stories of times of when we thought it was going to fall apart, and times we thought we got really close and didn't. When I look back on this stuff, I'm kind of surprised that John and Gerald trusted me to [keep] working on this. At this point now I have my own firm and my own team. My entire legal professional career I've worked on Little Shell. The tribe was my first independent client. So it's just nice to get where we are, through all the hoops."

The Little Shell have been fighting the US government in the courts since Ayabe-way-we-tung, the Chief Little Shell we are named after, lobbied to preserve who we are as a chief of the Pembina Chippewa, and then the Turtle Mountain Chippewa. Fortunes rose and fell from the founding of the Rocky Boy's reservation in 1916 and on through the thirties and forties. People kept at it, trying to make the government recognize who we are, what was done to us. Yet we remained, at best, unseen and landless, and at worst, erased from our role in history.

There's a long list of people on the front line of these decades of struggle besides Nicholas Vrooman who never saw their efforts rewarded. People like Joseph Dussome, president of the Landless Indians of Montana when Verne Dusenberry wrote his historic "Waiting for a Day That Never Comes" article in 1958. Dussome was already an old man then, speaking to Dusenberry from his cabin in the tiny Central Montana mining town of Zortman. Dussome, born in a camp on the Milk River, was of the last generation whose parents, like my great-great-grandparents, hunted wild buffalo on the plains. Dussome died in 1963 at the age of eighty-three. He devoted his life to finding a home for his people.

There was Raymond Gray, cousin of current Little Shell chairman Gerald Gray and cousin of Elaine Wiseman in Choteau, further proof of the interrelatedness of our people. He was the first Métis attorney to practice law in the state of Montana. He led a Helena-based organization called the Montana Organization of Landless Indians. He, too, devoted his life to his people.

There are many others who survive as ancestors to those of us who are witness to all these collected efforts paying off. It's a tribute to those efforts—the men and women meeting around kitchen tables in tar paper shacks; the bake sales to raise funds to send representatives to Washington, DC, to argue on our behalf; the endurance of so much poverty and sorrow—that people like Josh Clause, Gerald Gray, and all the members of our tribal council honored in keeping the effort alive, despite close calls and disappointments.

"One of the things that Chairman Gray always talked about is that this is about the dignity of our people, the dignity of our ancestors," Clause says. "It's gonna take time to build the infrastructure. I hope people are patient with the chairman and the council."

CHAPTER 20

2020

GREAT FALLS, MONTANA

It's an unseasonably warm January 25, 2020, on the high plains of Montana. I'm early when I arrive at the Holiday Inn in Great Falls, and the hallway outside the convention center is crammed with people. A harried hotel employee hollers from the end of the hallway that the doors won't open for another hour at least, and seems to urge the crowd to disperse. I can barely hear her over the drone of conversation. No one moves. Instead, many people take the opportunity to relax. The hotel seems to be in some intermediate phase of a remodel, and the lobby and this corridor are lined with long rolls of plastic-wrapped carpet about three feet tall. Pressed up against the wall, they make perfect couches.

We have gathered here to celebrate a singular occasion: the federal recognition of the Little Shell Tribe of Chippewa Indians.

Despite the festive atmosphere, my attitude could be better. I've had a chip on my shoulder for a couple weeks now in anticipation of the speeches from "dignitaries"—a parade of white politicians whom I, in my cynical nature, see as only being here to secure votes in various upcoming elections. I've seen the agenda and it looks tiresome. I want to take the high road, give these men the benefit of the doubt, but it's difficult. I almost talked myself out of coming at all, but I pushed through that ridiculousness. I'm often my own worst adviser. So here I am.

I find a spot against the wall to lean on and wait and watch the crowd. The delegation of Indians from Turtle Mountain, whom I met earlier, pass by with a hotel employee as escort. They're pushing a cart laden with boxes. "Gifts!" Merle St. Claire, a silver-haired former chairman, tells me with a grin. He's wearing a gorgeous buckskin vest sewn with beautiful beadwork, and I'm a little envious. "It's a bit much," he says when I express my admiration, "but it's good to bring it out on occasions like this."

Many people sport their finest. The male members of the Little Shell tribal council are mostly dressed in matching ribbon shirts, black with red, yellow, and white strips of ribbon sewed horizontally across the chest and back. Many of the women are in ribbon skirts. Kim McKeehan, my cousin and friend, approaches, and she's lovely in a long black skirt. She gives me a wide-eyed "Can you believe all this?!" expression when she hugs me and tells me she'll see me inside, then she disappears through a doorway into the room everyone is waiting to stampede. As a member of the tribal council, she enjoys such privileges.

I hear a clattering of small bells as Mike LaFountain, chair of the Little Shell Cultural Committee, makes his way through the crowd. He's a mountain of a man, and in full red, black, and yellow regalia hung with bells and feathers and beadwork, he seems to tower close to seven feet tall. He's an impressive, magnificent sight. His son, much smaller in matching regalia, follows close behind.

The media are here too. I see several folks wearing lanyards stamped with "Press" moving up and down the hallway. My friend Tailyr Irvine is here. Tailyr is a CSKT photojournalist working on a piece for *High Country News*, a highly regarded regional publication based in Colorado that focuses on the politics and people of the West. I'm thrilled she got the gig. Tailyr is smart, talented, and full of energy. She has her camera out, taking her angles, standing on the rolled carpet to get a higher view . . . she's working hard. I'm pleased I'm only here to observe and celebrate, not to work. At least not in the same way she is.

I experience a moment of sudden deep emotion. It comes in waves throughout the evening. These are my people, and many of these folks are likely related to me in one way or another. There's so much color—silk and ribbons and embroidery and beadwork and feathers—and so many Native faces I get a little verklempt. The crowd is also a wonderful cross section of the people of the northern plains, and what it might've been like traditionally when tribes intermingled. Many of my Blackfeet friends are here, and Salish friends. Crow friends. Friends who identify as solely Chippewa, and friends who identify as Cree. And then those of us who identify as Métis. Amazingly, we are likely the majority.

People have traveled from all across the country to be here. Earlier in the day I visited the Lewis and Clark National Historic Trail Interpretive Center and met a group of people from Michigan who were in town for the celebration. There are also people from California, Oregon, Minnesota, North Dakota, and who knows where else. Probably Canada, too, I expect. Not to mention folks from every corner of the state of Montana. It's stirring. The crowd continues to grow. It's hard to imagine everyone fitting into a single room.

My name is called in stage whisper. I turn and look to the left and there's Kim again. She gestures me toward her and the open doorway she called me from. She ushers me through and closes the door behind me. "I got you a seat at my table," she says. I'm relieved to know I'm guaranteed a place to enjoy the festivities.

With limited time—apparently the room was the location of a different event up until just a couple hours before—the people decorating the space have done a wonderful job. It's a large, warmly lit banquet room. There must be about forty round tables or so, arranged close together around the room, with eight or ten chairs and place settings each. Every table has a centerpiece in the shape of a teepee, and many of the tables have little cards indicating who they're reserved for, like the families of council members, or visiting guests. Small cards read, "Make sure to #LittleShell with any photos you take and post online at todays [sic] event." For some reason this tickles me to no end. The modern world comes crashing into Indian country, and I find it gleefully ridiculous. I can't resist posting an Instagram photo of the card, with the simple caption "#LittleShell."

A stage and lectern with a bank of microphones is set up in the center of the room. A large black banner emblazoned with the Little Shell emblem hangs behind it. To one side of the stage is a long table reserved for the tribal council. To the other is a table reserved for dignitaries. On the opposite wall across the room is another raised platform where three video cameras are placed, technicians preparing them for action.

The room is filling up already, even before the doors open. A number of the tables are partially occupied, and I greet and wave at several acquaintances—like my friend Al Wiseman, already seated as befits an elder of his stature, looking sharp in his vest and cowboy hat—as I make my way across the room. I drop into a chair at a table with a card that reads "Reserved for Council McKeehan Family."

Relaxing in my seat at the McKeehan table, waiting for the festivities to begin, I'm grateful to be sitting for a moment. I drink a glass of water, refill it from a sweating pitcher in the center of the table, and look around. I don't have much time to myself before Tailyr appears before me and smiles. We chat about the event, how it's all going for her so far. She points to my left hand, at a tattoo across my knuckles. Reading from index finger to pinkie, one symbol per knuckle, it says, "#574."

"Is that new?" she asks.

"Yes," I say.

"What is it?"

"It's to mark the occasion," I say. "We're the 574th tribe to gain federal recognition. I thought it would be a cool way to commemorate it."

"It's very cool," she says. "Can I get a picture?"

She leads me into a hallway in the back of the room, one mostly accessed by service people and staff. More celebrants are standing around here, chatting loudly. A contingent of Montana Highway Patrol troopers linger as well, their uniforms and armament a little unsettling to me. Indians and law enforcement have rarely mixed well. But there will be politicians here, and that means cops. I do my best to ignore them.

Tailyr directs me in front of some large windows where cool evening light still shines through. I hold my fist up and she moves around, snapping pictures, adjusting her settings. It feels a little awkward with so many bystanders watching.

"So how do you feel about federal recognition?" Tailyr asks when she finally lowers her camera.

I shrug. "I'm a little ambivalent about it, to be honest."

"Why?"

"Because I don't want to get all caught up in the idea that the feds have 'given' us something, like it's some kind of reward. It's not. The way I see it is an acknowledgment that they have been wrong all along, and federal recognition is the result of them admitting their mistake. We don't need their approval to be who we are."

"So it's bittersweet."

"I don't know that I'd call it that, necessarily."

"But you obviously care enough to get a tattoo."

She makes a point: there's some inconsistency here on my

part, I must admit. I'll think about it later. So after a moment I just say, "It's complicated."

As Tailyr and I part, a pair of highway patrol officers call me over. They want to see what she was photographing. I explain the tattoo, the significance. They smile.

~

The Little Shell have waited a long time for this opportunity. Depending on the date used for reference, I'll hear various speech givers throughout the evening cite anywhere from 100 to 150 years of waiting for "the day that never comes."

I choose to put our timeline for waiting at 156 years. That's the number of years that have passed since the Treaty of Old Crossing in 1863. That was the treaty involving mostly Minnesota Ojibwe originally signed by Little Shell II, our Little Shell's father, who then refused to sign a revised version that came out of Washington, DC. That was the event—his refusal to ever negotiate with the US government again—that to my thinking set in motion more than a century of landlessness.

Later, Kim Gottschalk, a Native American Rights Fund (NARF) attorney out of Boulder, Colorado, addresses the room. NARF has assisted the tribe since 1985 in the administrative process required to secure federal recognition. NARF is a nonprofit legal organization founded in 1970 that has "provided legal assistance to Indian tribes, organizations, and individuals nationwide who might otherwise have gone without adequate representation." In pursuit of Little Shell recognition they have, as of their last major submission of legal documents in 2005, provided over seventy thousand pages of documentation proving the legitimacy of the Little Shell claim and its people. Today is a celebration of their efforts as well. Gottschalk is a tall, soft-spoken speaker, but his words carry a century of weight.

"More than 94 percent of the present [Little Shell] membership were traced back to signers of the 1863 [Old Crossing] treaty," he says. "You were a sovereign nation before the 1863 treaty, you were a sovereign nation when you signed the 1863 treaty, you've been a sovereign nation ever since, and at long last the federal government recognizes that."

The room erupts.

~

The celebrations really began hours earlier at the Shawn Gilbert Event Center. This is the name the Little Shell cultural headquarters building was given the previous summer, in honor of the late son of former tribal chairman John Gilbert. Shawn was an active member of the tribe and died of cancer two years earlier. I attended the tribe's quarterly meeting when the new name was made official, and a sign bearing Shawn's portrait was unveiled. It was an emotional moment.

The event center is a metal-sided building that sits at the base of Hill 57. Today, the center will host a pipe ceremony scheduled for one o'clock this afternoon. I arrive early for this event as well and find the parking lot overflowing with cars, and people parking on the dirt road out front. This is when I first get an inkling that the day's events are going to be a bigger deal than I'd anticipated. I park and walk toward the building as cars continue to pull up.

It's an absolutely gorgeous day. The sun is out and bright, few clouds are in the sky, and it must be nearly forty degrees. Considering what the weather should be in this part of the state in January, the perfect conditions are more than anyone could've hoped for. The large, warehouse-style roll-up door in the side of the community center is wide open, and people mill about in the open in small knots. Their faces are mostly unfamiliar to me, and those I recognize don't come to me with names. A buzz of excitement surrounds the proceedings.

Kim McKeehan is the first familiar person I encounter, and she's in a tizzy because there are all these people and no one thought to bring water. So Alisa Herodes, another close friend and the woman responsible for decorating the Holiday Inn immediately after the pipe ceremony wraps up, has been dispatched to procure some.

"I need to just start always bringing water to these things," Kim says. "I hate bottled water because there's no plastic recycling in Great Falls, but people can't be here without any fucking water."

This is classic Kim, her first priority to see to everyone else's needs, even if the expression of her concern involves an f-bomb or two. It lightens my mood, and I laugh and give her a hug. As if on cue Alisa arrives, backing up her SUV to the open roll-up door and popping the hatchback. I help them unload several flats of bottled water. Kim and Alisa start passing bottles out while I muscle the cases inside.

It's the largest crowd I've ever seen for any event at the center, and the media are here in force too. The large open room where events are held is two-thirds full of folding metal chairs arranged in rows. At the back of the room is a large circle of chairs. When the ceremony begins, more people than can be accommodated are present. As the drums start and the rich scent of burning sage and pipe smoke fills the air, many observe from just outside the roll-up door.

It's a sacred ceremony. No cameras are allowed. It's quiet after an introduction and opening from Mike LaFountain, our spiritual leader. It's solemn and prayerful, prayers we are urged to make in silence. I sit, head bowed, just behind Alisa Herodes. I'm grateful to be near someone I know.

When the ceremony ends, it's like waking from a dream. There's more mingling and chatter. I have a moment to talk to Alisa.

"Did you see who was sitting next to me?" she asks.

"He looked familiar," I say.

"It was Matt Rosendale, ewww!" she says with a laugh.

Rosendale is a Republican politician originally from Baltimore, Maryland. He's now the Montana state auditor. Before that he served in the Montana House of Representatives and later the state senate. He ran against Jon Tester in 2018 to represent Montana in the United States Senate and lost. Now he's running for Montana's lone seat in the United States House of Representatives*. Later he'll post a selfie with Chairman Gray and a congratulatory shout-out to the Little Shell people to his Facebook.

But not all is as it seems. Rosendale is no friend to the Little Shell. As journalist Don Pogreba will point out the next day in the *Montana Post*, "In 2015, the Montana Legislature debated a joint resolution calling on the federal government to 'restore federal recognition to the Little Shell Tribe of Chippewa Indians of Montana.' The bipartisan measure was a single issue, with nothing attached to the bill. There were no costs associated with the bill. And Rosendale voted against it. Twice."

He was one of only thirteen Montana senators to do so. And here he is grinning and glad-handing at one of our sacred ceremonies?

This is why I'm suspicious of settler politicians.

The celebration at the Holiday Inn is a long and moving event. More people attend than the tribe ever imagined. Yes, the speeches are mostly tedious, but there are moments of joy as well. Music. Laughter and tears. What else is there to say about it? Instead, I'll share the prayer Mike LaFountain delivered to open

* He won that seat, but, as of this writing, he's being forced out of a campaign for reelection because even his own party figured out what a tool he actually is.

the festivities. It says a lot about who we are, and why we gather in celebration in the first place.

"It's been a long time," LaFountain began, his voice thick with emotion, his words slow. "We had a pipe ceremony today and it was in honor of our ancestors, all those that went home before us. They didn't get to be in this physical life and watch this day. But they're watching from up there, with their grandfathers and grandmothers, and I take comfort in that. I'm happy they're up there, smiling with us. They're up there, they're going to be dancing with us tonight, and that makes me happy. So I want to say thank you, Grandfather, for allowing us to walk in this beautiful day beside you. Grandfather, I pray for all my relations, the two legged and the four legged, the swimmers and the crawlers and the flyers. I want to give a special prayer to my mother Earth here, and ask her for her forgiveness, for the scars we put upon her every day. But I ask, and I thank her, for the life she gives us every day. Grandfather, watch over us as we celebrate this good time, this blessing in our life here today. Keep us healthy and happy and safe and in a good way. Look us up and down and have pity on us today, Grandfather. Let us get by in life with what we need. I ask you, Grandfather, and you, Mother Earth, to bless our old ones, and our young ones, with every step that they take upon you. Grandfather, let the young ones be young, run around and have fun, and be children. Let our old ones live to be old and teach us, teach us the way, the Native, the Indian way, so that it can be passed on to our young ones. Grandfather, we thank you for all that you give us. Thank you for all that you take from us. Thank you for the blessings that you give us every day. We love you, Grandfather, and we miss all our relations that are up there in the heavens with you. Thank you for this day."

Thank you, indeed. It was a good day.

I pass on an invitation to drinks and further socializing when the formal event ends. I retreat instead to my hotel room and get a pizza delivered. I drink some soda. I take out my journal and begin to make notes while the day's events remain fresh in my memory, but I'm too exhausted. I sit in the quiet and reflect on all that has happened. I wonder what will happen next, and how the coming weeks, months, and years will unfold. But that doesn't matter, not tonight. I close my notebook and trust I'll remember what's necessary when I come back to it. I just want to sit in my solitude and reflect.

My thoughts go back to the pipe ceremony a few hours earlier; it already seems like days ago. Mike LaFountain stands before the crowd and calls everyone into the room for the ceremony. He explains how it will work: only the people seated in the circle of chairs at the front of the room—maybe twenty or so men in all, representing the Little Shell and Turtle Mountain Chippewa—will actually interact with the pipes. They're powerful tools, carried only by those chosen for the honor, with specific rules for when and how they are used. The rest of us are encouraged to add our own, silent prayers to the proceedings, particularly prayers to our ancestors. There's a special kindness to his words that moves me, a gentleness he doesn't often display.

LaFountain tells us no cameras are allowed, no video. It's a sacred ceremony, and as such I won't describe what happens either. All I'll say is that the quiet, the weight of the ceremony, and the growing scent of burning sage and tobacco don't take long to create a magical state.

It's powerful. A room of over one hundred people, all praying in one form or another. It's times like this I can understand the attraction of attending services: the ritual, the solemnity all too lacking in day-to-day life. It always seems like a good idea right up until the guy in robes at the front of the room—and it's always a guy, isn't it?—opens his mouth. Then whatever good feeling I have about organized spiritual service comes crashing down. That doesn't happen here.

"Prayer" is a loaded word. For many, it brings to mind forced attendance at church or nods to organized religion in general. That's justified, but it's also unfortunate. I felt similarly up until recently, but I've come around. I pray. I don't pray to any god, I just pray to the universe. To the Great Mystery of life. I regularly thank that mystery for the beauty of this world and all the wondrous life that inhabits it. I pray that the universe looks after the people I care about. I sometimes pray for help in making my way in the world through all my fears and prejudices and petty resentments.

I pray during the ceremony. I sit there measuring my breaths, like I do when I meditate. I'm not asking for anything. I bring images to mind of my grandpa Leo, grandma Ruby—my father's parents, people I really didn't know. But I can see their faces clearly. I want them there to see what's happening.

I bring to mind my father. I can see him as if he's there before me. I invite him to join me, to sit in the chair beside me. I want him to find some comfort in what's happening here in the way I do. I know it would be hard for him, but it's hard for me too. I'm every bit the stubborn, headstrong man he was. My worst attributes are often the first ones to rise to any occasion, as seemed to be the case with him. But every moment of every day provides us the opportunity to try again, to be better.

I feel something. It's likely just the desire, the deep concentration on my dad, but I feel like his presence is here. He sits quietly beside me, honoring the moment, and he appreciates all I'm trying to do. Tears roll down my cheeks. I want the feeling to be real, and for several long moments, it's as real as anything.

I've dreamed of my dad many times since his death, but only one time have I ever felt his presence so vividly. That was in a dream—I call it a visitation—I had from him four years and three days after he died. He came to me in the early hours of the morning, in the stretch of time between waking, considering getting up, then dozing off again. It was on November 2, 2018, and was so momentous I wrote it down as best I could immediately after waking. I don't believe I got everything. He spoke to me, too, and I missed that. But this is enough.

The setting is the old house in Frenchtown, I think, but aspects of it remind me of the Six Mile house, mainly the verdancy brought on by the creek running through the backyard. There's a large bush or small tree (like a younger version of the big old cottonwood at the corner of the driveway in Frenchtown), and a weathered fence extends beyond to an old propane tank. We've hung seed feeders and hummingbird feeders from those thin, shepherd's crook–style feeder hangers, a small forest of them. There are also a couple cages for suet, only they are on the ground and large, like the size of a small dog kennel. There's a truck backed up, the old white pickup and topper my dad had for storing bags of garbage he hauled to the dump. Dad sits on the tailgate, which is folded open and flat. It's a young version of my dad: fit, healthy, and strong. Lucid.

As I approach, the little space is swarming with birds. The air hums with them. Brilliant green hummingbirds but large, like the size of my fist or larger. They zoom in and out. Many of the birds are fanciful, brilliantly colored, as if from an imaginary version of the tropics. There's a magpie inside one of the suet cages, feasting crazily. Robins, grosbeaks, blue jays. Birds my dad points out by name, but they're names I've never heard of and likely conjured from somewhere in my brain.

We're both happy and excited. In the grass at my feet are these small, bright, sky-blue orbs, like small balls half buried in the soil. I touch one with my finger and it kind of shivers and stands. It is also a bird! It lets me stroke it a couple times with my finger, then it flies off, and all the other little balls explode into the air as birds too. It fills me with joy.

I don't know what this dream means. My folks identified the birds that came to their house, and always had many feeders out. I think my dad might've participated a little, but it seemed to be more my mom's thing, at least in the later years. But still, Dad loved the wild ones who came around, more than he might've admitted. One of the last things I did for him was edit a photo he took of a raccoon hanging from the bird feeder in his backyard. The last time I looked at Facebook he still had a page there, and that image was his profile picture.

This is a significant morning to have and remember such a dream. This day of remembrance. This time when the veil between the worlds of the living and the dead is most transparent.

I'm happy my dad visited me.

Another story I tell of my dad: A friend asks me what I think of Idaho Spud candy bars. I tell her I resent them because of childhood trauma. Asked to explain, I say that when we were kids, my dad used to buy candy bars for my mom and stash them under her pillow. My sisters and I knew this was happening. Sometimes we would even investigate. But there was nothing we could do about it! So I (jokingly) resent Idaho Spuds because, at least in my memory, they were part of those secret little caches of untouchable candies.

My friend expresses surprise—this sweet little ritual doesn't fit with what I've said about my dad.

But it's true. For all his anger, there was a sweetness to my dad that he expressed, as best he could, toward his family. He did the best he could; both my parents did. And for all the traumas they carried, the apparent ones I can guess at and ones I have no clue about, they did a hell of a job, and I love them for it. I love my mother. I love my sisters. This is where I should say I only wish I knew my extended family better, those people my dad in particular didn't want in his life, but I'd be lying. I don't know any different, so not knowing the individuals who comprise that side of my family doesn't really bother me. The more I learn about my wider Little Shell family, though, the more I wish my dad was still around to meet them too. I like to think my presence would help him accept who he was a little better. I can only guess. I love knowing we are part of this big family, and that's enough for me.

If we believe our ancestors still walk among us, observing with love and curiosity to see what we do next, we must ask ourselves: Who will the Little Shell be? What kind of nation do we want to be? How do we want to show ourselves to the world?

"We are building a country, and we have to be patient," LaFountain says at our pipe ceremony. It's true. We have a unique opportunity to create ourselves, and that is a gift. I hope we remember what was done to us, and do all we can to make sure no other people have to endure what we have. I hope when it comes time to make these decisions, we all make the right ones.

It starts slowly in the days that follow—a meeting at a downtown coffee shop with a young journalist doing a story for a regional news magazine—but I soon find myself overwhelmed with requests for my time. A friend who teaches a journalism class at the University of Montana decides to devote the entire semester to stories about the Little Shell, and I'm inundated with requests for interviews from college students, for contact information for other Little Shell people, and more. It's good to tell our story, and it's fun . . . for a while.

I begin to feel irritated. Where was all this attention when we needed it, when we were still working against the crooked bureaucracy that made it so difficult for us to gain recognition in the first place? It begins to feel exploitive. I get defensive when I feel our elders and their time are being abused by journalists who just want to complete an assignment and forget about us. I begin getting close-lipped about providing contact information to people. It's not my finest hour. It's frustrating to me that everyone seems to want answers that don't exist yet. What will happen next? What are the Little Shell going to do? How much money do you get? There's no road map for this; federal recognition rarely happens, particularly for a tribe as large—just under 5,400 enrolled members—as ours. I can only imagine what Chairman Gray is going through, has been going through, in the weeks and months since recognition became fairly certain.

~

There's a new administration in Washington, DC, but we must continue to be wary. The same defense bill that granted the Little Shell federal recognition included funding for construction of a border wall along the American border with Mexico. That project was halted but problems along the southern border remain. People—families—fleeing persecution in their own countries are still being met with imprisonment in America. They're separated and herded into cages. Children are taken from their parents. These refugees are dying on our soil, or being sent back to persecution and death on their own. People who have been in America for years are being caught up in this dragnet as well, including American citizens.

How is what we are doing in America now to others any different from what was done to us as Chippewa Cree Métis people? How are these people not being made to suffer in the same ways our families have been made to suffer? These are Indigenous people, just like we are, just as we've always been. They deserve our love and compassion.

Now the Little Shell Tribe has a duty as a sovereign nation in a position to deal in strength with another nation that surrounds us on all sides, a nation we must never forget rarely has our best interests in mind. We must be alert, and we must be wary. We must be vigilant against any administration that shows signs of continuing the cruel policies the United States government often pursues—usually pursues—when it comes to its dealings with the poor and persecuted people of the world, within our borders or beyond them.

"I've been hearing the words 'federal recognition' since I could hear," Kim McKeehan tells me, a statement common among people who grew up with even distant ties to the tribe. "People are really hungry for community. They're hungry for knowledge, to know how they're connected to each other, and to the land."

Kim tells me there are many connections yet to be made to reconnect us to who we are. There are ceremonies, songs, and relationships to renew with relatives in Canada and North Dakota and probably Minnesota as well.

"I would hope this is the beginning of something beautiful," she says. "But I don't pretend to know what should happen." I don't think anyone does, which is why we need to forge our path forward together, a path always leaning toward compassion.

For the Little Shell Tribe, federal recognition opens a new era. The real work is just now beginning, and I'm intrigued to see how it plays out and curious as to what my role will be. The achievement of federal recognition for the Little Shell is the *end* of this first part of the story I've tried to tell. What happens next is the next one.

I'm no longer ambivalent about this recognition either. The joy of the long-suffering elders is palpable. Like Kim said, I've been hearing about "when we get recognition" for as long as I've known about the Little Shell. It was articles devoted to recognition efforts that helped me connect the dots of my own family back to where we came from. Of course we deserve to be seen by the feds, whatever the reasons for it. We never chose to be a diaspora. We never left our homeland; it was taken from us. We never chose to live on the fringes; we were pushed there. Finally being seen is necessary and important. I like to think such efforts would've made my dad proud, finally, of where he comes from too.

In researching and writing this book, I've become more involved with the tribe than I imagined I would when all this started. I've learned much of our history and met some wonderful people. It's so beautiful, and I'm so grateful to be part of it. I hope others feel the same way, even about the details I've probably misunderstood or gotten wrong. I'm so, so proud of who we are. I hope we're all proud of who we are. I'm here writing to urge you, anyone who has fought against and continues to fight against erasure, oppression, genocide, and hatred, to be proud. Look at what we Little Shell have done. It's been a fight at least 156 years in winning, but we've managed to outlast our opponents. All of them. We endured and we survived, and we triumphed. It's what we do. We are the Little Shell Tribe of Chippewa Indians, and we're the 574th federally recognized Indian tribe in the United States of America.

And I am Little Shell.

EPILOGUE

2021

BUTTE, MONTANA

I'M SITTING ALONE IN A LITTLE green house high on a hillside that overlooks Butte, Montana. I've been awarded a residency here, and I'm laboring through the final push to complete the first draft of this manuscript. It's mid-November 2021, and a storm is blowing in on howling winds that periodically extinguish the pilot light on the cranky old gas furnace that heats this place.

Nearly two years have passed since that fateful bill was signed that suddenly admitted to others what we already knew about ourselves. What happened in the interim? Federal recognition doesn't come very often, and there isn't any road map for it. Federal agencies most involved in the rollout—the BIA, the Indian Health Service (IHS)—are understaffed and underfunded. It's not like they have offices dedicated to assisting newly federally recognized tribes, especially ones with 5,300-plus enrolled members. Things don't happen overnight, and progress is glacial, especially when unexpected hurdles present themselves.

In November 2021, our tribe hadn't gathered officially since the recognition celebration in January 2020, even as enrollment swelled to over six thousand members and counting. Two summer powwows in a row were cancelled. There were no public quarterly meetings. All this was the result of the global coronavirus pandemic that took hold in the United States in March 2020.

The virus hit Native communities hard across the nation. In Montana specifically, "Native Americans account for 6.7% of Montana's population, but between March and October 2020, Indigenous people accounted for 19% of the state's COVID-19 cases and 32% of Montana's COVID-19 deaths."

I mentioned we wouldn't know the ramifications of federal recognition until after it happened. This is an example. In perhaps the most macabre instance of a silver lining emerging from as horrific a situation, even as the world reeled from its effects, the pandemic enabled the Little Shell Tribe to initiate projects that likely would've taken years, if not decades, to get up and running, and quickly. This is all because the tribe's federal recognition provided eligibility for COVID relief funds.

The Coronavirus Aid, Relief, and Economic Security (CARES) Act was passed by Congress and signed into law by President Donald Trump on March 27, 2020. This economic relief package amounted to more than $2 trillion. It's what earned many Americans $1,200 relief checks and small business loans and grants, and launched other assistance programs in an effort to keep the staggering US economy upright. It also included an unprecedented $8 billion for tribes.

"That $8 billion is the single largest investment in Indian country in the history of the United States," Josh Clause says when I speak to him in July 2020. "It was really important for parity with the states that the tribes received this, and I'm really proud that we [Clause's law firm] were able to be part of the team of lawyers and lobbyists here in DC who made it happen."

Clause says the CARES Act money sounds like a lot, and it was. But the need was also great, and the money's use was further complicated by the restrictions attached to it.

"There are very particular ways tribes may use the money," Clause says. "The three main requirements is that it has to be a cost incurred between March 1 and December 30 [, 2020]; you have to spend it within that time, and the work has to be done within that time. Finally, it has to be a necessary expenditure related to COVID."

For the Little Shell, the CARES Act money was akin to a miracle. We got busy, and things improved even more when the deadline for using the money was extended.

"We couldn't buy masks, we couldn't buy anything," Chairman Gerald Gray said of where the tribe was when the pandemic first hit. He'd hoped the tribe might get $1.5 million in CARES money so we could procure essential materials. We received $25 million. The amount was a shock, but it also created an incredible opportunity. Many opportunities.

A common misconception is that once the tribe received federal recognition, a switch would be thrown, and the Little Shell would be awash in federal money. That hasn't been the case. There's a morass of bureaucracy to overcome, and before the COVID relief the tribe hadn't received any money—nothing for operating costs, for putting together a governmental structure, nothing. Creating this infrastructure is a lot of work. The relief money allowed the tribe to move quickly on completing several tasks they had hoped to address when recognition happened.

The Little Shell bought a shuttered clinic in Great Falls, which has been remodeled to serve as a tribal health clinic. This is a huge step, and one Gray had wanted to accomplish since before the tribe gained recognition. The ribbon-cutting for it happened on November 12, 2021, with over a hundred people in attendance. The "10,000-square-foot clinic serves as a one-stop shop, offering comprehensive medical, dental, vision, radiology, pharmaceutical and behavioral health services. The tribe is also offering free shuttle services to help people access the clinic."

"For us to get a clinic from IHS," Gray says, "it would be impossible. They told us with current budget constraints, waiting lists, all of that, it would be over a hundred years before we would get our turn. So this is huge for us." By acquiring our own facility, we've expedited the process. IHS will still staff and operate the clinic for at least three years to satisfy federal requirements, but at least Little Shell members won't have to wait a couple generations for it to be built or acquired.

The tribe also purchased two delivery pickups and two passenger vans, one with a wheelchair lift. These vehicles, for example, enable leaders of the anti-tobacco awareness program to transport young people to events. They provide the tribe the option to drive elders to Rocky Boy's or Browning—the closest existing IHS health clinics—until our own facility is fully functional, or to take veterans to Helena for VA care or to other events, like a big Métis celebration in Helena—over an hour away from Great Falls—that I also attended in the fall of 2021.

The Little Shell have checked a few other things off our list too. The administrative building on Central Avenue in Great Falls got a new roof and phone system. The kitchen in the tribe's cultural center out at Hill 57 was remodeled to be certified as a commercial kitchen, and that building was finally connected to city water and sewer. The parking lot was redone, and a large vehicle barn for storing the new vehicles was built on the premises.

Besides the health care initiatives, other programs—and the people to run them—are under way to help with rental and mortgage assistance for people who lost income due to COVID and are struggling to catch up. And finally, the tribe purchased land on Hill 57 to begin a food sovereignty program that will include not only growing crops but raising cattle as well. These are all big, ambitious plans that aren't just being talked about, they're in process. There's more going on with the Little Shell than ever before.

Some of the things I complained about while I was trying to learn about the tribe and pursuing enrollment—the condition of the website, for example, or communications with members—have vastly improved. Now when tribal headquarters releases a news bulletin, it comes to me as a text. Sometimes.

An abundance of amazing work has been done, but there's still a long way to go. As always there are squabbles and drama from time to time such that it seems it could all fall apart at any moment. But what momentous change has never felt that way? They're growing pains from the birthing of a sovereign nation.

We have a long way to go, but we've already proven we're good over the distance.

It's October 30, 2023, and I'm putting the finishing touches on the third draft of this book before it goes to copyedits, then to advance reader copies, and finally to publication. Today is the nine-year anniversary of that terrible morning my mom called to tell me my dad was dead. Everything is different.

To call my father's death a "catalyst" would be a disservice to the enormity of it, but it's the best word I have. I could go on for another twenty thousand words about all the things in my life that have changed, and how I've changed. But I'll try to stick instead to who I am, which, as the bios I endlessly send out and my business cards say, is a Métis storyteller.

I travel all over the state doing presentations about the Little Shell and Métis people. I've been on NPR, radio programs in the UK, and a couple other programs I don't even remember, discussing Indigenous concerns. I teach children poetry on the Flathead reservation, and storytelling to university students as part of the creative writing department at the University of Montana. My schedule of speaking, workshopping, and teaching is busier than is probably good for me.

It's unlikely I would be doing this work, or anything like it, if I hadn't encountered Nicholas Vrooman and his *One Robe* book more than a decade ago. All those references to "Doney" and "La Tray" in its index awakened something in me I haven't let rest since. The Indigenous part of who I am is still blossoming, and I do my best to embody it every day. All too often, now, I'm someone people come to with questions about where they come from. They're farther back down the path of discovery than I am, but the trail is still all too familiar to me because I'm on it too. So I take my answers, my ability to answer, seriously.

I set out to write this book as a Little Shell person in service to my Little Shell people, but now I find myself a Little Shell person in service to the world. What we've faced, as I hope I've shown, is something more and more people face every day. I have a responsibility to make sure all the stories related to this struggle are told. I feel the light hands of my ancestors at my back, urging me forward, and they're with me when I falter and question the use of it all. It's hard.

But it's also a beautiful, beautiful life to be living.

NOTES

I read many books and essays and internet articles in preparation for writing this book. I also conducted lots of interviews, some formally with notebook and recorder and just as many, if not more, informally at picnic tables and folding tables and in conference rooms. Wherever I have referenced a specific publication or video, you will find it noted here. In the case of conversation and dialogue resulting from direct quotes from interviews, they are not noted; however, you will find a full list of the interviews relevant to the book in the bibliography that follows. There you will find texts mentioned here as well as others not specifically referenced but no less important to my learning and understanding.

CHAPTER 2

17 ***tools like pestles*** Frenchtown Historical Society, *Frenchtown Valley Footprints* (Missoula, MT: Mountain Press Publishing, 1976), 2.

18 ***sometime in the late 1840s*** *Frenchtown Valley Footprints*, 5.

19 ***a white-only population*** "Population Estimates, July 1, 2022, (V2022)," United States Census Bureau, accessed December 18, 2023, https://www.census.gov/quickfacts/fact/table/MT.

19 ***current population estimates*** "Missoula, MT," Data USA, accessed December 18, 2023, https://datausa.io/profile/geo/missoula-mt.

CHAPTER 4

38 ***The foundational issue*** Nicholas Vrooman, "The Whole Country Was . . . One Robe," CSPAN, October 8, 2013, video, https://www.c-span.org/video/?315917-1/the-country-wasone-robe. This is a quote I heard Nicholas Vrooman utter on many occasions. In addition, I've taken a few liberties to build the scene of watching Vrooman's presentation because, as I note in the chapter, I set aside my note-taking to just listen. However, this CSPAN video aired just days after the presentation I viewed, and much of what he says here is what he was saying in the presentation I was present for; to that extent, it is almost like having a video capture of the life-changing encounter I had with him in Missoula.

39 ***the oldest settlement*** *Frenchtown Valley Footprints*, 7.

43 ***relocated, dislocated, intermarried*** Vrooman, "The Whole Country."

CHAPTER 5

45 ***It is a truism*** Joseph Kinsey Howard, *Montana: High, Wide, and Handsome* (New Haven, CT: Yale University Press, 1943), 319.

45 ***effect a synthesis*** Howard, 319.

45 ***left Montanans*** Howard, 320.

46 ***the ill-starred Métis*** Howard, 320.

49 ***Thus there emerged*** Verne Dusenberry, "Waiting for a Day That Never Comes: The Dispossessed Métis of Montana," in *The New Peoples: Being and Becoming Métis in North America*, ed. Jacqueline Peterson and Jennifer S.H. Brown (St. Paul: Minnesota Historical Society Press, 2001), 120.

54 ***All of them have a blue*** William Hypolitus Keating, "Narrative of an Expedition to the Source of St. Peter's River . . . ," Library of Congress, accessed December 18, 2023, 44, https://tile.loc.gov/storage-services/service/gdc/lhbum/1607b/1607b.pdf.

54 ***When I do my teachings*** Lenard Monkman, "More Than a Fashion Statement, the Métis Sash Was Like 'Batman's Utility Belt,'" CBC News, February 17, 2020, accessed December 18, 2023, https://www.cbc.ca/news/indigenous/metis-sash-louis-riel-day-1.5465090.

54 ***Most men died*** Monkman.

60 ***started for Red River*** Nicholas C. P. Vrooman, "*The Whole Country Was . . . 'One Robe'": The Little Shell Tribe's America* (Helena, MT: Little Shell Tribe of Chippewa Indians of Montana and Drumlummon Institute, 2012), 134.

61 ***While the Canadian*** Adam Gaudry, "Métis," *The Canadian Encyclopedia*, last edited November 28, 2023, https://www.thecanadianencyclopedia.ca/en/article/metis.

CHAPTER 7

78 ***Peace, friendship and amity*** "Article 1," in "Treaty with the Blackfeet, 1855," Tribal Treaties Database, accessed December 18, 2023, https://treaties.okstate.edu/treaties/treaty-with-the-blackfeet-1855-0736.

78 ***the United States may*** "Article 8," in "Treaty with the Blackfeet, 1855."

CHAPTER 8

90 ***more than seven*** Antonio Regalado, "2017 Was the Year Consumer DNA Testing Blew Up," MIT Technology Review, February 12, 2018, https://www.technologyreview.com/2018/02/12/145676/2017-was-the-year-consumer-dna-testing-blew-up.

90 ***as many people purchased*** Regalado.

91 ***Genetic concepts further*** Kim TallBear, *Native American DNA: Tribal Belonging and the False Promise of Genetic Science* (Minneapolis: University of Minnesota Press, 2013), 26.

CHAPTER 9

Much of this chapter is based on a piece I wrote for the Fall 2017 issue of *Montana Quarterly* magazine. Quotes from individuals featured here are taken from transcripts of interviews with all of them in 2017; only quotes *not* gleaned from those interviews are noted here.

CHAPTER 10

All the quotes from Linda Watson occurred in a series of emails and phone conversations, and a couple brief face-to-face encounters, in the years they were mentioned.

115 ***Although it is*** "Red Lake Nation Alters Blood Quantum for Tribal Members," *Bemidji Pioneer*, October 11, 2019, https://www.bemidjipioneer.com/news/red-lake-nation-alters-blood-quantum-for-tribal-members.

CHAPTER 11

121 ***Almost every northern*** Dusenberry, "Waiting for a Day," 121.

121 ***It is simply*** "Red River Métis Cart," Métis Resource Centre, accessed December 18, 2023, https://www.cranbrookmetis.com/metis-culture.html.

125 ***290 army men, 340 mules*** Wikipedia, s.v. "Treaty of Old Crossing," last modified October 27, 2023, https://wikipedia.org/wiki/Treaty_of_Old_Crossing.

125 ***In 1863, the Red Lake Band*** David Treuer, *The Heartbeat of Wounded Knee: Native America from 1890 to the Present* (New York: Riverhead, 2019), 161.

126 ***each male adult*** Ella Hawkinson, "The Old Crossing Chippewa Treaty and Its Sequel," Minnesota History, vol. 15, no. 3 (September 1934), 294.

130 ***Little Shell III is probably*** Les LaFountain, "Chief Little Shell III," Makoche Studios, video, https://player.vimeo.com/video/354296107. As in chapter 4 when quoting Nicholas Vrooman, I've taken quotes from Les LaFountain from a different source in a similar context related to the very things we were talking about, simply because I wasn't taking notes or recording our time together, whether in Belcourt or via a couple phone calls we have had since.

131 ***forged between the*** Kade M. Ferris, "The Sweetcorn Treaty of 1858," Turtle Mountain Chippewa Heritage Center, November 13, 2019, http://www.chippewaheritage.com/heritage-blog/sweetcorn.

131 ***There was no reservation*** LaFountain, "Chief Little Shell III."

133 ***This reservation really*** LaFountain, "Chief Little Shell III."

135 ***Montana's native people*** Transcribed from a photograph I took of the actual sign.

137 ***The chief was eloquent*** W. E. Davis, "Tales of the Turtle Mountain Country, July 4, 1901," in Vrooman, *The Whole Country*, 134.

137 ***unsuccessful in his quest*** Vrooman, *The Whole Country*, 275.

137 ***Great leaders around*** LaFountain, "Chief Little Shell III."

CHAPTER 12

138 ***crude cottonwood carts*** Rick Graetz and Susie Graetz, *This Is Montana* (Helena, MT: Northern Rockies Publishing, 2003), 275.

139 ***First settlers along*** Howard, *Montana*, 122.

141 ***The final product*** Matthew L. Basso, *Meet Joe Copper: Masculinity and Race on Montana's World War II Home Front* (Chicago: University of Chicago Press, 2013), 5.

141 ***by the early twentieth century*** Basso, 48.

147 ***through Moccasin Flat*** Duane Reid, *Through the Lens of My Tribe: An Indigenous Archaeology Study on the Viability of the Little Shell Tribe* (Missoula, MT: Unpublished Manuscript, 2020), 18.

147 ***One Black Eagle*** Basso, *Meet Joe Copper*, 60.

CHAPTER 13

150 ***calculated to sandbag*** Mike Mansfield, "The American Stranger," NBC Kaleidoscope, 1958, video shared by Dave Boggess, October 27, 2014, on YouTube, https://www.youtube.com/watch?v=XYvBlWP2HAQ.

153 ***from the maps*** Mansfield, "The American Stranger."

158 ***it shall be*** American Indian Religious Freedom Act, Pub. L. No. 95–341, 92 Stat. 469 (1978), https://www.govinfo.gov/content/pkg/COMPS-5293/pdf/COMPS-5293.pdf.

CHAPTER 14

164 ***at least 710*** Scott D. Pierce, "In the Decade Before Gabby Petito Disappeared, 710 Indigenous People Went Missing in Wyoming," *Salt Lake Tribune*, September 23, 2021, https://www.sltrib.com/news/2021/09/23/decade-before-gabby.

165 ***The movement to*** Nick Estes, et al., eds., *Red Nation Rising: From Bordertown Violence to Native Liberation* (Oakland, CA: PM Press, 2021), 49.

165 ***do not count*** Estes et al., 49.

165 ***large, usually temporary*** Nick Estes, *Our History Is the Future: Standing Rock versus the Dakota Access Pipeline, and the Long Tradition of Native Resistance* (Brooklyn, NY: Verso, 2019), 8.

166 ***Practically to a man*** Sylvia Van Kirk, *Many Tender Ties: Women in Fur-Trade Society, 1670–1870* (Norman, OK: University of Oklahoma Press, 1983), 17.

166 ***the drudgery and hardship*** Van Kirk, 17.

169 ***a widespread and complex*** Van Kirk, 5.

171 ***having a relative*** *Demilitarization Is Decolonization*, Position Paper (Rapid City, SD: NDN Collective, February 2024), 1, https://ndncollective.org/wp-content/uploads/2024/02/demilitarization-is-decolonization-position-paper-min.pdf.

174 ***sinful and debased*** Van Kirk, *Many Tender Ties*, 145.

176 ***The 'new people'*** Dusenberry, "Waiting for a Day," 120.

CHAPTER 15

183 ***Like other Indigenous*** Émilie Pigeon, "Au Nom du Bon Dieu et du Buffalo: Metis Lived Catholicism on the Northern Plains" (dissertation, graduate program in history, York University, Toronto, Ontario, 2017), 93.

185 ***A voyageur canoe*** Peter Stark, *Astoria: Astor and Jefferson's Lost Pacific Empire* (New York: HarperCollins, 2015), 43.

186 ***Indigenous spiritual practices*** Pigeon, "Au Nom du Bon Dieu," 83.

187 ***The immediate gains*** Pigeon, 124.

188 ***investigate the experiences*** Denise K. Lajimodiere, *Stringing Rosaries: The History, the Unforgivable, and the Healing of Northern Plains American Indian Boarding School Survivors* (Fargo: North Dakota State University Press, 2019), 8.

189 ***I am a product*** Deb Haaland, "My Grandparents Were Stolen from Their Families as Children. We Must Learn About This History," *Washington Post*, June 11, 2021, https://www.washingtonpost.com/opinions/2021/06/11/deb-haaland-indigenous-boarding-schools.

189 ***a priest gathered*** Haaland.

190 ***Many of the boarding schools*** Haaland.

193 ***about acquiring new*** Jon M. Sweeney, *St. Francis of Assisi: His Life, Teachings, and Practice* (New York: St. Martin's, 2019), 42.

193 ***Is the purpose*** Sweeney, 42.

CHAPTER 16

201 ***Tirades appeared in*** Martha Harroun Foster, *We Know Who We Are: Métis Identity in a Montana Community* (Norman: University of Oklahoma Press, 2006), 77.

202 ***favorably impressed with*** Martha Harroun Foster, "'Just Following the Buffalo': Origins of a Montana Métis Community," in *Montana: A Cultural Medley*, ed. Robert R. Swartout Jr. (Helena, MT: Farcountry Press, 2015), 78.

208 ***precluded Métis economic*** Foster, 84.

CHAPTER 17

212 ***Pine Butte is part*** "Places We Protect: Pine Butte Preserve, Montana," The Nature Conservancy, accessed February 26, 2024, https://www.nature.org/en-us/get-involved/how-to-help/places-we-protect/pine-butte-swamp-preserve.

215 ***any group migration*** Dictionary.com, s.v. "Diaspora," accessed December 18, 2023, https://www.dictionary.com/browse/diaspora.

CHAPTER 18

232 ***By ignoring their long history*** Foster, "Just Following the Buffalo," 72.

CHAPTER 19

240 ***kicked down the road*** Jon Tester and Aaron Murphy, *Grounded: A Senator's Lessons on Winning Back Rural America* (New York: HarperCollins, 2020), 191.

240 ***There was a catch*** Tester and Murphy, 191.

240 ***I still keep Chairman Gray's*** Tester and Murphy, 191.

241 ***to enhance the quality*** "Bureau of Indian Affairs (BIA)," U.S. Department of the Interior, Indian Affairs, accessed December 18, 2023, https://www.bia.gov/bia.

241 ***an American Indian*** "Frequently Asked Questions," U.S. Department of the Interior, Indian Affairs, accessed December 18, 2023, https://www.bia.gov/frequently-asked-questions.

242 ***issued regulations governing*** "Frequently Asked Questions."

242 ***not enough evidence*** "Interior Finds Insufficient Evidence to Acknowledge the Little Shell Tribe of Chippewa Indians of Montana," U.S. Department of the Interior, Indian Affairs, October 27, 2009, https://www.bia.gov/as-ia/opa/online-press-release/interior-finds-insufficient-evidence-acknowledge-little-shell-tribe.

243 ***comprise a distinct community*** "Interior Finds Insufficient Evidence."

CHAPTER 20

253 ***provided legal assistance*** "About Us," Native American Rights Fund, accessed December 18, 2023, https://www.narf.org/about-us.

254 ***More than 94 percent*** Kim Gottschalk, quote from transcription of event, January 25, 2020.

256 ***In 2015, the Montana*** Don Pogreba, "Shameless Matt Rosendale Attends Little Shell Celebration Despite Voting Against Federal Recognition for the Tribe," *Montana Post*, January 26, 2020, https://themontanapost.com/blog/2020/01/26/shameless-matt-rosendale-attends-little-shell-celebration-despite-voting-against-federal-recognition-for-the-tribe.

257 ***It's been a long time*** Mike LaFountain, quote from transcription of event, January 25, 2020.

EPILOGUE

267 ***Native Americans account*** Nora Mabie, "Tribal Communities in Montana Receive More Than $2.6 Million in COVID-19 Relief," *Great Falls Tribune*, updated December 8, 2021, https://www.greatfallstribune.com/story/news/tribal-news/chippewa-cree-tribe/2021/12/08/montana-tribal-communities-chippewa-cree-salish-kootenai-receive-over-2-6-million-covid-19-relief/6435466001.

268 ***10,000-square-foot clinic*** Nora Mabie, "'A Really Exciting Time': Little Shell Tribe Opens Health Clinic in Great Falls," *Great Falls Tribune*, November 12, 2021, https://www.greatfallstribune.com/story/news/tribal-news/little-shell-tribe/2021/11/12/little-shell-tribe-opens-tribal-health-clinic-great-falls/8587922002.

BIBLIOGRAPHY

The following is a substantial but not all-inclusive list of books, articles, etc. that informed the writing of this book. There is a lot more out there, and I immersed myself in much of it.

BOOKS

Barman, Jean. *French Canadians, Furs, and Indigenous Women in the Making of the Pacific Northwest*. Vancouver: UBC Press, 2014.

Basso, Matthew L. *Meet Joe Copper: Masculinity and Race on Montana's World War II Home Front*. Chicago: University of Chicago Press, 2013.

Benton-Banai, Edward. *The Mishomis Book: The Voice of the Ojibway*. Minneapolis: University of Minnesota Press, 2010.

Cheney, Roberta Carkeek. *Name on the Face of Montana: The Story of Montana's Place Names*. Missoula, MT: Mountain Press, 1983.

Correia, David, Jennifer Nez Denetdale, Nick Estes, Melanie K. Yazzie. *Red Nation Rising: From Bordertown Violence to Native Liberation*. Oakland: PM Press, 2021.

Crutchfield, James. *It Happened in Montana: Remarkable Events That Shaped History*. New York: Globe Pequot, 2017.

Egan, Ken, Jr. *Montana 1889: Indians, Cowboys, and Miners in the Year of Statehood*. Helena, MT: Riverbend, 2017.

Estes, Nick. *Our History Is the Future: Standing Rock Versus the Dakota Access Pipeline, and the Long Tradition of Native Resistance*. Brooklyn: Verso, 2019.

Fiola, Chantal. *Rekindling the Sacred Fire: Métis Ancestry and Anishinaabe Spirituality*. Winnipeg: University of Manitoba Press, 2015.

Foster, Martha Harroun. *We Know Who We Are: Métis Identity in a Montana Community*. Norman, OK: University of Oklahoma Press, 2006.

Frenchtown Historical Society, *Frenchtown Valley Footprints*. Missoula, MT: Mountain Press Publishing, 1976.

Graetz, Rick and Susie Graetz. *This Is Montana*. Big Sky, MT: Northern Rockies Publishing, 2003.

Howard, Joseph Kinsey. *Montana: High, Wide, and Handsome*. New Haven, CT: Yale University Press, 1943.

Howard, Joseph Kinsey. *Strange Empire: A Narrative of the Northwest*. Minnesota: Minnesota Historical Society Press, 1994. First published 1952 by William Morrow (New York).

Krawec, Patty. *Becoming Kin: An Indigenous Call to Unforgetting the Past and Reimagining Our Future*. Minneapolis: Broadleaf, 2022.

Lajimodiere, Denise K. *Stringing Rosaries: The History, the Unforgivable, and the Healing of Northern Plains American Indian Boarding School Survivors*. Fargo: North Dakota State University Press, 2019.

Leeson, Michael A., ed. *History of Montana, 1739–1885*. Chicago: Warner, Beers, 1885.

Methot, Suzanne. *Legacy: Trauma, Story, and Indigenous Healing*. Toronto: ECW Press, 2019.

Nijhuis, Michelle. *Beloved Beasts: Fighting for Life in an Age of Extinction*. New York: W.W. Norton, 2021.

Peterson, Jacqueline and Jennifer S. H. Brown, eds. *The New Peoples: Being and Becoming Métis in North America*. St. Paul, MN: Minnesota Historical Society Press, 2001.

Pigeon, Émilie. "Au nom du Bon Dieu et du Buffalo: Metis Lived Catholicism on the Northern Plains." PhD diss., York University, Toronto, 2017.

Ratteree, Kathleen and Norbert Hill, eds. *The Great Vanishing*

Act: Blood Quantum and the Future of Native Nations. Arvada, CO: Fulcrum Publishing, 2017.

Reid, Duane. *Through the Lens of My Tribe: An Indigenous Archaeology Study on the Viability of the Little Shell Tribe Hill 57 Land Parcel as a National Register of Historic Places Nomination*. Unpublished manuscript, 2020.

Spritzer, Don. *Roadside History of Montana*. Missoula, MT: Mountain Press, 1999.

Stark, Peter. *Astoria: Astor and Jefferson's Lost Pacific Empire: A Tale of Ambition and Survival on the Early American Frontier*. New York: HarperCollins, 2015.

Stone, Arthur L. *Following Old Trails*. Stevensville, MT: Stoneydale, 2004.

Swartout, Robert R., Jr. *Montana: A Cultural Medley*. Helena, MT: Farcountry, 2015.

Sweeney, Jon M. *St. Francis of Assisi: His Life, Teachings, and Practice*. New York: St. Martin's, 2019.

TallBear, Kim. *Native American DNA: Tribal Belonging and the False Promise of Genetic Science*. Minneapolis: University of Minnesota Press, 2013.

Tester, Jon. *Grounded: A Senator's Lessons on Winning Back Rural America*. New York: HarperCollins, 2020.

Toole, K. Ross. *Montana: An Uncommon Land*. Norman, OK: University of Oklahoma Press, 1959.

Treuer, David. *The Heartbeat of Wounded Knee: Native America from 1890 to the Present*. New York: Riverhead, 2019.

Van Kirk, Silvia. *Many Tender Ties: Women in Fur-Trade Society, 1670–1870*. Norman, OK: University of Oklahoma Press, 1983.

Vrooman, Nicholas C. P. *"The Whole Country Was . . . 'One Robe'": The Little Shell Tribe's America*. Helena, MT: Drumlummon Institute and Little Shell Tribe of Chippewa Indians of Montana, 2012.

Yunkaporta, Tyson. *Sand Talk: How Indigenous Thinking Can Save the World*. New York: HarperCollins, 2020.

ARTICLES, ESSAYS, AND VIDEOS

Anderson, Vernon. "The La Tray Family and Their Part in Central Montana History." Term Paper, Lewistown College Center, College of Great Falls, December 1, 1975.

Bartsch, Don. "He Gave Hill 57 Its Name." *Great Falls Tribune*, November 17, 1963.

Dusenberry, Verne. "Waiting for a Day That Never Comes: The Dispossessed Métis of Montana." *Montana: The Magazine of Western History*, 1958.

Ferris, Kade. "The Rise of the Pembina Band." *Heritage* (blog), Turtle Mountain Chippewa Heritage Center, January 7, 2020. http://www.chippewaheritage.com/heritage-blog/the-rise-of-the-pembina-band.

Foster, Martha Harroun. "Just Following the Buffalo: Origins of a Montana Métis Community." *Great Plains Quarterly*, Summer 2006.

Hawkinson, Ella. "The Old Crossing Chippewa Treaty and Its Sequel," *Minnesota History*, 15, no. 3, September 1934.

Hornaday, William T. "The Extermination of the American Bison." Washington: Government Printing Office, 1887.

RECORDED INTERVIEWS

The following is merely a collection of audio recordings I accumulated from the myriad conversations I had in writing this book. Many, many conversations were had, and the list is far from conclusive.

Clause, Josh, in discussion with the author, December 19, 2019, telephone.

Clause, Josh, in discussion with the author, June 1, 2021, telephone.

Gray, Gerald, in discussion with the author, December 13, 2019, Billings, MT.

La Tray, Becky, in discussion with the author, March 16, 2019, Missoula, MT.

La Tray, Becky, in discussion with the author, March 12, 2020, Missoula, MT.

McKeehan, Kim, in discussion with the author, January 18, 2019, Great Falls, MT.

McKeehan, Kim, in discussion with the author, December 15, 2019, telephone.

Parenteau, Richard, in discussion with the author, October 18, 2020, telephone.

Reid, Duane, in discussion with the author, November 5, 2020, telephone.

Vrooman, Nicholas, in discussion with the author, June 21, 2018, Helena, MT.

Vrooman, Nicholas, in discussion with the author, October 17, 2018, Heritage Hall, Missoula, MT.

Watson, Linda, in discussion with the author, December 8, 2019, telephone.

Wiseman, Al, in discussion with the author, February 24, 2020, Choteau, MT.

ACKNOWLEDGMENTS

Anishinaabemowin—or you may call it Ojibwemowin or Ojibwe or even Chippewa—is the language of the Little Shell Tribe. When we want to say thank you, we say *miigwech*. Chi-miigwech means thank you very much. As languages go it is a relatively new word, coming into existence only after our Indigenous relatives began interacting with European traders more than three centuries ago. The story, such as I've learned it from my Turtle Mountain relative James Vukelich Kaagegaabaw, a person who has done more recently than just about anyone in educating folks about culture and language via his wonderful YouTube and Instagram interactions, is that the word's meaning was originally close to what we might call "enough." For example, in trading with the newcomers, as goods changed hands—say, beaver pelts for metal pots or tools—when the Anishinaabek person with the pelts received in exchange what they felt was sufficient for what they were offering, they would conclude the transaction by saying, "Miigwech." Enough. The European cultural understanding was that the word meant "thank you" for the exchange. The meaning stuck.

So, today I find myself wishing to express gratitude, thank you, miigwech, to a degree that will never be enough for a number of people without whom this book would not exist. There have been many people along the way who have been instrumental in helping me bring this story, or at least this part of it, to conclusion. If I have forgotten anyone, it is merely an oversight brought on by the overwhelm of finally being in this position. You live in these pages too.

Miigwech first to this land, this Turtle Island, for keeping and providing for all of us despite our proclivity toward distractions that raise barriers between us. May this book, inspired by my love for the world and all of the relatives I'm fortunate to share it with, be a small part in bringing more of us closer together again.

Miigwech to my immediate family: My mother, Becky La Tray, the keeper of our wonderful family's history; I've done my best to get it right. And to my sisters, Mitzi and Nikki. You lived all of this too; I hope I have done our shared memories justice, even if they vary in places. I love you all so much.

Miigwech to Sid, and to Julia, the people I have shared my life with longest, loved the longest, and without whom my time here would be far less beautiful. This book is for you too.

Miigwech to my Little Shell family, from Turtle Mountain and beyond, whose deep knowledge and stories and openness to discussing difficult histories made this book possible: Al Wiseman, Elaine Wiseman, John Gilbert, Duane Reid, Gerald Gray, Linda Watson, Richard Parenteau, Josh Clause, Les LaFountain, Kade Ferris, and everyone else I ever talked to. What a mighty people we are, and you are proof.

Miigwech to Kim McKeehan, my cousin, for the first taste of what real extended family feels like and for the love and support every inch of the way.

Miigwech to Alisa Herodes, whose efforts on behalf of the wider Métis and Little Shell community exemplifies what it means to be a Good Ancestor.

Miigwech to my friend Abby Travis, formerly of Milkweed, the first person I shared my idea for the book with and the first person from "the industry" to say, "Yes, I think we'd be interested . . ." Abby gave me the encouragement to push through my doubts and fears and to actually prepare a proposal.

Miigwech to Mara Panich, owner of Fact & Fiction Books in Missoula and, most importantly, my friend. You've been involved since the first time I talked about this book and every step of the way since and I'm so grateful to have you around for its emergence into the world.

Miigwech to my bookseller family. Barbara Theroux, friend and legendary founder of Fact & Fiction. To Bryn Agnew, my good friend, staunch supporter and, perhaps most importantly, my Dungeon Master. And to the other booksellers who picked up the slack during my time slinging books (once a bookseller, always a bookseller!) at F&F when I had to take time for residencies and various other writerly excursions; notably Hannah Dahl, Patrick Walrath, Joe Kirk, Apollo Uhlenbreck, and Danielle Clooney.

To Jimmy Rolle and Steve Jacobs, my bandmates in the dread American Falcon, who are always ready to join me in Rock-Based Volume Therapy.

Miigwech to the magnificent team at Milkweed Editions. Daniel Slager, Lauren Langston Klein, Mary Austin Speaker, Craig Popelars, Morgan LaRocca, Shannon Blackmer, Katie Hill, Jane Townsend, and Anna Thorsen. What a challenge we've taken on, and I can't imagine a better collection of folks to leap into the fray with.

Miigwech to copyeditor Anitra Budd, who with a tremendously gentle and invisible touch turned my raw manuscript into something special. When she didn't suggest changing reference to my beloved band of rock heroes "KISS" to "Kiss" I knew I was in excellent hands.

Miigwech to Amelia Hagen-Dillon for the beautiful map. You have no idea the gift you have given my people. And to Chris Chapman for the cover photo. Who knew how amazing that "You want to come over to my new studio so I can practice?" effort would be?

Miigwech to the brilliant Antonia Malchik, my great friend and inspiring example of how to look deeply and with fierce love at the world. And to Anne Helen Petersen for years of support and more inspiration for how to be a writer in this constantly changing landscape.

Miigwech to Selya Avila, whose kindness, good cheer, wisecracks, and willingness to check in on me as I lumbered down the stretch was irreplaceable. I couldn't have finished this without you.

Miigwech to Anna East, whose humility and deep care in keeping tremendous knowledge about the wider Native community in Montana, particularly as it relates to culture and education, is essential to every future thing I do in this undertaking that is my life's work. I couldn't do it without you.

Miigwech to the Mountain Words writing residency (Crested Butte, Colorado) and to the Dear Butte writing residency (Butte, Montana) for the time and space that was critical to finishing the first draft of this book.

Miigwech to the growing thousands of subscribers to my Irritable Métis newsletter, my so-called "Irritable Readers." Your enthusiasm for the eventual release of this book kept me going when I didn't think it was possible anyone would ever care about it.

Miigwech, finally, to my late friend and mentor Nicholas Vrooman. This book would not exist without his work and exuberant encouragement. I've tracked down the story as best I could, Nicholas. I hope I've done it justice.

CHRIS LA TRAY is a Métis storyteller, a descendent of the Pembina Band of the mighty Red River of the North, and an enrolled member of the Little Shell Tribe of Chippewa Indians. His book *One-Sentence Journal* won the Montana Book Award and a High Plains Book Award. La Tray is the Montana Poet Laureate and writes the weekly newsletter "An Irritable Métis." He lives near Frenchtown, Montana.

Founded as a nonprofit organization in 1980, Milkweed Editions is an independent publisher. Our mission is to identify, nurture, and publish transformative literature, and build an engaged community around it.

Milkweed Editions is based in Bdé Óta Othúŋwe (Minneapolis) within Mní Sota Makhóčhe, the traditional homeland of the Dakhóta people. Residing here since time immemorial, Dakhóta people still call Mní Sota Makhóčhe home, with four federally recognized Dakhóta nations and many more Dakhóta people residing in what is now the state of Minnesota. Due to continued legacies of colonization, genocide, and forced removal, generations of Dakhóta people remain disenfranchised from their traditional homeland. Presently, Mní Sota Makhóčhe has become a refuge and home for many Indigenous nations and peoples, including seven federally recognized Ojibwe nations. We humbly encourage our readers to reflect upon the historical legacies held in the lands they occupy.

milkweed.org

Milkweed Editions, an independent nonprofit literary publisher, gratefully acknowledges sustaining support from our board of directors, the McKnight Foundation, the National Endowment for the Arts, and many generous contributions from foundations, corporations, and thousands of individuals—our readers. This activity is made possible by the voters of Minnesota through a Minnesota State Arts Board Operating Support grant, thanks to a legislative appropriation from the arts and cultural heritage fund.

McKNIGHT FOUNDATION

Interior design by Mike Corrao

Typeset in Adobe Caslon Pro, a digital facsimile of William Caslon's 1722 typeface, inspired by the previous century's Dutch type foundries. It was revived for modern use in 1990 by the prolific Carol Twombly for the Adobe Originals program.